D0619645

Cascadia

MĀNOA 25:1   UNIVERSITY   HONOLULU
OF HAWAI'I
PRESS

Cascadia

THE LIFE AND BREATH OF THE WORLD

Frank Stewart

EDITOR

Trevor Carolan

GUEST EDITOR

Editor   Frank Stewart

Managing Editor   Pat Matsueda

Designer and Art Editor   Barbara Pope

Associate Editor   Sonia Cabrera

Assistant Editor   Nelson Rivera

Staff   Madoka Nagadō, Noah Perales-Estoesta

Consulting Editors   Barry Lopez, W. S. Merwin, Carol Moldaw, Michael Nye, Naomi Shihab Nye, Gary Snyder, Arthur Sze, Michelle Yeh

Corresponding Editors for Asia and the Pacific
CAMBODIA   Sharon May
CHINA   Fiona Sze-Lorrain
HONG KONG   Shirley Geok-lin Lim
INDONESIA   John H. McGlynn
JAPAN   Leza Lowitz
KOREA   Bruce Fulton
NEW ZEALAND AND SOUTH PACIFIC   Vilsoni Hereniko
PACIFIC LATIN AMERICA   H. E. Francis, James Hoggard
PHILIPPINES   Alfred A. Yuson
SOUTH ASIA   Sukrita Paul Kumar, Alok Bhalla
WESTERN CANADA   Charlene Gilmore

Advisors   William H. Hamilton, Robert Shapard, Robert Bley-Vroman

Founded in 1988 by Robert Shapard and Frank Stewart

Interior images from the sketchbooks of Emily Carr
courtesy of Royal British Columbia Museum, British Columbia Archives.

Additional copyright information and permissions are located on page 222.

Mānoa is published twice a year. Subscriptions: U.S.A. and international—individuals $30 one year, $54 two years; institutions $50 one year, $90 two years; international airmail add $24 per year. Single copies: U.S.A. and international—individuals $20; institutions $30; international airmail add $12 per copy. Call toll free 1-888-UHPRESS. We accept checks, money orders, Visa, or MasterCard, payable to University of Hawai'i Press, 2840 Kolowalu Street, Honolulu, HI 96822, U.S.A. Claims for issues not received will be honored until 180 days past the date of publication; thereafter, the single-copy rate will be charged.

Mānoa gratefully acknowledges the support of the University of Hawai'i Administration and the University of Hawai'i College of Languages, Linguistics, and Literature; and additional support from the National Endowment for the Arts, the Hawai'i State Foundation on Culture and the Arts, the Mānoa Foundation, and the University of the Fraser Valley, located in traditional Stó:lō territory.

manoajournal.hawaii.edu
uhpress.hawaii.edu/journals/manoa
muse.jhu.edu (Project Muse)
jstor.org

CONTENTS

Editors' Note

Languages and literature—primarily poetry, song, and narrative, whether oral or written—bring us close to the truth of a place. In *Cascadia: The Life and Breath of the World,* they help us to experience the bio-cultural region called Cascadia. The name for this region was made popular in the 1970s, when it was used by geologist Bates McKee. It was taken up in the 1990s by William Henkel, who in his article "Cascadia: A State of (Various) Minds" noted that thinking in terms of ecological regions, such as Cascadia, had inspired a group of loosely associated philosophers, poets, biologists, conservationists, and social activists—all referred to now as bio-regionalists. Influenced by First Nations, eco-spiritual activists, and trans-Pacific thought, this diverse group has stimulated an international appreciation of the region's languages, literature, ecological practices, and environmentalism. As Vancouver Island poet Kim Goldberg has pointed out, their writing is not so much "nature-minded" as "ecologically sensitive," meaning that their ecological aesthetics and poetics are socially, politically, and spiritually engaged.

For decades, thinkers such as agronomist Wes Jackson and poet Gary Snyder have stressed the importance of regional languages in building bio-cultural communities, networks, and coalitions. Poet John Carroll, of British Columbia's Fraser Valley, says that writers attuned to the ecology of the Pacific Northwest come together through the "tradition of a shared vocabulary . . . ; like rain absorbed into the soil, it becomes intimate with the essence of the land." Olympic Peninsula sculptor and poet Tom Jay writes that "A word is a clipped breath, a bit of spirit—*inspire, expire*—wherein we hear the weather. Our 'tongues' taste the world we eat."

Many Cascadian poets and writers belong to an intercultural literary ecology—what poet, linguist, typographer, and translator Robert Bringhurst refers to as an eco-linguistics for the global age. In their work, these authors give palpable meaning to concepts of *place* and seek to create conversations that nourish, fortify, and prepare our communities for the inevitable cultural turns ahead. By blurring artificially constructed political borders—while remaining mindful of an old world heritage—they are fostering a new world ecological awareness that is fundamentally a spiritual awareness. In *The Tree of Meaning,* Bringhurst reminds us that

Cannery. 1929. Graphite on paper by Emily Carr. Royal British Columbia Museum, British Columbia Archives. PDP08744

Cultures don't mingle by watering each other down. They mingle by thickening the soup, infusing one another with a richer store of references and models, adding facets and dimensions to each other.

Geographically, Cascadia's western boundary begins in southwest Alaska, follows the coastline of British Columbia and the Pacific Northwest states of Washington and Oregon, and terminates at Cape Mendocino, in northern California. The southern border snakes northeast, back into Oregon, then bends southeast into Nevada and eastward into Wyoming, according to David McCloskey, founder of the Cascadia Institute and regarded by some as the "father" of Cascadia's bio-region. Though Cascadia's precise eastern border is disputed, McCloskey and others suggest that it follows the Continental Divide northwest, into the region that includes the salmon runs in the Yukon River.

Recently, Washington State poet Bill Yake elaborated on the understanding of Cascadia as a cultural region in Alfred L. Kroeber's 1939 book *Cultural and Natural Areas of Native North America:*

> [Kroeber] imagines the northwest coast as cultures ranging from the Tlingit of southern Alaska to the Yurok, Karok and Hupa of the lower Klamath River drainage of northwestern California. These cultures grew out of settings that provided similar foods including salmon and other sources of marine fat and protein and natural materials: mussel shell knives and harpoon valves, a similar range of forest materials including cedar, medicines, berries. There would undoubtedly be similar approximations from other geographic regions around the Cascadia-Pacific world.

Yake also notes that Gary Snyder defines the region by the range of the Douglas-fir, which he calls "the definitive tree of the Pacific Northwest."

> This outline, [Snyder] says, has its "northern limit...around the Skeena River in British Columbia. It is found west of the [Cascade Mountain Range] crest through Washington, Oregon, and Northern California. The southern coastal limit of Douglas Fir is about the same as that of salmon, which do not run south of the Big Sur River.... [This] outline describes the boundary of a larger natural region that runs across three states and one international border."

In "Reinhabitation," Snyder suggests that communities in Cascadia think in a way that transcends political boundaries and is unified by their experience with and knowledge of local flora and fauna, and the water, air, mineral, and nutrient cycles that are shared within the region.

Experiencing the intensity and power of the wilderness inevitably leads to consciousness of the devastation of old-growth forests, salmon breeding grounds, pristine lakes, and other icons of the region. It was perhaps no accident that the Greenpeace movement was founded in Cascadia.

The importance of preserving the wilderness has always been recognized by the First Nations peoples. Chief William Sepass, for example, recited stories of the creation and the proper relationship between humans and the non-human world. More recently, Chief Dan George and Louis Owens, among others, have spoken for the wilderness. To properly appreciate Cascadia, we need to understand the profound and abiding relationships that First Nations peoples have with their environment.

From this perspective, we recognize our bio-cultural commonalities, and these commonalities in turn transform us into whole human beings who are *at home*. "Critical thinking and a heart of compassion," Snyder says, "value a sense of 'all beings' and the sense of the deep interconnections of all phenomena."

Chinese poet Stonehouse, who lived in the fourteenth century, expresses a belief in interconnectedness similar to that of the Coast Salish culture. As made vivid by Cascadian translator Red Pine, Stonehouse's poems express a notion like that of *shexwli,* which in Halq'eméylem—a language of British Columbia's lower Fraser River region—suggests the essence of all life, the spirit in everything. Red Pine is not out of place among the many writers in Cascadia who are steeped in traditional Buddhist thought; Snyder's influence has been instrumental in encouraging an awareness of Asian concepts, the principles of dharma, and Gaian Deep Ecology.

The writings in this volume, forged in Cascadia and the Pacific Northwest, offer ways to reimagine culture, community, ecology, language, knowledge, and the life of the spirit. *Cascadia: The Life and Breath of the World* addresses the wasteful and destructive practices of the present and proposes creating a community of goodwill that will collectively advocate the preservation of Cascadia and our planet, in all their bio-cultural depth and breadth. In the words of theologian Richard Neuhaus, "We change a culture by creating a community."

As Rex Weyler reminds us in his piece, "Nature's Apprentice: A Metanarrative for Aging Empires,"

> Nature is not a "thing," but a process, a set of relationships among dynamic systems that are co-creative, coevolutionary, and interdependent. Nature is a system of systems, and the complexity unfolds at orders of magnitude and in eons of time beyond our conventional awareness.

In order to grasp nature in all its complexity—in order to understand the region in all its temporal, biological, and physical multiplicity—we need to hear Cascadia's poetry and songs, listen to its stories, and preserve and share them.

First Nations poet Lee Maracle, granddaughter of Chief Dan George, speaks in her poem "I'm Home Again" of coming back to her culture and rediscovering it through the ways of her elders. The "urgent watery alone-ness / only writers feel,"

> Weaving snippets of dream words we selected to play with into the
> loom of our
> imaginations
> harnessing language
> to plough new soil,
> create new story, is thick, omnipresent here.

She expresses thanks for the "consideration and hospitality" of her elders:

> Haitchka for leading me here
> Haitchka my dead for fussing over language for me
> Haitchka to those who came before me,
> for story,
> for song,
> for dance.

Cascadia: The Life and Breath of the World is an attempt to discover the possibilities of a future that is shaped deliberately, instead of one that relies upon the happenstance of technology to undo our mistakes and mindless destructiveness. We start with language, with stories, poems, and narrative, to map the truth of this place called Cascadia.

Mahalo to the following individuals, who were critically helpful in different ways: Yvon Dandurand, Paul Falardeau, Linda Dahl, Michelle Rhodes, Brad Whittaker, Wayne Martin, Joseph Blake, and Bill Yake.

Trevor Carolan
University of the Fraser Valley
Abbotsford, British Columbia

There are many kinds of activism. One of the most powerful is activism of the ethical imagination, when writers and artists change people's minds by reflecting the world back to them with fresh clarity. They remind us why we need to restore ethics and reverence in our lives, and demonstrate through song and narrative how to be honorable companions with the non-human world.

The majority of authors and artists in this volume on Cascadia are activists of the imagination, which also means they strengthen our conviction that conserving and protecting habitats, species, languages, and cultures are urgent enterprises. They do this, as a first step, by deepening our bonds of affection—our emotional and empathic ties—with this extraordinary bio-cultural region.

After searching for an appropriate subtitle of this collection, we settled upon *The Life and Breath of the World*. The words *breath* and *life* have several levels of significance. *Breath* recognizes the respiration of the trees, animals, mountains, rivers, fishes, fungi, and microscopic creatures in Cascadia. *Breath* also refers to the songs, languages, and stories of the inhabitants—both Native and non-Native—when they speak for and with this world.

The Secwepemc Nation (also known as the Shuswap people) traditionally say that language is a gift from the Creator to humans and non-humans alike. Secwepemc stories maintain that the natural world speaks to humans in its own languages, and provides us with important information if we listen. This concept may seem fanciful or sentimental to the Western mind. To the Secwepemc, however, its validity is proven in the way the cricket announces when it is time to begin catching salmon; the way the seasonal blossoming of the wild strawberry says that a certain type of fish is ready to be caught; and the way the vegetation, by stating its various names, tells a traveler where he is.

In the days before Western contact, the Secwepemc comprised thirty bands, and their traditional territory in the interior plateau was vast: from the western slopes of the Rocky Mountains to the Fraser River, and from the upper Fraser in the north to the Arrow Lakes in the south. One of their traditional stories is about the time Coyote went into the mountains for a gathering of the animals. (This tale came from John Jules, of the Kamloops band of the Secwepemc Nation, and was translated by the late Ida Williams, of the North Thompson band.) In the games the animals played, Coyote defeated all of them. Raven, a fellow trickster, retaliated by stealing Coyote's eyes so that he wouldn't be able to find his way home. Blindly, Coyote felt around until he found some kinnikinnick berries and put them in his eye sockets. They helped only a little as Coyote stumbled down the slope. He asked the trees and plants their names, and their answers told him where he was on the mountain, how close he was to water, and other things about his location. When the Saskatoon bush told Coyote its name, he realized he was almost home. This story illustrates ecological intelligence: when we listen to nature, we don't need a calendar, map, or almanac to find our way home. As Tom Jay writes in his essay "The Salmon of the Heart," humans and non-humans in mythic time belonged to "an ethical system that resounded in every corner of their locale. The Aboriginal landscape was a democracy of spirits where everyone listened, careful not to offend the *resource* they were a part of."

The cover of this volume shows a photograph of a Secwepemc woman, taken in 1898 near Kamloops, in the Thompson Valley. The place is near the confluence of the north and south branches of the Thompson River, about two hundred miles northeast of Vancouver. The valley is very unlike western Cascadia. Many of the pieces in this volume focus on the west: the grandeur of the ancient forests, waterfalls, rivers, and rugged coastline. There, on the Pacific Ocean side of the Coast Mountains, moist air flowing off the sea encounters the high mountain ranges and turns to rain, creating one of the wettest places in North America: the average annual rainfall in the snowy peaks of the Coast Mountains is ninety inches.

The Secwepemc woman places us to the east, on the Interior Plateau. Here, in the rain shadow of the high coastal ranges, the climate becomes markedly drier. On the upper parts of the plateau are subalpine fir, Englemann spruce, larch, and whitebark pine. But at lower elevations, in the Thompson and Okanagan valleys, the landscape is arid, with an annual rainfall of only nine inches. Farther east are shrub-steppe and prairie lands that extend to the edge of the Columbia Basin. The grasslands of the Southern Interior once stretched into Washington, Montana, and North Dakota, merging with the Great Prairies.

When the photograph was taken, the woman's appearance was probably not typical of most Secwepemc women, and she probably is posing for the ethnographer who took her picture. In fact, by 1898, the Secwepemc people had barely survived the coming of European settlers—the Gold Rush migrants in the 1850s, followed closely by horse and cattle ranchers who encouraged the establishment of reservations to keep Native people off their fenced land. The introduction of cattle destroyed the grasslands. In pre-contact days, the bunchgrass was said to have been for miles upon miles "belly-high to a horse," and the eastern-facing watersheds had healthy wetlands that supported great biological, and cultural diversity. The ranching, overgrazing, fencing, and diversion of water from high on the slopes changed all this. The riparian, belly-high grasslands were replaced with low-growing shrubs, rough fescue, bluegrass, and weeds. By 1900, most of the grassland was gone.

On this land, the Secwepemc and other First Nations tribes had hunted elk, moose, and caribou and harvested over a hundred species of plants for food, medicine, ceremonial purposes, and daily use. Today, we would call such peoples "low-impact agriculturists," fishermen, and hunters. The white settlers brought not only bad land management, but also smallpox. In two generations—between 1850 and 1903—epidemics reduced the Secwepemc populations by seventy percent. Of the original thirty bands, only seventeen survived.

A 2007 census counted a population of only 8,475 Secwepemc. Because the population was decimated, the language, Secwepemctsin, also became endangered. A 1999 survey reported that fewer than four percent of the population were native speakers of their own language.

But Secwepemctsin is being revitalized by programs such as the Chief Atahm School on the Adams Lake reserve, where students get full immersion from kindergarten through grade seven. Many enter Chief Atahm

School from the Cseyseten Family Language Centre, a Secwepemctsin "language nest" for infants and preschoolers. Typically, about fifty students attend Chief Atahm School each year. And while many children cannot speak Secwepemctsin at home, because their parents are not fluent, the school has been operating for over twenty years and progress is being made. The Secwepemcs' situation is not unlike that of many other First Nations people in Canada and the United States.

The story in this volume that gives a sense of the Southern Interior Plains of Cascadia is "In the Great Bend of the Souris River," by Barry Lopez. The grassland of the Southern Interior Plains, between the Rocky Mountains and the Coast Ranges, includes the vast Secwepemc Territory. To the east are the Great Plains of Alberta and to the south the Northern Plains of the United States. Wild horses were plentiful in Secwepemc Territory by 1807, and First Nations people of the Interior Plains were master horsemen, following the grasslands south on distant journeys to visit, hunt, and trade.

The men Adrian Whippet encounters in Lopez's story are entirely at home in this landscape, and he regards them with the same respect he feels for the place; they belong to it in a fundamental way, as he does not. In them, however, he recognizes fully an image of what his spirit longs for: to inhabit this place with his whole being. Whippet experiences—call it grace—an intersection with a world that is past but, potentially, not entirely lost. Through the power of his attention and ethical imagination, there is the possibility that in some essential sense it can be recovered.

Many people have our gratitude for generously supporting this volume. Among them are the original publishers of some of the pieces reprinted in *Cascadia: The Life and Breath of the World.* We also wish to acknowledge the University of the Fraser Valley, located in traditional Stó:lō territory, for its support and help in distributing *Cascadia* to First Nations community centers and libraries in British Columbia. To all, we extend our thanks.

We would also like to acknowledge the project coordinated by Judith Berman, of the University of Victoria, and Aaron Glass, of the Bard Graduate Center, to create an annotated digital edition of Franz Boas's 1897 monograph *The Social Organization and the Secret Societies of the Kwakiutl Indians.* Their work led us to the image on our back cover of an important mask of the Nuxalk (Bella Coola) people. For a more complete description of the image and the project, please see the note at the back of this volume.

Frank Stewart
Honolulu, Hawai'i

Beach. 1929?
Graphite on paper by Emily Carr.
Royal British Columbia Museum,
British Columbia Archives.
PDP05695

Maps of Dreams

The rivers of northeast British Columbia are at their most splendid in the early fall. The northern tributaries of the Peace achieve an extraordinary beauty; they, and their small feeder creeks and streams, are cold yet warm—perfect reflections of autumn. The banks are multi-colored and finely textured; clear water runs in smooth, shallow channels. The low water of late summer reveals gravel and sand beaches, textures and colors that are at other times of the year concealed. Such low water levels mean that all these streams are easily crossed, and so become the throughways along the valleys that have always been at the heart of the Indians' use of the land. In October those who know these creeks can find corners, holes, back eddies where rainbow trout and Dolly Varden abound.

The hunter of moose, deer, caribou (and in historic times, buffalo) does not pursue these large animals without regard to more abundant and predictable, if less satisfying, sources of food. The man who tracks and snares game, and whose success depends on his constant movement, cannot afford to fail for much more than two days running. On the third day of hunger he will find it hard to walk far or fast enough: hunger reduces the efficiency of the hunt. Hunger is inimical to effective hunting on foot; yet continuance of the hunt was, not long ago, the only means to avoid hunger. This potential source of insecurity for a hunter is resolved by his ability to combine two kinds of hunting: he pursues large ungulates in areas and with movements that bring him close to locations where he knows rabbits, grouse, or fish are to be found. These are security, but not staples. Hunting for large animals is the most efficient, the most rational activity for anyone who lives in the boreal forest. But such a hunter would be foolhardy indeed to hunt for the larger animals without a careful and strategic eye on the availability of the smaller ones.

In October, only a month after Joseph Patsah [elder of the Beaver clan] and his family first spoke to us about their lives, they suggested that I go hunting with them—and, of course, fishing. By now the rainbow trout would surely be plentiful and fat. Joseph said that he also hoped we could go far enough to see the cross [a medicine cross carved into a tree]. One evening, then, he proposed that we should all set out the next day for Blue-stone Creek.

Between a proposal to go hunting and actual departure there is a large and perplexing divide. In the white man's world, whether urban or rural, after such a proposal there would be plans and planning; conversation about timing and practical details would also help to build enthusiasm. In Joseph's household, in all the Indian households of northeast British Columbia, and perhaps among hunters generally, planning is so muted as to seem nonexistent. Maybe it is better understood by a very different name, which is still to suppose that planning of some kind does in fact take place.

Protests against the hunting way of life have often paid hostile attention to its seemingly haphazard, irrational, and improvident nature. Before the mind's eye of agricultural or industrial man loom the twin spectres of hunger and homelessness, whose fearsome imminence is escaped only in the bright sunlight of planning. Planners consider many possibilities, weigh methods, review timing, and at least seek to deduce what is best. To this end they advocate reason and temperance, and, most important, they are thrifty and save. These ideas and dispositions, elevated to an ideal in the economics of nineteenth-century and secular Puritanism, live on in the reaction of industrial society to hunters—and in the average Canadian's reaction to Indians. And a reaction of this kind means that a person, even if inclined to be sympathetic to hunters and hunting, has immense difficulty in understanding what planning means for hunters of the North.

Joseph and his family float possibilities. "Maybe we should go to Copper Creek. Bet you lots of moose up there." Or, "Could be caribou right now near Black Flats." Or, "I bet you no deer this time down on the Reserve . . ." Somehow a general area is selected from a gossamer of possibilities, and from an accumulation of remarks comes something rather like a consensus. No, that is not really it: rather, a sort of prediction, a combined sense of where we *might* go "tomorrow." Yet the hunt will not have been planned, nor any preparations started, and apparently no one is committed to going. Moreover, the floating conversation will have alighted on several irreconcilable possibilities, or have given rise to quasi-predictions. It is as if the predictions are all about other people—or are not quite serious. Although the mood is still one of wait and see, at the end of the day, at the close of much slow and gentle talk about this and that, a strong feeling has arisen about the morning: we shall go to Bluestone, maybe as far as the cross. We shall look for trout as well as moose. A number of individuals agree that they will go. But come morning, nothing is ready. No one has made any practical, formal plans. As often as not—indeed, more often than not—something quite new has drifted into conversations, other predictions have been tentatively reached, a new consensus appears to be forming. As it often seems, everyone has changed his mind.

The way to understand this kind of decision making, as also to live by and even share it, is to recognize that some of the most important variables are subtle, elusive, and extremely hard or impossible to assess with finality. The Athapaskan hunter will move in a direction and at a time that are determined by a sense of weather (to indicate a variable that is easily grasped, if all too easily oversimplified by the one word) and by a sense of rightness. He will also have ideas about animal movement, his own and others' patterns of land use . . . But already the nature of the hunter's decision making is being misrepresented by this kind of listing. To disconnect the variables, to compartmentalize the thinking, is to fail to acknowledge its sophistication and completeness. The hunter considers variables as a composite, in parallel, and with the help of a blending of the metaphysical and the obviously pragmatic. To make a good, wise, sensible hunting choice is to accept the interconnection of all possible factors, and to avoid the mistake of seeking rationally to focus on any one consideration that is held as primary. What is more, the decision is made in the doing: there is no step or pause between theory and practice. As a consequence, the decision—like the action from which it is inseparable—is always alterable (and therefore may not properly even be termed a decision). The hunter moves in a chosen direction; but, highly sensitive to so many shifting considerations, he is always ready to change his direction.

Planning, as other cultures understand the notion, is at odds with this kind of sensitivity and would confound such flexibility. The hunter, alive to constant movements of nature, spirits, and human moods, maintains a way of doing things that repudiates a firm plan and any precise or specified understanding with others of what he is going to do. His course of action is not—must not be—a matter of predetermination. If a plan constitutes a decision about the right procedure or action, and the decision is congruent with the action, then there is no space left for a "plan," only for a bundle of open-ended and nonrational possibilities. Activity enters so far into this kind of planning as to undermine any so-called plans.

All this is by way of context or background for the seemingly straightforward proposal that we should set out the next morning to hunt moose and fish for trout at Bluestone Creek. Since there are many such apparent decisions, it is important that they be understood for what they are: convenient—but often misleading—reductions to a narrative convention of intimate and unfamiliar patterns of hunters' thought and behavior.

"The next morning" came several times before we set out in the direction of Bluestone. Several individuals said they would come, but did not; others said they would not come, but did. Eventually, we drove in my rented pickup to a stretch of rolling forests, where hillsides and valley were covered by dense blankets of poplar, aspen, and birch, and occasional stands of pine or spruce. After studied consideration of three places, Joseph and Atsin chose a campsite a short walk from a spring that created a narrow pool of good water in a setting of damp and frosted leaves. There we camped, in a complex of shelters and one tent around a long central fire. It was a place the hunters had often used, and it had probably been an Indian campsite off and on for centuries. It was a clearing among thin-stemmed pine, a woodland tangled and in places made dense by a great number of deadfalls lying at all heights and angles to the ground.

Night fell as we completed the camp. The fire was lit and was darkly reflected by these dead trees that criss-crossed against the forest. Long before dawn (it cannot have been later than five o'clock), the men awoke. The fire rekindled, they sat around it and began the enormous and pro-tracted breakfast that precedes every day's hunting: rabbit stew, boiled eggs, bannock, toasted slices of white bread, barbecued moose meat, whatever happens to be on hand, and cup after cup of strong, sweet tea. A little later, women and children joined the men at the fire and ate no less heartily.

As they ate, the light changed from a slight glimmer, the relief to predawn blackness, to the first brightness that falters without strength at the top of the trees. As the light grew, the men speculated about where to go, sifting evidence they had accumulated from whatever nearby places they had visited since their arrival. Everyone had walked to fetch water, cut wood, or simply to stretch the legs a little. Atsin, at the end of a short walk that morning, returned with a rabbit. He had taken it in a snare evi-dently set as soon as we arrived the evening before. It was white already, its fur change a dangerously conspicuous anticipation of a winter yet to come. Conversation turned to rabbits. All the men had noticed a prolifera-tion of runs and droppings. It was an excellent year for rabbit, the fifth or sixth in a cycle of seven improving years. It might be a good idea to hunt in some patches of young evergreens, along trails that led towards the river. There could be more rabbits there. Lots of rabbits. Always good to eat lots of rabbit stew. And there could be rainbow trout in that place, below the old cabin, and in other spots. Or maybe it would be good to go high up in the valley . . . This exchange of details and ideas continued off and on throughout the meal. When it had finally ended and everyone had reflected a good deal on the day's possibilities, the men set off. Perhaps it was clear to them where and why, but which possibilities represented a starting point were not easily understood by an outsider.

Atsin's younger brother Sam set off alone, at right angles to a trail that led to the river by way of a place said to be particularly good for rabbits. Two others, Jimmy Wolf and Charlie Fellow—both relations of Joseph's wife, Liza—also set off at an angle, but in the opposite direction. I fol-lowed Atsin along another, more winding trail. Liza and her oldest child, Tommy, together with two other women and their small children, made their way behind the men on the main trail; Atsin's son David attached himself to Brian Akattah and his ten-year-old nephew Peter. The choice of partner and trail was, if possible, less obviously planned than direction or hunting objective. Everyone was plainly free to go where and with whom he or she liked. As I became more familiar with this kind of hunt, though, I found that some individuals nearly always hunted alone, whereas others liked a companion, at least at the outset. A sense of great personal freedom was evident from the first. No one gives orders; everyone is, in some fundamental way, responsible to and for himself.

The distance between camp and the particular bend in the river that had been selected as the best possible fishing place was no more than a mile and a half. No time had been appointed for a rendezvous. Indeed, clock time is of no significance here. (Only Joseph had a watch, and it was never used for hunting purposes.) Everyone nonetheless appeared from the woods and converged on the fishing spot within minutes of one another. This coordination of activities is not easily understood, although it testified to the absence of big game, of moose, deer, or bear. If any of the hunters had located fresh tracks, he would have been long gone into the woods. Atsin, who seemed to be an expert at the job, appeared with two rabbits he had shot after glimpsing their helpless whiteness in the dun-colored undergrowth. But fishing was going to supply the next meal.

The river at this place flows in a short curve around a wooded promontory that juts from the main forest. Both sides are deeply eroded banks, where sandy rubble is given some short-lived firmness by exposed tree roots. On the far side the landscape is barer, with meadowy, more open land for fifty yards before the forested slopes rise towards the mountains. Where the trail meets the creek (sometimes no wider than ten rushing yards), it deepens into a pool. There, the water is held back by a shallow rib of rock over which it quickens and races to the next pool.

The fishing spot itself turned out to be a platform of jumbled logs that must have been carried by the stream in flood, and then piled by currents until they reshaped the banks themselves. The sure-footed can find precarious walkways across this latticework platform. At their ends the logs offer a view down into the deepest part of the hole. Through the sharp clearness of this water, rainbow trout could be seen, dark shadows hovering or moving very slowly among long-sunken logs and roots. Joseph studied the water and the fish, then produced a nylon line. It was wound tightly around a small piece of shaped wood—a spool that he carried in his pocket—wrapped in cloth. Along with the line were four or five hooks (size 6 or 8) and a chunk of old bacon. On his way along the trail he had broken off a long thin branch, and by the time we had arrived at the creek, he had already stripped off its side twigs, peeled away the bark, and broken it to the right length. He tied some line to this homemade rod and handed other lengths to Brian and David. The three of them then clambered along the log platform, found more or less firm places at its edge, and began to fish.

The baited hooks were lowered straight down until they hung just above the streambed. They did not hover there for long. Almost immediately the fish were being caught. The men could watch a trout swim towards a bait and, with one firm turn of its body, part suck and part grab the hook. The fisherman, with a single upward swing of the rod, would pull it straight out of the water and onto the logs. Then each fish was grabbed at and missed, fell off the hook among the logs, was grabbed at again . . . The fish, and the fishermen, could easily slip between the gaps of the platform. As the trout thrashed and leaped about, there were shouts of excitement, advice, and laughter.

The trout were plentiful, as Joseph had said they would be, and fat. One after the other they came flying through the air into someone's hands, then to shore, where Atsin and Liza gutted them. A dozen or more fish, of one or two pounds each, every one of them with a brilliant red patch on its gills and red stripes along its sides—rainbow trout at their most spectacular. Then the fishing slowed down. Enough had been caught. Joseph, Brian, and David climbed back to the bank. We sat around the fires to eat rabbit stew and cook some of the fish.

By this time it was early afternoon, but the meal was unhurried. Perhaps the success of the moose hunt was doubtful, while a good supply of rabbit and fish had already been secured. Conversation turned again to places where it might be worth hunting, directions in which we might go; many possibilities were suggested, and no apparent decision was made. But when the meal ended, the men began to prepare themselves for another hunt. Having eaten and apparently rested and stared into the fire, one by one the hunters, unhurried and apparently indecisive, got up, strolled a little way, and came back. Then each began to fix his clothes, check a gun—began to get ready. By the time the last of the hunters was thus occupied, some had begun to drift away in one direction or another. After a last conversation, the rest of them left, except for Joseph, Brian's wife, Mary, Liza, and the children, who stayed by the fire. Perhaps the afternoon was going to be long and hard.

This time a group of men walked in single file, Atsin in front. After a short distance, one went his own way, then others did so, until each of them had taken a separate direction. I again stayed close to Atsin, who made his way—often pushing his way—through dense bushes and small willows, along the riverbank. He said once, when we paused to rest and look around and think, that it was disappointing to find so few signs of moose, but there might be more fishing.

It must have been an hour before the men regrouped, this time on a high and eroded sandbar. The beach here was strewn with well-dried driftwood. Atsin and Robert Fellows began to gather enough of this wood to make a large fire. Brian fetched water for tea. Atsin's brother Sam, together with Jimmy Wolf, cut fishing poles, fixed up lines, went a short way upstream to a spot where the water turned and deepened against the bank, and began to fish. Their lines hung in the water, baits out of sight and judged to be close to the bottom. From time to time they changed the angle of their rods to adjust the depth at which they fished; and by taking advantage of the pole's being longer than the line, they periodically pulled the bait clear of the water, checked that all was well in place, and then dropped it easily back to where the fish should be.

But the fish were not there, or not hungry, or not to be fooled. Sam and Jimmy waited. There were no sudden upward whips of the pole, no bites, no shouts, no laughter. The others sprawled around the fire, watching the two fishermen, drinking tea, limiting themselves to an occasional squinting look towards the river and remarks about the dearth of game. The afternoon was warm and still. There seemed to be no reason for any great activity. Soon Jimmy decided to abandon the river in favor of a rest beside the fire. Sam forded the stream, crossed the sandbar, and tried his luck on the other side. From where we sat and lay we could see his head and shoulders, and the lift and drop of his long rod. It was easy enough to tell whether or not he was catching anything; he was not. Moments, minutes, even hours of complete stillness: this was not time that could be measured. Hunters at rest, at ease, in wait, are able to discover and enjoy a special form of relaxation. There is a minimum of movement—a hand reaches out for a mug, an adjustment is made to the fire—and whatever is said hardly interrupts the silence, as if words and thoughts can be harmonized without any of the tensions of dialogue. Yet the hunters are a long way from sleep; not even the atmosphere is soporific. They wait, watch, consider. Above all they are still and receptive, prepared for whatever insight or realization may come to them, and ready for whatever stimulus to action might arise. This state of attentive waiting is perhaps as close as people can come to the falcon's suspended flight, when the bird, seemingly motionless, is ready to plummet in decisive action. To the outsider, who has followed along and tried to join in, it looks for all the world as if the hunters have forgotten why they are there. In this restful way hunters can spend many hours, sometimes days, eating, waiting, thinking.

The quality of this resting by the fire can be seen and felt when it is very suddenly charged, just as the nature of the falcon's hover becomes clear when it dives. Among hunters, the emergence from repose may be slow or abrupt. But in either case a particular state of mind, a special way of being, has come to an end. One or two individuals move faster and more purposively, someone begins to prepare meat to cook, someone fetches a gun to work on, and conversation resumes its ordinary mode.

This transformation took place that afternoon around the fire on the pebbled beach at just the time Sam gave up his fishing and began to walk back towards us. Atsin, Jimmy, and Robert all moved to new positions. Robert stood with his back to us, watching Sam's approach, while Atsin and Jimmy squatted where they could look directly at me.

In retrospect it seems clear that they felt the right time had come for something. Everyone seemed to give the few moments it took for this change to occur some special importance. Plainly the men had something to say, and in their own time, in their own way, they were going to say it. Signs and movements suggested that the flow of events that had begun in Joseph's home and Atsin's cabin, and continued with the fishing at Bluestone Creek, was about to be augmented. Something of significance to the men here was going to happen. I suddenly realized that everyone was watching me. Sam joined the group, but said nothing. Perhaps he, as a younger man, was now leaving events to his elders: to Atsin, Jimmy, and Robert. There was a brief silence made awkward by expectancy, though an awkward pause is a very rare thing among people who accept that there is no need to escape from silence, no need to use words as a way to avoid one another, no need to obscure the real.

Atsin broke this silence. He spoke at first of the research: "I bet some guys make big maps. Lots of work, these maps. Nobody knows that. White men don't know that." Silence again. Then Robert continued: "Yeah, lots of maps. All over this country we hunt. Fish too. Trapping places. Nobody knows that. White men don't know that." Then Jimmy spoke: "Indian guys, old-timers, they make maps too." With these words, the men introduced their theme. The tone was friendly, but the words were spoken with intensity and firmness. The men seemed apprehensive, as if anxious to be very clearly understood—though nothing said so far required such concern. Once again, it is impossible to render verbatim all that they eventually said. I had no tape recorder, and memory is imperfect. But even a verbatim account would fail to do justice to their meaning. Here, then, in summaries and glimpses, is what the men had in mind to say.

Some old-timers, men who became famous for their powers and skills, had been great dreamers. Hunters and dreamers. They did not hunt as most people now do. They did not seek uncertainly for the trails of animals whose movements we can only guess at. No, they located their prey in dreams, found their trails, and made dreamkills. Then, the next day, or a few days later, whenever it seemed auspicious to do so, they could go out, find the trail, re-encounter the animal, and collect the kill. Maybe, said Atsin, you think this is all nonsense, just so much bullshit. Maybe you don't think this power is possible. Few people understand.

The old-timers who were strong dreamers knew many things that are not easy to understand. People—white people, young people—yes, they laugh at such skills. But they do not know. The Indians around this country know a lot about power. In fact, everyone has had some experience of it. The fact that dream-hunting works has been proved many times.

A few years ago a hunter dreamed a cow moose kill. A fine, fat cow. He was so pleased with the animal, so delighted to make this dreamkill, that he marked the animal's hooves. Now he would be sure to recognize it when he went on the coming hunt. The next day, when he went out into the bush, he quickly found the dream-trail. He followed it and came to a large cow moose. Sure enough, the hooves bore his marks. Everyone saw them. All the men around the fire had been told about the marks, and everyone on the Reserve had come to look at those hooves when the animal was butchered and brought into the people's homes.

And not only that fat cow moose—many such instances are known to the people, whose marks on the animal or other indications show that there was no mistaking, no doubts about the efficacy of such dreams. Do you think this is all lies? No, this is power they had, something they knew how to use. This was their way of doing things, the right way. They understood, those old-timers, just where all the animals came from. The trails converge, and if you were a very strong dreamer you could discover this, and see the source of trails, the origin of game. Dreaming revealed them. Good hunting depended upon such knowledge.

Today it is hard to find men who can dream this way. There are too many problems. Too much drinking. Too little respect. People are not good enough now. Maybe there will again be strong dreamers when these problems are overcome. Then more maps will be made. New maps.

Oh yes, Indians made maps. You would not take any notice of them. You might say such maps are crazy. But maybe the Indians would say that is what your maps are: the same thing. Different maps from different people—different *ways*. Old-timers made maps of trails, ornamented them with lots of fancy. The good people. None of this is easy to understand. But good men, the really good men, could dream of more than animals. Sometimes they saw heaven and its trails. Those trails are hard to see, and few men have had such dreams. Even if they could see dream-trails to heaven, it would be hard to explain them. You draw maps of the land, show everyone where to go. You explain the hills, the rivers, the trails from here to Hudson Hope, the roads. Maybe you make maps of where the hunters go and where the fish can be caught. That is not easy. But easier, for sure, than drawing out the trails to heaven. You may laugh at these maps of the trails to heaven, but they were done by the good men who had the heaven dream, who wanted to tell the truth. They worked hard on their truth.

Atsin had done most of the talking thus far. The others interjected a few words and comments, agreeing or elaborating a little. Jimmy told about the cow moose with marked hooves. All of them offered some comparisons between their own and others' maps. And the men's eyes never ceased to remain fixed on me: were they being understood? Disregarded? Thought ridiculous? They had chosen this moment for these explanations, yet no one was entirely secure in it. Several times, Atsin paused and waited, perhaps to give himself a chance to sense or absorb the reaction to his words. These were intense, but not tense, hiatuses. Everyone was reassuring himself that his seriousness was being recognized. That was all they needed to continue.

The longest of these pauses might have lasted as much as five minutes. During it the fire was rebuilt. It seemed possible, for a few moments, that they had finished, and that their attention was now returning to trout, camp, and the hunt. But the atmosphere hardly altered, and Jimmy quite abruptly took over where Atsin had left off.

The few good men who had the heaven dream were like the Fathers, Catholic priests, men who devoted themselves to helping others with that essential knowledge to which ordinary men and women have limited access. (Roman Catholic priests have drifted in and out of the lives of all the region's Indians, leaving behind fragments of their knowledge and somewhat rarefied and idealized versions of what they had to preach.)

Most important of all, a strong dreamer can tell others how to get to heaven. We all have need of the trail, or complex of trails, but, unlike other important trails, the way to heaven will have been seen in dreams that only a few, special individuals have had. Maps of heaven are thus important. And they must be good, complete maps. Heaven is reached only by careful avoidance of the wrong trails. These must also be shown so that the traveler can recognize and avoid them. How can we know the general direction we should follow? How can anyone who has not dreamed the whole route begin to locate himself on such a map? When Joseph, or any of the other men, began to draw a hunting map, he had first to find his way. He did this by recognizing features, by fixing points of reference, and then, once he was oriented to the familiar and to the scale or manner in which the familiar was reproduced, he could begin to add his own layers of detailed information. But how can anyone begin to find a way on a map of trails to heaven, across a terrain that ordinary hunters do not experience in everyday activities or even in their dream-hunts?

The route to heaven is not wholly unfamiliar, however. As it happens, heaven is to one side of, and at the same level as, the point where the trails to animals all meet. Many men know where this point is, or at least some of its approach trails, from their own hunting dreams. Hunters can in this way find a basic reference, and once they realize that heaven is in a particular relation to this far more familiar centre, the map as a whole can be read. If this is not enough, a person can take a map with him; some old-timers who made or who were given maps of the trails to heaven choose to have a map buried with them. They can thus remind themselves which ways to travel if the actual experience of the trail proves to be too confusing. Others are given a corner of a map that will help reveal the trail to them. And even those who do not have any powerful dreams are shown the best maps of the route to heaven. The discoveries of the very few most powerful dreamers—and some of the dreamers have been women—are periodically made available to everyone.

The person who wishes to dream must take great care, even if he dreams only of the hunt. He must lie in the correct orientation, with his head towards the rising sun. There should be no ordinary trails, no human pathways, between his pillow and the bush. These would be confusing to the self that travels in dreams towards important and unfamiliar trails which can lead to a kill. Not much of this can be mapped—only the trail to heaven has been drawn up. There has been no equivalent need to make maps to share other important information.

Sometime, said Jimmy Wolf, you will see one of these maps. There are some of them around. Then the competence and strength of the old-timers who drew them will be unquestioned. Different trails can be explained, and heaven can be located on them. Yes, they were pretty smart, the men who drew them. Smarter than any white man in these parts and smarter than Indians of today. Perhaps, said Atsin, in the future there will be men good enough to make new maps of heaven—but not just now. There will be changes, he added, and the people will come once again to understand the things that Atsin's father had tried to teach him. In any case, he said, the older men are now trying to explain the powers and dreams of old-timers to the young, indeed to all those who have not been raised with these spiritual riches. For those who do not understand, hunting and life itself are restricted and difficult. So the people must be told everything, and taught all that they need, in order to withstand the incursions presently being made into their way of life, their land, and into their very dreams.

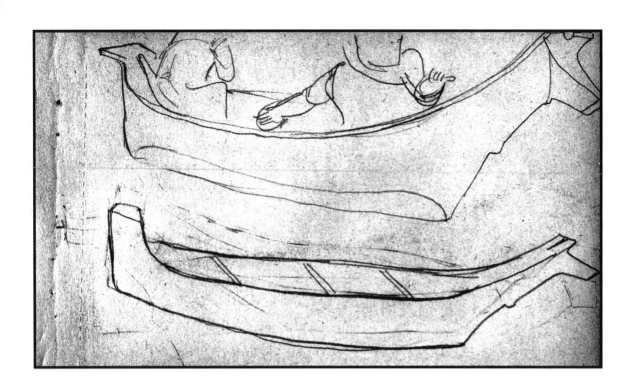

Canoe studies. 1929.
Graphite on paper by Emily Carr.
Royal British Columbia Museum,
British Columbia Archives.
PDP08797

Among the Beautiful

The following is a talk Chief Dan George gave at Western Washington State College (now known as Western Washington University) on May 5, 1971, when he was seventy-one years old. By then, he was nationally recognized for his film and television roles and for speaking out against the dishonorable treatment of First Nations peoples. On June 25, 1971, about seven weeks after this talk was given, he was awarded the prestigious Order of Canada for "services both as an actor and an interpreter of his people."

My very good dear friends, was it only yesterday that men sailed around the moon and it is today they stand upon its barren surface? You and I marvel that men should travel so far and so fast, but if they have travelled far, then I farther. If they have travelled fast, then I faster. For I was born a thousand years ago, born in the culture of bows and arrows. Yet within the space of half a lifetime I was flown across the ages to the culture of the atom bomb; and from bows and arrows to atom bomb is a distance far beyond a flight to the moon.

I was born in an age that loved the things of nature and called it beautiful names like Teslelwhat instead of dried up names like Burrard Inlet. I was born in an age when people loved the things of nature and spoke to it as though it has a soul. I can remember going up the north arm to Indian River with my dad when I was very small. I can remember him watching the sun light fires on Mount Penany as it rose to its peak. I can remember him saying his thanks to it, as he often did, with the Indian word *Hey-mus-hey-snocum*. And then the people came. More and more people came. Like a crushing, rushing wave they came, hurling the years aside, and suddenly I found myself a young man in the midst of the twentieth century.

I found myself and my people adrift in this new age, but not a part of it. Engulfed by its rushing tide but only as a captive eddy, round and round. On little reserves, on plots of land we floated in a kind of gray unreality, unsure of who we were or where we were going, uncertain of our grip on the present, weak in our hope for the future. And that is where we pretty well stand today.

I had a glimpse of something better than this. I knew my people when they lived the old way. I knew them when there was still a dignity in our lives, and a feeling of worth in our outlook. I knew them when there was unspoken confidence in the home, a certain knowledge of the path we walked upon. But we were living on the dying energy of a dying culture—a culture that was slowly losing its forward thrust.

I think it was the suddenness of it all that hurt us so. We did not have time to adjust to the startling upheaval around us. We seemed to have lost what we had without a replacement of it. We did not have time to take this twentieth-century progress and eat it little by little and digest it. It was forced feeding from the start, and our stomachs turned sick.

Do you know what it is like to be without moorings? Do you know what it is like to be in a surrounding that is strange, while all around you, you see strange things? It depresses man, for man must live among the beautiful if his soul is to grow.

Do you know what it's like to have your race belittled, and to come to learn that you are only a burden to the country? Maybe we did not have the skills to make a meaningful contribution, but nobody would wait for us. We were shoved aside, because we were dumb and could not learn.

Do you know what it is like to be without pride in your race, pride in your family, pride and confidence in yourself? What is it like? You do not know. You have never tasted its bitterness.

I shall tell you what it is like. It is like not caring for tomorrow, because what does tomorrow matter? It is like having a reserve that looks like a junkyard, because the beauty of the soul is dead, and why should the soul express an external beauty that does not match it? It is like getting drunk, and for a few brief moments escaping from the ugly reality and feeling a sense of importance. It is most of all like awakening the next morning to the guilt of betrayal because the alcohol did not fill the emptiness, but only dug it deeper.

And now you hold out your hand and you beckon to me to come across the street. But how can I come? I am naked and ashamed. How can I come in dignity? I have no treasures, I have no gifts. What is there in my culture that you value? My poor treasures you can only scorn. Am I then to come as a beggar and receive all from your omnipotent hand?

No! Somehow I must wait. I must delay. I must find myself, I must find my treasure. Then I can say to my wife and to my family, "Listen: they are calling me; they need me. I must go." Then I can walk across the street. I will hold my head high for I can meet you as an equal. I will not scorn you for your demon gifts, and you will not receive me in pity. Pity I can do without. My manhood I cannot do without. I can only come as Chief Capalano came to Captain Vancouver: one sure of his authority, certain of his worth, master of his house, leader of his people.

I shall not come as a cringing object of your pity. I shall come in dignity, or I shall not come at all. And now you talk big words of integration. Does it really exist? Can we talk of integration until there is social integration?

Unless there is integration in hearts and minds, you only have a physical presence and the walls are as high as the mountaintops. Come with me to the playgrounds of an integrated high school. See how ugly and flat the blacktop is. Now listen. The bell rings; it is recess time. The doors open, and the students pour out of the doors. Soon over there is a group of white students, and over there by the fence is a group of native students. But now look: the blacktop is no longer there.

Mountain ranges rising, valleys falling, and a great chasm is opening up between the two groups: yours and mine. And no one seems to be capable of crossing over. Why? God in heaven, why? Why?

I know what you must be saying: "Tell us, what do you want?" Yes, what do we want? We want first of all to be respected and to feel that we are people of worth. We want equal job opportunities for our students. We want guidance and counselling. We want to feel that we are a people of worth.

Let no one forget this: we are a people with special rights guaranteed to us by promises and treaties. We do not beg for these rights, nor do we thank you. We do not thank you because we paid for them. God help us, the price we paid was exorbitant. We paid for them with our culture, pride, and self-respect. We paid, we paid, and we paid until we became a beaten race, poverty stricken and conquered. But you have been kind to listen to me, and I know that in your hearts you wish you could help.

I wonder if there is much you can do, and yet there is a lot you can do. When you meet my children in your classrooms, respect each one for what he is: a child of our Father in heaven, and your brother. Maybe it boils down to just that.

Dunjau Jas

whale
Skidigate

Two Poems

WEST WIND

West wind's grass dance
Issues forth promise
Not dulled by repetition

East wind pulls up belief
Re-searches the world of grass
Nurtures winded promise

Grass blades succumb to north wind's song
Trees surrender to being buffeted by cold
Stilled by winter's sleep

South wind exalts
Pulls water in small miracles
From the edge of dreaming rivers

In this ceremony
Of wind song and dance
New life is born

Whale,
Skidegate.
1928. Graphite
on paper by
Emily Carr.
Royal British
Columbia
Museum,
British
Columbia
Archives.
PDP08737

I'M HOME AGAIN

Blue-hued dark, green islands jut up to reach the sky
Still looking as though they are struggling to become flatlands
valleys and lush green meadows
They didn't quite make it most of them
They remain cedar and fir-decked
mountain edges of earth
tied to the deep.

The sea holds these her baby lands
bathing them in her white-capped evening water
rocking them as though it were the ferry standing still
and the islands moving
Memory pulls at my skin,
images punch holes in this moment
of awe over the vista—the not-quite-born islands make.
My body knows these islands

The story of this corridor belongs to Suquamish boatmen
ferrying families from one end of its territory
to the other. Cedar and ermine-skin-clad women ancestors
stand regal in the canoes while brown-skinned men
Dip and sing through the slate under-bellied
Blue-green water.

Conquest silenced these boatmen
stilling the story of canoes for a time to waken in the first year
of my birth. This meander feels so familiar
I have to wonder whether or not I am impressed.

I'm home again.
This journey from Squamish, BC, post-cultural prohibition
in 1951 to Hedgebrook in the summer of 2000,
thirty-eight years after our emancipation
is fraught with the urgent watery aloneness
only writers feel.
The aloneness of paddling about in our
various sociological and historical swamps,
Weaving snippets of dream words we selected to play with into the
        loom of our
                    imaginations
harnessing language
to plough new soil,
create new story, is thick, omnipresent here.

I'm home again.
My pathway here is strewn with sharp stones
singing confusing songs of yearning.
My bones,
my personal stones,
sing back songs of yearning—Tsuniquid's
yearning.
I watch myself highstep my way to this language

This pen
This paper
this place.

The stones' razored edges bleed white as the faces of my dead
emerge, embossed by the shadows in the center of each stone.
Between the stones holding their faces, ribbons of light flicker
Snippets of my busyness shine inside each ribbon of light.
I watch myself steal moments to create art.
Coolly and deliberately I let go of Lucucid
Grieve the parking of my original language
And bury it inside my bones.

I pick up the volumes of books cradling the text of this language.
I feel the sandpapering this language once was and re-watch as my
     body
smoothes the rough edges as the words journey through me
See-yah becomes saskatoon,
si-siutl becomes sea serpent,
Tsuniquid becomes the mother of thought
Thought becomes hidden being,
Hidden being becomes a spiral down to a moment of peace and
     recognition
Knowing becomes a spiral out to meet the world.
This sea, this new Tsuniquid forms the structure of my being.

I'm home again.
Killer whales sidle their litheness alongside the ferry.
Cedar bows acknowledging my return

Raven calls out a cackled hello.
Berries look ready to greet me.
Even the sea peels back its tide
To permit a trek across her mud just as I land
I can see the wetlands from the hill near my cottage
The tears come.

I'm home, Momma.
Haitchka for leading me here
Haitchka my dead for fussing over language for me
Haitchka to those who came before me,
for story,
for song,
for dance.
You paved my journey home with light and alacrity.

I am home again.
Suquamish voices are everywhere here.
I am so totally old and so completely new here.
I pull fragments from old file cabinets,
splinters of memory,
Bind them together to re-shape my world.
I weave this imagined dream world onto old
Squamish blankets,
history-hole-punched and worn—
to re-craft today,
to re-member future in this new language
And I sing I am home again.

Two Poems

FIFTY BELOW

I remember one time in Fort Rae
I was walking with my cousins,

four girls, who were walking with me.
They were laughing at me, those girls,
and I was wearing my father's boots
two sizes too big for me.

And these four girls,

these four cousins,

they laughed at me as I dragged my boots.

　　"You girls," I said. "What's so funny?"

One girl,
one cousin,

stopped and pointed to my feet:

　　"Auntie told us, if you're going to marry a man,
　　listen to his feet when you walk with him.

　　If he drags his feet when he walks

　　you must not marry him:

　　he is lazy—

　　no good.

He won't be a good father.

He won't be a good husband."

And those four girls,
those four cousins,

They ran far ahead of me laughing.

And this time

when I ran after them

I lifted my feet as high as I could.

THE DENE SPEAK

Someone is throwing snow to look like paper, the way it
swirls like puppets on strings caught up in wind, I remember
these words whispered to me by a Cree woman who

could put the taste of a spring thaw in her bannock, so

soft was the bite that it led me to bliss:

"Do you see the snow on the trees?

That is the breath of the caribou—

they are so close."

A Yellowknife Métis, over coffee, told me something that again
wonderfully haunts me:

"I have seen the wolves run on their hind legs in the

barren lands. Like humans they ran.

You will never see that in any textbook
and I haven't heard it anywhere else
but I have seen it!

I have seen it!

I have once watched *Noh-gah,* the wolverine,

stand on a winter lake,

Like a man it stood on its hindquarters
it shielded its eyes with its paws
shielded them against the sun.

When it saw that I was watching he went back

    to all fours

and dove into the snowbank, under it.
Maybe I should not have seen that

but I did!

    I did!"

A Chippewa elder told this to me as she sewed pieces of sky
and earth into one of her quilts:

"A rabbit screams like a child when it's snared.
A bear screams like a woman when shot.

So do moose.

So do deer.

You can't tell me we're not animals.

You can't tell me we're not cousins."

This is something I wanted to share, something I've picked up and never wanted to put down, something that's yours, ours, hers and his, something worth waiting for, something worth living for.

Mahsi
Mahsi . . .

The Laughing One:
Word Sketches from Klee Wyck

Born in Victoria, British Columbia, in 1871, Emily Carr is well known in Canada. A university of art and design and an elementary school in Vancouver are named in her honor, as are a public library in Victoria, a middle school in Ottawa, and public schools in Ontario. Her many paintings of the landscape and First Nations cultures of British Columbia and Alaska—influenced by the Post-Impressionists and Fauvists, whom she'd studied in Paris, New York, and elsewhere—are saturated with color. The keenness of her eye for nature and the way she renders shapes have been compared with the style of Georgia O'Keefe, whom she met. Carr was greatly encouraged by her association with the famous Group of Seven, Canadian landscape artists active in the 1920s and 1930s.

When her poor health made it impossible to travel and paint anymore, she began writing. Her first book, Klee Wyck, was published in 1941, when she was sixty-nine, by Oxford University Press. The book is a collection of stories—she modestly referred to them as "sketches"—which she wrote in notebooks over a number of years. To Carr's surprise, Klee Wyck won the 1941 Governor General's Award for literature. Robertson Davies praised the book. "Completely free of fripperies and self-conscious fine writing. . . . Every unnecessary word has been purged from her descriptions, every thought is as clear as a bell." And he predicted that Carr would soon be "recognized as one of the foremost among the few important writers that Canada has produced." She published three other books of stories before she died in 1945; a few more were published posthumously.

In 1951, Clarke, Irwin and Company purchased the rights to Klee Wyck from Oxford and was given permission by Ira Dilworth, Carr's literary executor, to republish the book as part of a series for schools. But in editing Klee Wyck, Clark, Irwin expurgated over twenty-five hundred words—all considered unflattering of the missionaries or too explicit in depicting the cruelty shown First Nations people and their culture. In the first story, "Ucluelet," Carr writes about a visit she made at age fifteen to a Mission School near the Nuu-chah-nulth First Nations community of Ucluelet. The publisher cut

eight hundred words, including the last two pages. As Carr's executor, Dil-
worth was furious but could do nothing about it.

For the next fifty-two years, Canadian and world readers knew Klee Wyck
only in the expurgated version published by Clark, Irwin and Company, and
were not informed that it had been edited. Kathryn Bridge, however, an
archivist with the British Columbia Archives, holder of the Emily Carr papers,
examined the original manuscripts and compared them to Clark, Irwin's ver-
sion. She was "taken aback" by what she found. The copyright ownership of
Carr's work had expired, so a new version of Klee Wyck *could be released. In*
a handsome edition from Douglas & McIntyre, the book was reprinted in its
entirety in 2003. After two generations, readers could become acquainted with
the real Emily Carr: a strong and amazing woman who rendered vividly and
honestly the wild places of British Columbia and the conditions of First
Nations people, culture, and daily lives. In literature as well as painting, Carr
did this at a time when too many people valued neither.

Ucluelet

The lady Missionaries expected me. They sent an enormous Irishman in a tiny canoe to meet the steamer. We got to the Ucluelet wharf
soon after dawn. Everything was big and cold and strange to me, a fifteen-
year-old school girl. I was the only soul on the wharf. The Irishman did
not have any trouble deciding which was I.

It was low tide, so there was a long, sickening ladder with slimy rungs to
climb down to get to the canoe. The man's big laugh and the tippiness of
the canoe were even more frightening than the ladder. The paddle in his
great arms rushed the canoe through the waves.

We came to Toxis, which was the Indian name for the Mission House.
It stood just above high-tide water. The sea was in front of it and the forest
behind.

The house was of wood, unpainted. There were no blinds or curtains. It
looked, as we paddled up to it, as if it were stuffed with black. When the
canoe stuck in the mud, the big Irishman picked me up in his arms and set
me down on the doorstep.

The Missionaries were at the door. Smells of cooking fish jumped out
past them. People lived on fish at Ucluelet.

Both the Missionaries were dignified, but the Greater Missionary had
the most dignity: the Lesser Missionary was fussy. They had long pale
faces. Their hair was licked back from their foreheads into buns on the
scruffs of their necks. They had long noses straddled by spectacles, thin
lips, mild eyes, and wore straight, dark dresses buttoned to the chin.

There was only two of everything in the kitchen, so I had to sit on a
box, drink from a bowl, and eat my food out of a tin pie-dish.

After breakfast came a long Presbyterian prayer. Outside the kitchen window, just a few feet away at the edge of the forest, stood a grand balsam pine tree. It was very tall and straight.

The sizzling of the Missionaries' "trespasses" jumped me back from the pine tree to the Lord's Prayer just in time to "Amen." We got up from our knees to find the house full of Indians. They had come to look at me.

I felt so young and empty standing there before the Indians and the two grave Missionaries! The Chief, old Hipi, was held to be a reader of faces. He perched himself on the top of the Missionaries' drug cupboard; his brown fists clutched the edge of it, his elbows taut and shoulders hunched. His crumpled shoes hung loose as if they dangled from strings and had no feet in them. The stare of his eyes searched me right through. Suddenly they were done; he lifted them above me to the window, uttered several terse sentences in Chinook, jumped off the cupboard, and strode back to the village.

I was half afraid to ask the Missionary, "What did he say?"

"Not much. Only that you had no fear, that you were not stuck up, and that you knew how to laugh."

Toxis sat upon a long, slow lick of sand, but the beach of the Indian village was short and bit deep into the shoreline. Rocky points jutted out into the sea at either end of it.

Toxis and the village were a mile apart. The schoolhouse was half-way between the two and, like them, was pinched between sea and forest.

The schoolhouse called itself "church house" on Sundays, and looked as Presbyterian as it could under the circumstances.

It had a sharp roof, two windows on each side, a door in front, and a woodshed behind.

The school equipment consisted of a map of the world, a blackboard, a stove, crude desks and benches, and, on a box behind the door, the pail of drinking-water and a tin dipper.

The Lesser Missionary went to the school first and lit the fire. If the tide were high she had to go over the trail at the forest's edge. It was full of holes where high seas had undermined the big tree roots. Huge upturned stumps necessitated detours through hard-leafed salal bushes and skunk cabbage bogs. The Lesser Missionary fussed her way jumpily. She hated putting her feet on ground which she could not see, because it was so covered with growing green. She was glad when she came out of the dark forest and saw the unpainted schoolhouse. The Greater Missionary had no nerves and a long, slow stride. As she came over the trail she blew blasts on a cow's horn. She had an amazing wind, the blasts were stunning, but they failed to call the children to school, because no voice had ever suggested time or obligation to these Indian children. Then the Greater Missionary went to the village and hand-picked her scholars from the huts.

Totem poles at Kitwancool. 1928?
Graphite on paper by Emily Carr.
Royal British Columbia Museum,
British Columbia Archives.
PDP05802

Kitwancool. 1928.
Graphite on paper by Emily Carr.
Royal British Columbia Museum,
British Columbia Archives.
PDP05795

On my first morning in Ucluelet there was a full attendance at school because visitors were rare. After the Lord's Prayer the Missionaries duetted a hymn while the children stared at me.

When the Missionary put A–B–C on the board, the children began squirming out of their desks and pattering down to the drinking bucket. The dipper registered each drink with a clank when they threw it back.

The door squeaked open and shut all the time, with a second's pause between opening and closing. Spitting on the floor was forbidden, so the children went out and spat off the porch. They had not yet mastered the use of the pocket-handkerchief, so not a second elapsed between sniffs. The Lesser Missionary twitched as each sniff hit her ear.

Education being well under way, I slipped out to see the village.

When I did not return after the second's time permitted for spitting, the children began to wriggle from the desks to the drinking bucket, then to the spitting step, looking for me. Once outside, their little bare feet never stopped till they had caught me up. In the empty schoolroom the eyes of the Lesser Missionary waited upon those of the Greater as the shepherd's dog watches for the signal to dash.

"That is all for today," the older woman said quietly and they went home.

After that I was shut up tight at Toxis until school was well started; then I went to the village, careful to creep low when passing under the school windows.

On the point at either end of the bay crouched a huddle of houses—large, squat houses made of thick, hand-hewn cedar planks, pegged and slotted together. They had flat, square fronts. The side walls were made of driftwood. Bark and shakes, weighted with stones against the wind, were used for roofs. Every house stood separate from the next. Wind roared through narrow spaces between.

Houses and people were alike. Wind, rain, forest, and sea had done the same things to both—both were soaked through and through with sunshine, too.

I was shy of the Indians at first. When I knocked at their doors and received no answer, I entered their houses timidly, but I found a grunt of welcome was always waiting inside and that Indians did not knock before entering. Usually some old crone was squatted on the earth floor, weaving cedar fibre or tatters of old cloth into a mat, her claw-like fingers twining in and out, in and out, among the strands that were fastened to a crude frame of sticks. Papooses tumbled around her on the floor for she was papoose-minder as well as mat-maker.

Each of the large houses was the home of several families. The door and the smoke-hole were common to all, but each family had its own fire with its own things round it. That was their own home.

The interiors of the great houses were dim. Smoke teased your eyes and throat. The earth floors were not clean.

It amused the Indians to see me unfold my camp stool, and my sketch sack made them curious. When boats, trees, houses appeared on the paper, jabbering interest closed me about. I could not understand their talk. One day, by grin and gesture, I got permission to sketch an old mat-maker. She nodded and I set to work. Suddenly a cat jumped in through the smoke-hole and leaped down from a rafter onto a pile of loose boxes. As the clatter of the topple ceased there was a bestial roar, a pile of mats and blankets burst upwards, and a man's head came out of them. He shouted and his black eyes snapped at me and the old woman's smile dried out.

"Klatawa" (Chinook for "Go") she shouted, and I went. Later, the old wife called to me across the bay, but I would not heed her call.

"Why did you not reply when old Mrs. Wynook called you?" the Missionary asked.

"She was angry and drove me away."

"She was calling, 'Klee Wyck, come back, come back,' when I heard her."

"What does 'Klee Wyck' mean?"

"I do not know."

The Mission House door creaked open and something looking like a bundle of tired rags tumbled onto the floor and groaned.

"Why, Mrs. Wynook," exclaimed the Missionary, "I thought you could not walk!"

The tired old woman leaned forward and began to stroke my skirt.

"What does Klee Wyck mean, Mrs. Wynook?" asked the Missionary.

Mrs. Wynook put her thumbs into the corners of her mouth and stretched them upwards. She pointed at me; there was a long, guttural jabber in Chinook between her and the Missionary. Finally the Missionary said, "Klee Wyck is the Indians' name for you. It means 'Laughing One.'"

The old woman tried to make the Missionary believe that her husband thought it was I, not the cat, who had toppled the boxes and woke him, but the Missionary, scenting a lie, asked for "straight talk." Then Mrs. Wynook told how the old Indians thought the spirit of a person got caught in a picture of him, trapped there so that, after the person died, it had to stay in the picture.

"They have such silly notions," said the Missionary.

"Tell her that I will not make any more pictures of the old people," I said. It must have hurt the Indians dreadfully to have the things they had always believed trampled on and torn from their hugging. Down deep we all hug something. The great forest hugs its silence. The sea and the air hug the spilled cries of sea-birds. The forest hugs only silence; its birds and even its beasts are mute.

When night came down upon Ucluelet the Indian people folded themselves into their houses and slept.

At the mission house candles were lit. After eating fish, and praying aloud, the Missionaries creaked up the bare stairs, each carrying her own tin candlestick. I had a cot at the foot of their wide wooden bed and quickly scrambled into it. Blindless and carpetless, it was a bleak bedroom even in summer.

The Missionaries folded their clothes, paired their shoes, and put on stout nightgowns. Then, one on each side of the bed, they sank to their knees on the splintery floor and prayed some more, this time silent, private prayers. The buns now dangled in long plaits down their backs and each bowed head was silhouetted against a sputtering candle that sat on an upturned apple-box, one on either side of the bed, apple-boxes heaped with devotional books.

The room was deathly still. Outside, the black forest was still, too, but with a vibrant stillness tense with life. From my bed I could look one storey higher into the balsam pine. Because of his closeness to me, the pine towered above his fellows, his top tapering to heaven like the hands of the praying Missionaries.

Every day might have been a Sunday in the Indian village. At Toxis only the seventh day was the Sabbath. Then the Missionaries changed their "undies" and put lace jabots across the fronts of their "ovies," took an hour longer in bed in the morning, doubled their doses of coffee and prayers, and conducted service in the schoolhouse which had shifted its job to church as the cow's horn turned itself into a church bell for the day.

The Indian women with handkerchiefs on their heads, plaid shawls round their shoulders, and full skirts billowing about their legs, waddled leisurely towards church. It was very hard for them to squeeze their bodies into the children's desks. They took two whole seats each, and even then the squeezing must have hurt.

Women sat on one side of the church. The very few men who came sat on the other. The Missionaries insisted that men come to church wearing trousers, and that their shirt tails must be tucked inside the trousers. So the Indian men stayed away.

"Our trespasses" had been dealt with and the hymn, which was generally pitched too high or too low, had at last hit square, when the door was swung violently back, slopping the drinking bucket. In the outside sunlight stood old Tanook, shirt tails flapping and legs bare. He entered, strode up the middle of the room, and took the front seat.

Quick intakes of horror caught the breath of the women; the Greater Missionary held on to her note, the Lesser jumped an octave.

A woman in the back seat took off her shawl. From hand to hand it travelled under the desks to the top of the room, crossed the aisle, and passed into the hand of Jimmy John, old Tanook's nephew, sitting with the men. Jimmy John squeezed from his seat and laid the shawl across his uncle's bare knees.

The Missionary's address rolled on in choppy Chinook, undertoned by a gentle voice from the back of the room which told Tanook in pure Indian words what he was to do. The Lesser Missionary's eyes popped with indignation. The Greater Missionary's voice went straight on.

With a defiant shake of his wild hair old Tanook got up; twisting the shawl about his middle he marched down the aisles, paused at the pail to take a loud drink, dashed back the dipper with a clank, and strode out.

The service was over, the people had gone, but a pink print figure sat on in the back seat. Her face was sunk down on her chest. She was waiting till all were away before she slunk home. It is considered more indecent for an Indian woman to go shawl-less than for an Indian man to go bare-legged. The woman's heroic gesture had saved her husband's dignity before the Missionaries but had shamed her before her own people.

The Greater Missionary patted the pink shoulder as she passed.

"Disgusting old man!" muttered the Lesser Missionary.

"Brave woman!" said the Greater Missionary, smiling.

One day I walked upon a strip of land that belonged to nothing.

The sea soaked it often enough to make it unpalatable to the forest. Roots of trees refused to thrive in its saltiness.

In this place belonging neither to sea nor to land I came upon an old man dressed in nothing but a brief shirt. He was sawing the limbs from a fallen tree. The swish of the sea tried to drown the purr of his saw. The purr of the saw tried to sneak back into the forest, but the forest threw it out again into the sea. Sea and forest were always at this game of toss with noises.

The fallen tree lay crosswise in this "nothing's place"; it blocked my way. I sat down beside the sawing Indian and we had dumb talk, pointing to the sun and to the sea, the eagles in the air and the crows on the beach. Nodding and laughing together I sat and he sawed. The old man sawed as if aeons of time were before him, and as if all the years behind him had been leisurely and all the years in front of him would be equally so. There was strength still in his back and limbs but his teeth were all worn to the gums. The shock of hair that fell to his shoulders was grizzled. Life had sweetened the old man. He was luscious with time like the end berries of the strawberry season.

With a final grin, I got up and patted his arm—"Goodbye!" He patted my hand. When he saw me turn to break through the forest so that I could round his great fallen tree, he ran and pulled me back, shaking his head and scolding me.

"Swaawa! Hiyu swaawa!" Swaawa were cougar: the forest was full of these great cats. The Indians forbade their children to go into the forest, not even into its edge. I was to them a child, ignorant about the wild things which they knew so well. In these things the Indian could speak with authority to white people.

No one disturbed the Indian dead. Their place was a small, half-cleared spot, a little off from the village and at the edge of the forest. When an

Indian died, no time was lost in hurrying the body away. While death was approaching, a box was got ready. Sometimes, if they owned one, a trunk was used. The body did not lie straight and stark in the box. It was folded up; often it was placed in the box before it really was a corpse. When life had quite gone, the box was closed, some boards were broken from the side wall of the house, and it was taken away through the hole which was later mended so that the spirit should not remember how it got out and come bothering back.

The people never went to the dead's place except to carry another dead body there and then they would hurry back to make dreadful mourning howls in the village.

One day I went to the place of the dead to sketch. It was creepy. At first I did not know whether I could bear it or not. Bones lay about—human bones—skulls, staring from their eye hollows, stuck out from under the bracken; ribs and thigh bones lay among the roots of the trees where coffin boxes had split. Many "dead-boxes" were bound to the high branches of the pines. The lower limbs of the trees were chopped away. Sometimes a Hudson's Bay blanket would be bound around the box, and flapped in the wind as the tree rocked the box. Up there in the keen air, the body disintegrated quickly. The sun and the rain rotted the ropes that bound the box to the tree. They broke and the bones were flung to earth where greenery soon hid them.

It was beautiful how the sea air and sun hurried to help the corpses through their horror. The poor, frail boxes could not keep the elements out; they were quick to make the bones clean and white.

Sometimes, Indians used the hollow boles of ancient cedar trees as grave holes, though life was still racing through the cedar's outer shell.

In one of these hollow trees the Indians had lately buried a young woman. They had put her in a trunk. There was a scarlet blanket over the top. Scattered upon that were some beads and bracelets. There was a brass lamp and her clothes too. The sun streamed in through the split in the side of the tree and sparkled on her dear things. This young, dead woman lay in the very heart of the living cedar tree. As I stood looking, suddenly twigs crackled and bracken shivered behind me. My throat went dry and my forehead wet—but it was only Indian dogs.

Up behind Toxis the forest climbed a steep hill and here in the woods was one lonely grave, that of "our only professed Christian Indian," according to the Missionaries. The Missionaries had coffined him tight and carried him up the new-made trail with great difficulty. They put him into the earth among the roots of the trees, away from all his people, away from the rain and the sun and the wind which he had loved and which would have rushed to help his body melt quickly into the dust to make earth richer because this man had lived.

Kitwancool

When the Indians told me about the Kitwancool totem poles, I said: "How can I get to Kitwancool?"

"Dunno," the Indians replied.

White men told me about the Kitwancool poles too, but when I told them I wanted to go there, they advised me—"Keep out." But the thought of those old Kitwancool poles pulled at me. I was at Kitwangak, twenty or so miles from Kitwancool.

Then a halfbreed at Kitwangak said to me, "The young son of the Kitwancool chief is going in tomorrow with a load of lumber. I asked if he would take you; he will."

"How can I get out again?"

"The boy is coming back to Kitwangak after two days."

The chief's son Aleck was shy, but he spoke good English. He said I was to be at the Hudson's Bay store at eight the next morning.

I bought enough food and mosquito oil to last me two days; then I sat in front of the Hudson's Bay store from eight to eleven o'clock, waiting. I saw Aleck drive past to load his lumber. The wagon had four wheels and a long pole. He tied the lumber to the pole and a sack of oats to the lumber; I was to sit on the oats. Rigged up in front somehow was a place for the driver—no real seat, just a couple of coal-oil boxes bound to some boards. Three men sat on the two boxes. The road was terrible. When we bumped, the man on the down-side of the boxes fell off.

A sturdy old man trudged behind the wagon. Sometimes he rode a bit on the end of the long pole, which tossed him up and down like a see-saw. The old man carried a gun and walked most of the way.

The noon sun burnt fiercely on our heads. The oat-sack gave no support to my back, and my feet dangled. I had to clutch the corner of the oat-sack with one hand to keep from falling off—with the other I held my small griffon dog. Every minute I thought we would be pitched off the pole. You could seldom see the old man because of clouds of yellow dust rolling behind the wagon. The scrub growth at the road-side smelt red hot.

The scraggy ponies dragged their feet heavily; sweat cut rivers through the dust that was caked on their sides.

One of the three men on the front seat of the wagon seemed to be a hero. The other men questioned him all the way, though generally Indians do not talk as they travel. When one of the men fell off the seat, he ran round the wagon to the high side and jumped up again and all the while he did not stop asking the hero questions. There were so many holes in the road and the men fell off so often that they were always changing places, like birds on a roost in cold weather.

Suddenly we gave such an enormous bump that we all fell off together, and the horses stopped. When the wheels were not rattling anymore, we

group of Kitwancool.
Poles.

could hear water running. Then the old man came out of the clouds of dust behind us and said there was a stream close by.

We threw ourselves onto our stomachs, put our lips to the water, and drank like horses. The Indians took the bits out of their horses' mouths and gave them food. Then the men crawled under the wagon to eat their lunch in its shade; I sat by the shadiest wheel. It was splendid to put my legs straight out and have the earth support them and the wheel support my back. The old man went to sleep.

After he woke and after the horses had pulled the wagon out of the big hole, we rumbled on again.

When the sun began to go down, we were in woods, and the clouds of mosquitoes were as thick as the clouds of dust, but more painful. We let them eat us because, after bumping for seven hours, we were too tired to fight.

At last we came to a great dip where the road wound around the edge of a ravine shaped like an oblong bowl. There were trees growing in this earth bowl. It seemed to be bottomless. We were level with the tree-tops as we looked down. The road was narrow—its edges broken.

I was afraid and said, "I want to walk."

Aleck waved his hand across the ravine. "Kitwancool," he said, and I saw some grey roofs on the far side of the hollow. After we had circled the ravine and climbed the road on the other side, we would be there, unless we were lying dead in that deep bowl.

I said again, "I want to walk."

"Village dogs will kill you and the little dog," said Aleck. But I did walk around the bend and up the hill, until the village was near. Then I rode into Kitwancool on the oat-sack.

The dogs rushed out in a pack. The village people came out too. They made a fuss over the hero-man, clustering about him and jabbering. They paid no more attention to me than to the oat-sack. All of them went into the nearest house taking Aleck, the hero, the old man, and the other man with them, and shut the door.

I wanted to cry, sticking alone up there on top of the oats and lumber, the sagging horses in front and the yapping dogs all round, nobody to ask about anything—and very tired. Aleck had told me I could sleep on the verandah of his father's house, because I only had a cot and a tent-fly with me, and bears came into the village often at night. But how did I know which was his father's house? The dogs would tear me if I got down and there was no one to ask, anyway.

Suddenly something at the other end of the village attracted the dogs. The pack tore off and the dust hid me from them.

Aleck came out of the house and said, "We are going to have dinner in this house now." Then he went in again and shut the door.

Kitwancool. 1928. Graphite on paper by Emily Carr. Royal British Columbia Museum, British Columbia Archives. PDP05801

The wagon was standing in the new part of the village. Below us, on the right, I could see a row of old houses. They were dim, for the light was going, but above them, black and clear against the sky, stood the old totem poles of Kitwancool. I jumped down from the wagon and came to them. That part of the village was quite dead. Between the river and the poles was a flat of green grass. Above stood the houses, grey and broken. They were in a long, wavering row, with wide, windowless fronts. The totem poles stood before them there on the top of a little bank above the green flat. There were a few poles down on the flat too, and some graves that had fences round them and roofs over the tops.

When it was almost dark I went back to the wagon.

The house of Aleck's father was the last one at the other end of the new village. It was one great room like a hall, and was built of new logs. It had seven windows and two doors; all the windows were propped open with blue castor-oil bottles.

I was surprised to find that the old man who had trudged behind our wagon was Chief Douse—Aleck's father.

Mrs. Douse was more important than Mr. Douse; she was a chieftainess in her own right, and had great dignity. Neither of them spoke to me that night. Aleck showed me where to put my bed on the verandah and I hung the fly over it. I ate a dry scrap of food and turned into my blankets. I had no netting, and the mosquitoes tormented me.

My heart said into the thick dark, "Why did I come?"

And the dark answered, "You know."

In the morning, the hero-man came to me and said, "My mother-in-law wishes to speak with you. She does not know English words so she will talk through my tongue."

I stood before the tall, cold woman. She folded her arms across her body and her eyes searched my face. They were as expressive as if she were saying the words herself instead of using the hero's tongue.

"My mother-in-law wishes to know why you have come to our village."

"I want to make some pictures of the totem poles."

"What do you want our totem poles for?"

"Because they are beautiful. They are getting old now, and your people make very few new ones. The young people do not value the poles as the old ones did. By and by there will be no more poles. I want to make pictures of them, so that your young people as well as the white people will see how fine your totem poles used to be."

Mrs. Douse listened when the young man told her this. Her eyes raked my face to see if I was talking "straight." Then she waved her hand towards the village.

"Go along," she said through the interpreter, "and I shall see." She was neither friendly nor angry. Perhaps I was going to be turned out of this place that had been so difficult to get into.

The air was hot and heavy. I turned towards the old village with the pup Ginger Pop at my heels. Suddenly there was a roar of yelpings, and I saw my little dog putting half a dozen big ones to rout down the village street. Their tails were flat, their tongues lolled, and they yelped. The Douses all rushed out of their house to see what the noise was about, and we laughed together so hard that the strain, which before had been between us, broke.

The sun enriched the old poles grandly. They were carved elaborately and with great sincerity. Several times, the figure of a woman that held a child was represented. The babies had faces like wise little old men. The mothers expressed all womanhood—the big wooden hands holding the child were so full of tenderness they had to be distorted enormously in order to contain it all. Womanhood was strong in Kitwancool. Perhaps, after all, Mrs. Douse might let me stay.

I sat in front of a totem mother and began to draw—so full of her strange, wild beauty that I did not notice the storm that was coming, till the totem poles went black, flashed vividly white and then went black again. Bang upon bang, came the claps of thunder. The hills on one side tossed it to the hills on the other; sheets of rain washed over me. I was beside a grave down on the green flat; some of the pickets of its fence were gone, so I crawled through onto the grave with Ginger Pop in my arms to shelter under its roof. Stinging nettles grew on top of the grave with mosquitoes hiding under their leaves. While I was beating down the nettles with my easel, it struck the head of a big wooden bear squatted on the grave. He startled me. He was painted red. As I sat down upon him my foot hit something that made a hollow rattling noise. It was a shaman's rattle. This then must be a shaman's, a medicine-man's grave, and this the rattle he had used to scare away evil spirits. Shamen worked black magic. His body lay here just a few feet below me in the earth. At the thought I made a dash for the broken community house on the bank above. All the Indian horses had got there first and taken for their shelter the only corner of the house that had any roof over it.

I put my stool near the wall and sat upon it. The water ran down the wall in rivers. The dog shivered under my coat—both of us were wet to the skin. My sketch sack was so full of water that when I emptied it on to the ground it made the pool we sat in bigger.

After two hours the rain stopped suddenly. The horses held their bones stiff and quivered their skins. It made the rain fly out of their coats and splash me. One by one they trooped out through a hole in the wall. When their hooves struck the baseboard, there was a sodden thud. Ginger Pop

Kitwancool.
1928? Graphite
on paper by
Emily Carr.
Royal British
Columbia
Museum,
British
Columbia
Archives.
PDP05778

shook himself too, but I could only drip. Water poured from the eyes of the totems and from the tips of their carved noses. New little rivers trickled across the green flat. The big river was whipped to froth. A blur like boiling mist hung over it.

When I got back to the new village, I found my bed and things in a corner of the Douses' great room. The hero told me, "My mother-in-law says you may live in her house. Here is a rocking-chair for you."

Mrs. Douse acknowledged my gratitude stolidly. I gave Mr. Douse a dollar and asked if I might have a big fire to dry my things and make tea. There were two stoves—the one at their end of the room was alight. Soon, mine too was roaring and it was cosy. When the Indians accepted me as one of themselves, I was very grateful.

The people who lived in that big room of the Douses were two married daughters, their husbands and children, the son Aleck, and an orphan girl called Lizzie. The old couple came and went continually, but they ate and slept in a shanty at the back of the new house. This little place had been made round them. The floor was of earth and the walls were of cedar. The fire on the ground sent its smoke through a smoke-hole in the roof. Dried salmon hung on racks. The old people's mattress was on the floor. The place was full of themselves—they had breathed themselves into it as a bird, with its head under its wing, breathes itself into its own cosiness. The Douses were glad for their children to have the big fine house and be modern but this was the right sort of place for themselves.

Life in the big house was most interesting. A baby swung in its cradle from the rafters; everyone tossed the cradle as he passed and the baby cooed and gurgled. There was a crippled child of six—pinched and white under her brown skin; she sat in a chair all day. And there was Orphan Lizzie who would slip out into the wet bushes and come back with a wild strawberry or a flower in her grubby little hand, and, kneeling by the sick child's chair, would open her fingers suddenly on the surprise.

There was no rush, no scolding, no roughness in this household. When anyone was sleepy he slept; when they were hungry they ate; if they were sorry they cried, and if they were glad they sang. They enjoyed Ginger Pop's fiery temper, the tilt of his nose, and particularly the way he kept the house free of Indian dogs. It was Ginger who bridged the gap between their language and mine with laughter. Ginger's snore was the only sound in that great room at night. Indians sleep quietly.

Orphan Lizzie was shy as a rabbit but completely unselfconscious. It was she who set the food on the big table and cleared away the dishes. There did not seem to be any particular meal-times. Lizzie always took a long lick at the top of the jam-tin as she passed it.

The first morning I woke at the Douses', I went very early to wash myself in the creek below the house. I was kneeling on the stones brushing my teeth. It was very cold. Suddenly I looked up—Lizzie was close by me, watching. When I looked up, she darted away like a fawn, leaving her water pails behind. Later, Mrs. Douse came to my corner of the house, carrying a tin basin; behind her was Lizzie with a tiny glass cream pitcher full of water, and behind Lizzie was the hero.

"My mother-in-law says the river is too cold for you to wash in. Here is water and a basin for you." Everyone watched my washing next morning. The washing of my ears interested them most.

One day after work I found the Douse family all sitting round on the floor. In the center of the group was Lizzie. She was beating something in a pail, beating it with her hands; her arms were blobbed with pink froth to the elbows. Everyone stuck his hand into Lizzie's pail and hooked out some of the froth in the crook of his fingers, then took long delicious licks. They invited me to lick too. It was "soperlallie," or soap berry. It grows in the woods; when you beat the berry it froths up and has a queer, bitter taste. The Indians love it.

For two days, from dawn till dark, I worked down in the old part of the village. On the third day Aleck was to take me back to Kitwangak. But that night it started to rain. It rained for three days and three nights without stopping; the road was impossible. I had only provisioned for two days, had been here five, and had given all the best bits from my box to the sick child. All the food I had left for the last three days was hard tack and raisins. I drank hot water, and rocked my hunger to the tune of the rain beating on the window. Ginger Pop munched hard tack unconcerned— amusing everybody.

The Indians would have shared the loaf and jam-tin with me, but I did not tell them that I had no food. The thought of Lizzie's tongue licking the jam-tin stopped me.

When it rained, the Indians drowsed like flies, heavy as the day itself.

On the sixth day of my stay in Kitwancool the sun shone again, but we had to wait a bit for the puddles to drain.

I straightened out my obligations and said goodbye to Mr. and Mrs. Douse. The light wagon that was taking me out seemed luxurious after the thing I had come in on. I climbed up beside Aleck. He gathered his reins and "giddapped."

Mrs. Douse, followed by her husband, came out of the house and waved a halt. She spoke to Aleck.

"My mother wants to see your pictures."

"But I showed her every one before they were packed."

At the time I had thought her stolidly indifferent.

"My mother wishes to see the pictures again."

I clambered over the back of the wagon, unpacked the wet canvases, and opened the sketchbooks. She went through them all. The two best poles in the village belonged to Mrs. Douse. She argued and discussed with her husband. I told Aleck to ask if his mother would like to have me give her pictures of her poles. If so, I would send them through the Hudson's Bay store at Kitwangak. Mrs. Douse's neck loosened. Her head nodded violently and I saw her smile for the first time.

Repacking, I climbed over the back of the seat to Aleck.

"Giddap!"

The reins flapped: we were off. The dust was laid; everything was keen and fresh; indeed the appetites of the mosquitoes were very keen.

When I got back to Kitwangak the Mounted Police came to see me.

"You have been in to Kitwancool?"

"Yes."

"How did the Indians treat you?"

"Splendidly."

"Learned their lesson, eh?" said the man. "We have had no end of trouble with those people—chased missionaries out and drove surveyors off with axes—simply won't have whites in their village. I would never have advised anyone going in—particularly a woman. No, I would certainly have said, 'Keep out.'"

"Then I am glad I did not ask for your advice," I said. "Perhaps it is because I am a woman that they were so good to me."

"One of the men who went in on the wagon with you was straight from jail, a fierce, troublesome customer."

Now I knew who the hero was.

Reinhabitation

The following is based on a talk given at the Reinhabitation Conference at North San Juan School, sponsored by the California Council on the Humanities, August 1976. It was published in The Old Ways *(City Lights, 1977) and reprinted in* A Place in Space *(Counterpoint, 1995).*

I came to the Pacific slope by a line of people that somehow worked their way west from the Atlantic over 150 years. One grandfather ended up in the Territory of Washington and homesteaded in Kitsap County. My mother's side were railroad people down in Texas, and before that they'd worked the silver mines in Leadville, Colorado. My grandfather being a homesteader and my father a native of the state of Washington put our family relatively early in the Northwest. But there were people already there, long before my family, I learned as a boy. An elderly Salish Indian gentleman came by our farm once every few months in a Model T truck, selling smoked salmon. "Who is he?" "He's an Indian," my parents said.

Looking at all the different trees and plants that made up my second-growth Douglas fir forest plus cow pasture childhood universe, I realized that my parents were short on a certain kind of knowledge. They could say, "That's a Doug fir, that's a cedar, that's bracken fern," but I perceived a subtlety and complexity in those woods that went far beyond a few names.

As a child I spoke with the old Salishan man a few times over the years he made these stops—then, suddenly, he never came back. I sensed what he represented, what he knew, and what it meant to me: he knew better than anyone else I had ever met *where I was*. I had no notion of a white American or European heritage providing an identity; I defined myself by relation to the place. Later I also understood that "English language" is an identity—and later, via the hearsay of books, received the full cultural and historical view—but never forgot, or left, that first ground, the "where" of our "who are we?"

There are many people on the planet now who are not "inhabitants." Far from their home villages; removed from ancestral territories; moved into town from the farm; went to pan gold in California—work on the pipeline— work for Bechtel in Iran. Actual inhabitants—peasants, paisanos, paysan, peoples of the land, have been dismissed, laughed at, and overtaxed for centuries by the urban-based ruling elites. The intellectuals haven't the least notion of what kind of sophisticated, attentive, creative intelligence it takes to "grow food." Virtually all the plants in the gardens and the trees in the orchards, the sheep, cows, and goats in the pastures were domesticated in the Neolithic, before "civilization." The differing regions of the world have long had—each—their own precise subsistence pattern developed over millennia by people who had settled in there and learned what particular kinds of plants the ground would "say" at that spot.

Humankind also clearly wanders. Four million years ago those smaller protohumans were moving in and out of the edges of forest and grassland in Africa—fairly warm, open enough to run in. At some point moving on, catching fire, sewing clothes, swinging around the arctic, setting out on amazing sea voyages. During the middle and late Pleistocene, large-fauna hunting era, a fairly nomadic grassland-and-tundra hunting life was established, with lots of mobility across northern Eurasia in particular. With the decline of the Ice Age—and here's where we are—most of the big-game hunters went out of business. There was possibly a population drop in Eurasia and the Americas, as the old techniques no longer worked.

Countless local ecosystem habitation styles emerged. People developed specific ways to *be* in each of those niches: plant knowledge, boats, dogs, traps, nets, fishing—the smaller animals and smaller tools. From steep jungle slopes of Southwest China to coral atolls to barren arctic deserts—*a spirit of what it was to be there* evolved that spoke of a direct sense of relation to the "land"—which really means, the totality of the local bioregion system, from cirrus clouds to leaf mold.

Inhabitory peoples sometimes say, "This piece of land is sacred"—or "all the land is sacred." This is an attitude that draws on awareness of the mystery of life and death, of taking life to live, of giving life back—not only to your own children but to the life of the whole land.

Abbé Breuil, the French prehistorian who worked extensively in the caves of southern France, has pointed out that the animal murals in those twenty-thousand-year-old caves describe fertility as well as hunting—the birth of little bison and cow calves. They show a tender and accurate observation of the qualities and personalities of different creatures, implying a sense of the mutuality of life and death in the food chain and what I take to be a sense of the sacramental quality of that relationship.

Inhabitation does not mean "not traveling." The term does not of itself define the size of a territory. The size is determined by the bioregion type. The bison hunters of the great plains are as surely in a "territory" as the Indians of northern California, though the latter may have seldom ventured farther than thirty miles from where they were born. Whether a vast grassland or a brushy mountain, the Peoples knew their geography. Any member of a hunting society could recall and visualize any spot in the surrounding landscape and tell you what was there, how to get there. "That's where you'd get some cattails." The bushmen of the Kalahari Desert could locate a buried ostrich egg full of emergency water in the midst of a sandy waste— walk right up and dig it out: "I put this here three years ago, just in case."

As always, Ray Dasmann's terms are useful to make these distinctions: "ecosystem-based cultures" and "biosphere cultures." By that Dasmann means societies whose life and economies are centered in terms of natural regions and watersheds, as against those who discovered—seven or eight thousand years ago in a few corners of the globe—that it was "profitable" to spill over into another drainage, another watershed, another people's territory, and steal away its resources, natural or human. Thus, the Roman Empire would strip whole provinces for the benefit of the capital, and villa-owning Roman aristocrats would have huge slave-operated farms in the south using giant wheeled plows. Southern Italy never recovered. We know the term *imperialism*—Dasmann's concept of "biosphere cultures" helps us realize that biological exploitation is a critical part of imperialism, too: the species made extinct, the clear-cut forests.

All that wealth and power pouring into a few centers had bizarre results. Philosophies and religions based on fascination with society, hierarchy, manipulation, and the "absolute." A great edifice called "the state" and the symbols of central power—in China what they used to call "the true dragon"; in the West, as Mumford says, symbolized perhaps by that Bronze Age fort called the Pentagon. No wonder Lévi-Strauss says that civilization has been in a long decline since the Neolithic.

So here in the twentieth century we find Occidentals and Orientals studying each other's wisdom, and a few people on both sides studying what came before both—before they forked off. A book like *Black Elk Speaks,* which would probably have had zero readership in 1900, is perceived now as speaking of certain things that nothing in the Judeo-Christian tradition, and very little in the Hindu-Buddhist tradition, deals with. All the world religions remain primarily human-centered. That next step is excluded or forgotten—"well, what do you say to Magpie? What do you say to Rattlesnake when you meet him?" What do we learn from Wren, and Hummingbird, and Pine Pollen, and how? Learn what? Specifics: how to spend a life facing the current; or what it is perpetually to die young; or how to be huge and calm and eat *anything* (Bear). But also, that we are many selves looking at each other, through the same eye.

The reason many of us want to make this step is simple, and is explained in terms of the forty-thousand-year looping back that we seem to be involved in. Sometime in the last twenty years the best brains of the Occident discovered to their amazement that we live in an Environment. This discovery has been forced on us by the realization that we are approaching the limits of something. Stewart Brand said that the photograph of the earth (taken from outer space by a satellite) that shows the whole blue orb with spirals and whorls of cloud was a great landmark for human consciousness. We see that it has a shape, and it has limits. We are back again, now, in the position of our Mesolithic forebears—working off the coasts of southern Britain, or the shores of Lake Chad, or the swamps of Southeast China, learning how to live by the sun and the green at that spot. We once more know that we live in a system that is enclosed in a certain way, that has its own kinds of limits, and that we are interdependent with it.

The ethics or morality of this is far more subtle than merely being nice to squirrels. The biological-ecological sciences have been laying out (implicitly) a spiritual dimension. We must find our way to seeing the mineral cycles, the water cycles, air cycles, nutrient cycles as sacramental—and we must incorporate that insight into our own personal spiritual quest and integrate it with all the wisdom teachings we have received from the nearer past. The expression of it is simple: feeling gratitude to it all; taking responsibility for your own acts; keeping contact with the sources of the energy that flow into your own life (namely dirt, water, flesh).

Another question is raised: is not the purpose of all this living and studying the achievement of self-knowledge, self-realization? How does knowledge of place help us know the Self? The answer, simply put, is that we are all composite beings, not only physically but intellectually, whose sole individual identifying feature is a particular form or structure changing constantly in time. There is no "self" to be found in that, and yet oddly enough, there is. Part of you is out there waiting to come into you, and another part of you is behind you, and the "just this" of the ever-present moment holds all the transitory little selves in its mirror. The Avatamsaka ("Flower Wreath") jeweled-net-interpenetration-ecological-systems-emptiness-consciousness tells us no self-realization without the Whole Self, and the whole self is the whole thing.

Thus, knowing who we are and knowing where we are are intimately linked. There are no limits to the possibilities of the study of *who* and *where*, if you want to go "beyond limits"—and so, even in a world of biological limits, there is plenty of open mind-space to go out into.

Summing Up

In Wendell Berry's essay "The Unsettling of America," he points out that the way the economic system works now, you're penalized if you try to stay in one spot and do anything well. It's not just that the integrity of Native American land is threatened, or national forests and parks; it's *all* land that's under the gun, and any person or group of people who tries to stay there and do some one thing well, long enough to be able to say, "I really love and know this place," stands to be penalized. The economics of it works so that anyone who jumps at the chance for quick profit is rewarded—doing proper agriculture means *not* to jump at the most profitable chance—proper forest management or game management means doing things with the far future in mind—and the future is unable to pay us for it right now. Doing things right means living as though your grandchildren would also be alive, in this land, carrying on the work we're doing right now, with deepening delight.

I saw old farmers in Kentucky last spring who belong in another century. They are inhabitants; they see the world they know crumbling and evaporating before them in the face of a different logic that declares, "Everything you know, and do, and the way you do it, mean nothing to us." How much more the pain and loss of elegant cultural skills on the part of the nonwhite Fourth World primitive remnant cultures—who may know the special properties of a certain plant or how to communicate with dolphins, skills the industrial world might never regain. Not that special, intriguing knowledges are the real point: it's the sense of the magic system, the capacity to hear the song of Gaia *at that spot,* that's lost.

Reinhabitory refers to the tiny number of persons who come out of the industrial societies (having collected or squandered the fruits of eight thousand years of civilization) and then start to turn back to the land, back to place. This comes for some with the rational and scientific realization of interconnectedness and planetary limits. But the actual demands of a life committed to a place, and living somewhat by the sunshine green-plant energy that is concentrating in that spot, are so physically and intellectually intense that it is a moral and spiritual choice as well.

Mankind has a rendezvous with destiny in outer space, some have predicted. Well: we are already traveling in space—this is the galaxy, right here. The wisdom and skill of those who studied the universe firsthand, by direct knowledge and experience, for millennia, both inside and outside themselves, are what we might call the Old Ways. Those who envision a possible future planet on which we continue that study, and where we live by the green and the sun, have no choice but to bring whatever science, imagination, strength, and political finesse they have to the support of the inhabitory people—natives and peasants of the world. In making common cause with them, we become "reinhabitory." And we begin to learn a little of the Old Ways, which are outside of history, and forever new.

The Tree of Meaning and the Work
of Ecological Linguistics_____

This lecture was given at the Conference on Environmental Ethics, Yukon College, Whitehorse, 19 July 2001.

I.

When the European invasion of the Americas began, there were about sixty languages being spoken in the territory now known as Canada, another sixteen, more or less, in Alaska, and at least two hundred twenty in what are now the forty-eight contiguous states of the U.S.A. Some of these straddle the borders, of course. I count a total of about two hundred eighty in North America north of the Rio Grande. There were another two hundred or more from the Rio Grande to the Isthmus of Panama. About five hundred, you could say, in North America as a whole. More than that—perhaps in the vicinity of seven hundred—were spoken in South America. That's a total of twelve hundred or so in the Americas, out of six thousand or more in the world as a whole.

Other things being equal—which of course they never are—it is probably true that language density increases as biomass increases. In practice, languages go where speakers go, and speakers go, when they can, where the living is good. They also go where migration routes allow them to go, and in difficult times, they go where refugees are suffered to exist. So there are some interesting pockets of aboriginal language density on the map of North America. California was a magnet for immigrants in precolonial times, the same as it is now, and in the year 1500 it had more human languages per unit of land than anywhere else north of Oaxaca. This pattern held right up the coast, to the southern tip of Alaska. The West Coast of North America, not the East Coast, was the most densely peopled region before the Europeans arrived. As an old migration corridor, the West Coast acquired more languages per unit of population as well as more humans per unit of land. And the languages that lived on the West Coast were more varied—they represented a much wider taxonomic range—than on the East Coast or elsewhere on the continent.

It's wrong, of course, to speak about these things in the past tense, but present tense is not entirely right either. Of about three hundred languages formerly spoken in all the native nations gobbled up by the U.S.A. and Canada, about one hundred seventy still survive. That is a little over half. But most of those surviving languages have fewer than five percent of the number of speakers they used to have. Most of those languages are eroding, simplifying, losing the rich vocabularies and grammars they had acquired over centuries of relatively peaceful maturation, and the odds are very good that most of these languages will vanish in your lifetime.

A lot of effort is going into language revival and language maintenance nowadays—very important effort, which needs all the support and all the encouragement it can get. But languages, like all living things, have to live within environments, to which they must adapt. A language that only survives in the classroom, like a plant that only survives in a flowerpot, or an animal that only survives in the laboratory or the zoo, is a different thing—and in some respects a lesser thing—than one that survives in the wild.

For a language, life "in the wild" means life as a functioning part of a cultural ecosystem, where chatter, laughter, conversations, stories, songs, and dreams are as continuous as breathing. It means the luxury of *being taken for granted*, in the same way that a tree is taken for granted by the birds that perch in its branches, by the earth, water, light, and air it grows in, and by the beetles, lichens, and mosses growing upon it.

Life in the wild, for a language as for any living entity—animal, plant, fungus, protozoan, or bacterium—means a dependable and nourishing interconnection with the rest of life on the planet. It means a place in the food chain. It means a sustaining, sustainable habitat. That perennial connection to biological and physical reality is what feeds and shapes and calibrates a language. In conditions of natural equilibrium, languages have ranges, no more permanently fixed than the ranges of plants and animals, but also no less vital, no less real. The native range of a language is the domain it keeps up to date with: a territory it inevitably shares but one it can't and doesn't take for granted. It is the portion of the world which that language ceaselessly catalogues and explores. A language can only do this, of course, with the help of its speakers.

Its speakers are in a sense the lungs of the language. Without them it will neither speak nor breathe. But without that other nourishing attachment—not to its speakers but to the world that surrounds them—the ability to speak would be of little value. A language severed from the world might go on talking, but the memory of its referents would fade, and its standards of truth and beauty would wither. After a time we would find it had nothing of substance to say.

A language, you may say, cannot have living speakers and yet have no connection to the world, because its speakers also have to eat and breathe. But they can eat and breathe indoors, and if they do that all the time, their language shrinks. The indoor world becomes the only world it knows.

Because the number of speakers has, in most cases, shrunk, and because the world of those speakers has, in most cases, stiffened and contracted, the languages native to North America are endangered now in nonpolitical as well as political ways and have much less security than before the colonization. Teaching them in the schools doesn't change that. Raising the GNP doesn't change it either. On the contrary, raising the GNP appears to endanger languages severely.

You all know something about the accelerated destruction of plant and animal species that began with the European colonization. You know that some species—Steller's sea cow and the passenger pigeon for instance—have been exterminated, while many others, including the buffalo, the whooping crane, and the Port Orford cedar, have come very close. You also know that the process—habitat destruction and species annihilation—is still galloping along in North America and elsewhere in the world.

The strange thing is this: there are more humans alive than ever before—more, it seems, than the planet can comfortably tolerate—and yet human languages and cultures rank right up near the top of that list of threatened beings. Over a space of four centuries, from 1500 to 1900, while the immigrant population was steadily rising, the total indigenous population of North America fell by more than ninety percent. Given that much death, and the forced dislocation, missionization, and cultural transformation that went with it, it's astounding that over half of the languages spoken in North America five centuries ago are still spoken today.

When you wipe out a community, a culture, and leave five or ten or twenty speakers of the language, you can claim that the language survives, that it isn't extinct. But what happens is every bit as terrible as when you clearcut a forest and leave a strip of trees along the edge, to hide the clearcut from the highway. In both cases, something will eventually grow back—but what was there before is gone forever.

A language is an organism: a weightless, discontinuous organism that lives in the minds and bodies of those who speak it—or from the language's point of view, in the bodies and minds of those *through whom it is able to speak*. Languages change over time, and eventually they perish, like other living things. But in a state of environmental health, when languages die, other languages—neighbors and children of those that are dying—are growing up to replace them. When you kill a language off and replace it with an import, you kill part of the truth. A language is a means of seeing and understanding the world, a means of talking with the world. Never mind talking *about* the world; that's for dilettantes. A language is a means of talking *with* the world. When you kill a language off—even a language with only one speaker—you make the entire planet less intelligent, less articulate, less capable, and so decidedly less beautiful than it was.

What is it that people say when they're conversing with the world? They sing songs and tell stories. They make poems, in other words: lyric poems and narrative poems. And wherever there is language, that is what happens. Wherever in nature there are humans, there are human languages, and wherever in nature there are languages, there are stories. If we dress that statement up so it sounds like it belongs in the university, it will say, *Every natural human language has a literature.* But in its own unprintable way, every *nonhuman* language has a literature too. If something speaks well, literature is what it has to say. (If you prefer a more self-centered definition, we can also put it this way: any well-told story, and maybe even any earnest statement, turns out to have literary properties when you pay it close attention.)

In Europe, China, and other regions of the earth where industrial technology has become a fetish, many people seem to believe that literature is a rare and special achievement, only created by "advanced civilizations." Some historians claim that great literatures are only created by great empires. It is true that the resources of empire can do a lot to increase literary *quantity* or literary *storage capacity,* but literary *quality* is independent of that.

Literature, in fact, is as natural to language as language is to human beings—and for human beings, language is as natural as walking. Language, in fact, is as natural as eating, which all living creatures do. Humans have a proven ability to out-talk and out-eat everything else on the planet, at least in the short term, and some people seem immensely proud of that. Why, I'm not quite sure.

Scripture—that is, writing—is a technology, but a seemingly simple technology, like fire. Unlike fire, however, writing is not—and in the long run can't be—a cultural universal. This may be why mythographers (myth *writers,* as distinguished from mythtellers) usually say that writing wasn't stolen from the gods but was freely given to humans instead.

Any society that wants this technology can obtain it, but only those prepared to pay the price, in social self-absorption and bureaucratic overhead, can keep it. And like other potent technologies, writing radically alters every society into which it is introduced. It involves, after all, a kind of ritual mutilation of the intellect, a sort of cerebral circumcision. To this day there are missionary agencies, both secular and religious, going about the world attempting to spread literacy, claiming that this technology will empower and enfranchise and enrich all those to whom it is given. What these missionary agencies are doing in actual fact is exterminating the earth's last oral cultures. Those who seek to improve human welfare by

exterminating ancient oral cultures are in need of greater wisdom—just like those who seek to improve human welfare by clearcutting the earth's last virgin forests.

II.

People often notice that language helps them think—and then they sometimes ask, *Are there other ways to think besides in language?* Doubtless a good question; but that, I think, is not the way to ask it. What the question means is, *Are there languages to think in other than the ones in which we talk?* And the answer is, *Of course!* There are the languages of mathematics, the languages of music, languages of color, shape, and gesture. Language is *what something becomes when you think in it.* Life as we know it thinks, it seems, in nucleic acids. The forest thinks in trees and their associated life forms: asters, grasses, mosses, fungi, and the creatures who move through them, from annelids and arthropods to thrushes, jays, and deer. Humans often, but not always, think in words and sentences.

Ideas, according to Marx, do not exist apart from language. Many others say the same. They are asserting that the only way to think is in the speech of human beings. The entire natural world stands as proof that this is false. Yet in a broader sense—a sense that is equally alien both to Marxist and capitalist values—I suspect the claim is true: where there are ideas, there is language. Mythtellers, however, are prone to remember (and writers to forget) that the languages of words are not the only kind of human language, and that the languages spoken by humans are only a small subset of language as a whole. Some deeply human stories tell us this is so.

In the hands of an expert mythteller, stories are a form of wisdom. In the hands of anyone else, they may be nothing more than narrative clichés. Here as elsewhere, everything depends on the tradition—yet everything depends on the individual as well. If you treat the stories with respect, you have to learn to hear them in their language—their tradition—but also in the voices of the real individuals who are telling them.

The anthropologist Franz Boas, who spent half a century taking dictation in Native American languages and studying the results—and who inspired a whole tribe of able people to do likewise—often tried to separate the tale from the teller. For much of his career, it seemed to him unscientific to do otherwise. Though Boas never said so, he apparently believed that stories underwent an evolutionary change, akin to speciation, as they passed from language to language and culture to culture. If that were so, then to study the comparative anatomy of stories, we would have to disregard individual performances as such, and individual artistry. We'd have to find the holotypes instead: the canonical "Haida version," "Tlingit version," "Tagish version," and so on for each story. Some of Boas's students—Alfred Kroeber and Robert Lowie in particular—swallowed this unspoken idea whole. And it is wonderful to see, through their footnotes, personal letters, and other remarks, how they all—Boas and Lowie especially—chafed at the constraints of this self-imposed, untenable assumption.

As long as they sat in the classroom or the library, reading synopses and translations, they could believe in the ethnic speciation of stories. What taught them otherwise? Love of their work, and love of reality. Repeated trips to the field, hearing storytellers speak in their own languages. There they heard and saw and felt the incredible variation—anatomical, physiological, and behavioral—with which stories can unfold, depending on who's telling and who's listening. Ethnicity, language, and culture have no more effect on the speciation of stories than on the speciation of people.

It does, however, seem to me that a course in literary history ought to begin with linguistic geography: a close look at the map and the calendar, to see what languages are spoken in what places, and whose words have been transcribed and when and where and under what conditions. If we taught North American literatures that way, we would be well into the course before we came to the moment in history when Spanish, English, French, and the other colonial languages were imported to this continent and the big colonial literatures started to build. Most people teaching literature in the U.S.A. and Canada teach only the top layer and forget to even mention the foundations.

There is in fact no boundary, so far as I'm concerned, between linguistics and literary history. Linguistics is a branch of natural history—the branch that focuses, let us say, on the statements made by speaking creatures, and on the stories that they tell—in the same way that conchology focuses on the shells made by shell-making creatures, and osteology on the bones made by creatures that possess internal skeletons. This approach frightens many linguists away. Many of them don't know what "literature" is, but they know it sounds awfully subjective and unscientific, so they'd like to think it has nothing to do with their field. And to some scholars of literature, "linguistics" sounds morbidly objective, technical, and dry.

I prefer to think about literature and language as a continuum that includes everything from birdsong to linear algebra and symbolic logic. Most of that continuum, or all of it, is occupied with stories.

So linguistics, as I understand it, deals with the stories creatures tell. But what about the stories creatures *are?* Can we do a linguistics of that? I don't see why not. What kind of linguistics would it be? It would be biology. If that's the case, it appears not only that linguistics is a branch of natural history, but that natural history is a branch of linguistics.

Now maybe we're getting somewhere. That is, maybe we're getting to where we are, which is deep in a net of stories and interconnections from which, even in death, there is no escape. Each of us tells stories, and each of us *is* a story. Not just each of us humans, but each of us creatures—spruce trees and toads and timber wolves and dog salmon. We all tell stories to ourselves and to each other—within the tribe, within the species, and way beyond its bounds. Roses do this when they flower, finches when they sing, and humans when they speak, walk, sing, dance, swim, play a flute, build a fire, or pull a trigger.

A lot of the messages humans send are audible messages, transmitted by the fancy apparatus of the mouth, received by the even fancier apparatus of the ear. Those are the sorts of messages most linguists choose to study. But a number of Native American languages—including American Sign Language (ASL), the Langue de signes de Québec (LSQ), and their Latin American relatives—are altogether silent. These exceptions prove a very important rule. The words *language* and *linguistics* are made, of course, from *lingua,* which is the Latin name for the tongue. But language isn't limited to the tongue. People speak with their hands, arms, shoulders, heads, faces as well as their voices. Speakers of LSQ and ASL speak with these silent organs exclusively. This tells us that the terms *language, linguistics, syllable, phoneme, phonetics,* and so on—all those words fixated on sounds and on the tongue—are really metaphors. So is the dichotomy *oral* versus *written,* which invites us all to choose up sides and have a tournament or a war between the People of the Mouth and the People of the Hand. Talking and writing are different, it's true, but those are only two of many ways to speak, and they can enter into many sorts of partnerships and collusions—which, by the way, is what is happening here and now.

Language isn't confined to the system of mouth and ear any more than emotions are restricted to the heart or dancing to the feet. There isn't any one organ or one anatomical process to which language is confined. Nor any human language to which certain forms of stories are confined.

III.

Humans, in any case, send messages. Analytical linguists parse these messages into components—phonemes, morphemes, suffixes, prefixes, infixes, roots, particles, words, phrases, clauses, sentences. A lot of linguists stop there, just at the point where, for me, the study of language gets most interesting.

A story is to the sentence as a tree is to the twig. And a literature is to the story as the forest is to the tree. Language—that metaphor—is the wood the tree is made of, an engineer might say, but a biologist would notice something else. The wood the tree is made of is created by the tree. Stories make the language they are made of. They make it and keep it alive. You can kill the tree and take the wood, kill the story and take the language, kill the earth and take the ore, kill the river and take the water—but if you really want to understand the wood, the water, the minerals, and the rocks, you have to visit them at home, in the living trees, the rivers, the earth. And if you really want to understand the language, you have to encounter it in the stories by which it was made.

What's more, if you really want to understand the tree, you have to encounter it in the forest. If you want to understand the river, you have to explore the watershed. If you want to understand the story, you have to go beyond it, into the ecosystem of stories.

If you'll forgive me, I'll make a little detour here into the dreary realm of terminology. I have not lived for the thousand years it would take to become conversant with all five hundred Native North American languages, but as far as I've been able to make out, most of these languages distinguish two major kinds of stories: those that occur in mythtime and those that occur in human time or historical time. In Cree, for example, the former are called *âtayôhkan* or *âtayôhkêwin* and the latter *âcimôwin*. In Haida, the former are *qqaygaang* and the latter *gyaahlghalang*. In Kwakwala, the former are called *nuyem* and the latter *q'a'yoł*. In Osage, the former are *hígo,* the latter *úthage.* In Winnebago, they are *waiką* and *worak.* These are not the only names for literary genres in any of these languages, but this basic distinction between two kinds of time, and two kinds of story, seems to be important. Like the distinction between oral and written, it's a distinction we should be careful not to get trapped in. The Cree mythteller Kâ-kîsikâw-pîhtokêw loved to play around with this pair of terms in Cree, calling the same stories *âtayôhkêwin* at one moment and *âcimôwin* the next, teasing his student, the linguist Leonard Bloomfield, and anyone else who tried to pin these notions down.

The etymology of these terms naturally differs from one language family to another, but consider the two Cree words for example. The word *âcimôwin,* meaning a story set in human time or historical time, comes from the verb *âcimo-,* which means to tell, to explain, to report. The word *âtayôhkan,* meaning a myth, a sacred story, a story set in mythtime, is related to—in fact, on the surface, it is identical to—one of the words for spirit being or guardian spirit. Is such a story merely "something told"? Its name appears to mean it has a little more reality than that.

It's easy to get into trouble translating these terms into English. One reason is that English is a very acquisitive language that keeps putting words in the bank. We have a surplus of terms: *myth, story, tale, legend, reminiscence, memoir, history, tradition, chronicle, epic, fiction, narrative, novel, travelogue,* and so on, not to mention compound terms such as *fairy tale, true story, science fiction,* and the rest. In the real life of language, these terms overlap; in fact, they sprawl all over each other like teenagers lounging around on the couch. A pedant could make them all sit up straight and proper and measure off the space assigned to each, but the moment the pedant left the room, that order would dissolve. And while we have that surplus of words for different kinds of stories, there are some other equally basic terms we lack.

We have the word *myth,* in any case, and we can use it for any kind of story, any kind of narrative, happening in mythtime. A *mythology,* then, is an ecosystem of myths, a forest of language where those kinds of stories are dominant. What do we call an ecosystem made of the other kind of stories, the ones that are sited in human time? This kind of language forest embraces both history and fiction. The English word *history* had that larger sense once upon a time, but we would have to do some work to get it back. And what about the larger ecosystem, including mythology, history, and fiction? I've been using the word *literature* for that kind of ecosystem, even though I know the term *literature* has been tainted by academic use. I need a name for the big watershed of stories, human and nonhuman, and that's the most suitable term I have found.

This detour into terminology is all in aid of making a simple point. A story—whether it's myth or fiction or history—typically has a beginning, a middle, and an end. We may not start at the beginning and may never get to the end, but we expect them to exist, like head and foot. This is a sign that stories, like sentences, are individual organisms more than they are communities. An ecosystem is different. A forest has an *edge,* it has a *boundary,* and it may, vaguely speaking, have a *middle,* but it has no beginning and no end, because it isn't a linear structure. It simply starts wherever you enter it and ends wherever you come out. The same is true of a mythology. History may or may not be linear, like a river, as many people claim. Mythology, like the forest, clearly is not.

IV.

Trees grow in and on the earth. Where do stories grow? They grow in and on storytelling creatures. Stories are epiphytes: organisms that grow on other organisms, in much the same way staghorn ferns and tree-dwelling lichens—Alectoria, Bryoria, Letharia, and so on—grow on trees.

I have a hunch that from a lichen's point of view, the basic function of a tree is to provide a habitat for lichens. I have a hunch that from a story's point of view, the function of storytelling creatures—humans for example—is to provide a habitat for stories. I think the stories might be right. That's what you and I are really *for:* to make it possible for certain kinds of stories to exist.

We don't know very much, strange to say, about the biology of stories. Aristotle studied their anatomy, but not much more was done, in a scientific way, until the twentieth century. The comparative work of Boas and Lowie and Stith Thompson added a little. Then Vladimir Propp, Claude Lévi-Strauss, and linguist Dell Hymes began to study the anatomy and physiology of stories more intensely. One of the first things Propp and Hymes discovered is that, whatever the language they're told in, stories tend to have branching, fractal structures, very much like trees.

Those trees, the trees of meaning we call stories, grow in your brain and the rest of your body. And there seems to be a symbiotic relation between those trees of meaning and ourselves. What the stories get out of it is that they get to exist. What we get out of it is guidance. Stories are one of the fundamental ways in which we understand the world. They are probably our best maps and models of the world—and we may yet come to learn that the reason for this is that stories are some of the basic constituents of the world.

Most of you, I suspect, are familiar with a twentieth-century proverb, *The map is not the territory.* We owe this statement to a linguist by the name of Alfred Korzybski. (Semantics, Korzybski's field, is of course a subdivision of linguistics, though Korzybski did his best to make it sound like something else.)

Thirty years ago, in a lecture in honor of Korzybski, Gregory Bateson proposed an idea that startled and frightened his audience. The idea was simple enough. It was that *the units of biological evolution and the units of mind are one and the same.* This thesis owes something to Darwin, of course, and something to Lamarck—an often vilified biologist for whom Bateson had a refreshing degree of respect. And it owes something to Parmenides, the pre-Socratic poet who said, among other things, τὸ γὰρ αὐτὸ νοεῖν ἔστιν τε καὶ εἶναι. This is a short, sweet, simple Greek sentence which no equally sweet and short and simple English sentence matches. It takes more than one English map, in other words, to portray this little parcel of Greek territory. Here are two approximate translations: (1) *To be and to think are the same;* (2) *To be and to have meaning are the same.* The implication of the Greek verb νοεῖν (*noeîn*) is that thought and meaning form a unit which ought not to be dissolved.

The English words *noesis, knowledge,* and *narration* all stem from the same root. Thought and meaning are connected not just to each other but to storytelling too. What Parmenides is saying extends to what he's doing. *To be and to tell a story are the same.* Or: *To be is to be a story.* Or: *I am, therefore I think*—and not the other and more arrogant way around.

Put the Greek philosopher-poet Parmenides and the English biologist Charles Darwin in the same room for a moment and you have the makings of Bateson's thesis, positing the unity of biological evolution and mind. Put Parmenides and the Haida philosopher-poet Skaay together for a moment in the same canoe and you have the implicit beginnings of what I like to call ecological linguistics.

I have a hunch that fields of learning worth their salt grow up from their own subject matter. I don't imagine they can be generated by lightning bolts of theory hurled from above. But lightning storms are welcome now and then, if only for the glory of the show, and Bateson's thesis looks to me like an illuminating flash, giving an instantaneous glimpse of what ecological linguistics ought to be.

Bateson was sixty-five years old when he delivered his Korzybski Lecture, and this was the time of his own awakening. I'd happily quote you the whole lecture, but here two paragraphs will do:

> If you put God outside and set him vis-à-vis his creation, and if you have the idea that you are created in his image, you will logically and naturally see yourself as outside and against the things around you. And as you arrogate all mind to yourself, you will see the world around you as mindless and therefore not entitled to moral or ethical consideration. The environment will seem to be yours to exploit. Your survival unit will be you and your folks or conspecifics against the environment of other social units, other races and the brutes and vegetables.
>
> If this is your estimate of your relations to nature *and you have an advanced technology,* your likelihood of survival will be that of a snowball in hell. You will die either of the toxic byproducts of your own hate, or, simply, of overpopulation and overgrazing.

An idea, as Bateson says, is *a difference that makes a difference.* A *meaningful* difference in other words. A thought worth thinking is a meaning. A tree of meaning is a story. A forest of such stories is a mind. So is a tree with birds in its branches. So is a human with ideas (plural) perching in its brain.

V.

We owe many things to David Abram, not the least of which is the rallying cry, *The rejuvenation of oral culture is an ecological imperative.*

Why is oral culture a key to our continued coexistence with the world?

Because oral culture means much more and less than simply talking. Rekindling oral culture means rejoining the community of speaking beings—sandhill cranes, whitebark pines, coyotes, wood frogs, bees, and thunder.

Oral culture also means much more than telling stories. It means learning how to hear them, how to nourish them, and how to let them live. It means learning to let stories swim down into yourself, grow large in there, and rise back up again. It does not—repeat, does *not*—mean memorizing the lines so you can act the script you've written or recite the book you've read. Oral culture—and any culture at all—involves, as nature does, a lot of repetition. But rote memorization and oral culture are two very different things.

If you embody an oral culture, you are a working part of a place, a part of the soil in which stories live their lives. There will in that event be stories you know by heart—but when the stories come out of your mouth, as when the trees come out of the ground, no two performances will ever be the same. Each incarnation of a story is itself. What rests in the mythteller's heart are the seeds of the tree of meaning. All you can tape or transcribe is a kind of photograph or fossil of the leaves: the frozen forms of spoken words.

To put it in other terms, the text is just the map; the story is the territory. The story, however, is also a map—a map of the land, a map of the mind, a map of the heart, a map of the language in which the story is told. Every map is also a territory, and every territory a map—*but not its own.* To be and to mean and to think and to tell are the same, yet all of them rest on that tissue of interconnection. The story that you tell and are is you *but not your own.*

You find the words by walking through the vision, which may be in the heart that is there inside your body, or it may be in the heart that is out there in the land. You learn the trail if you walk it many times, but every time you walk it, you reinvent the steps. There may, of course, be steep and narrow stretches where you memorize the moves—those places in the story often crystallize as songs—but they are subject, even then, to variation and erosion and other forms of change. And they connect you to yourself and to the world.

In an oral culture, stories are given voice. They are also given the silence in which to breathe. Very rarely in oral cultures do you meet people *who talk all the time.* In literate societies, I meet them rather often. Here, what's more, I am in danger of becoming one myself. I therefore beg to be excused.

JAN ZWICKY

Five Poems

INTO THE DARK

Was there a time I did not know you? The continents
had other names and shapes, perhaps; the days
before the feather was invented; before
the sea was blue. Even then

the muscles of your shoulders could not
lift the world. Though
I think you tried: this scar, here; the long bruise
you never talk about

that never fades. How beautiful
you must have been then, bronze and flashing,
for how beautiful you are: though now
the birds are falling from the sky, the terrifying rain

has washed the cliff away. This back of yours,
what it still bears. You are
the one I've always walked towards, the one I've sensed
as salt, as wind, as answer. Now, at last, you turn from me,

the soft whuff of your sleeping self,
the white wisps of your hair like tufts of silk,
like so much that I love:
strewn, fragile, mortal, gleaming.

LATE LOVE

At the end, far into the afternoon,
I'd walk the same trail, when I could,
up to the ridge. For often then,
but only at that time of day, there would be
sun. The creeks still overflowing and the path

still slick, but what gushed
among the rocks and deadfall was alight,
the droplets flashing in the firs—gold, emerald,
rose—their sharp glint echoed
in the polished tangle of the overgrown salal.

And I saw that it was true,
what you had taught me: beauty
insists: it is connexion
with the real. Even on the days I couldn't tell my sorrow
from the world's: the sudden calm
that was your touch, how I was trued
inside your glance. The long and level shaft of light
at day's end, reaching from the planet's edge
beneath its lid of cloud. That clarity.
Brief brightness on the earth.

SECURING THE HOUSE

What is it we are trying
to achieve? That we will learn
before we die to make
our leaving orderly? Imagine

turning down the heat
and walking out, not even
locking up, imagine
coming back weeks later. Ah,

the list of failures: unpaid bills,
the missing jewellery, plant leaves
browning on the window sills.

And the dust. What of the dust?

MEDITATION LOOKING WEST FROM THE BERKELEY HILLS

Then, even the work dissolves—
whatever it was. The great ships
motionless in the enormous bay,
gone the next time you look up.

And have you ever really wanted anything
except that disappearing act,
the open ocean, all horizon,
just the other side of the bridge?

Its vastness makes it comprehensible, frames
the restlessness, reduces it
to stationary shimmer. Who wouldn't
want to let go. Who wouldn't choose

those distances. They're too big
to get the mind around, too big
even for the heart. Though we try each day,
falling more and more silent.

It's love, in the end, that we learn, learning also
that it isn't ours. Inexplicably, unsummoned,
the world rises to fill its own emptiness. You feel it
reaching through you—a voice, a hand,

a greenness not your own—
and are buoyed up momentarily, amazed,
before you find your feet again,
or drown.

DESIRE

Desire, you who lift us each morning,
        rough as the disc of the sun,
you who bind us, who drag us half senseless
        through the gift of our pain,

who leap without thought, who climb
        with the climber who seizes the air
in the fists of his lungs, drinking
        the light with the lungs of his eyes,

tell me: even the dead do not know,
        even those who are ashes and sleeping now
under the lake, their extravagance
        earns them no answer.

You, who live high in the mountains,
        where being itself empties down like the falls,
sometimes in tumult, here glassy with weight, its pour
        as though motionless: see

how the air, the melodious air,
        fills the clearing: floating the grass
and the palm-bright leaves. Their breathing
        like sleep, and the year that completes itself in them.

If I go down on my knees, if I go down
        in the burnt yellow grass, in the somnolent leaves,
what will this serve? No appeal,
        no assuaging the centuries,

the droughts and the floods, the poisoned and vanished
        that pile up and stagger against the horizon.
The sick sky won't swallow me, its sick heat
        won't melt the scab of my fear.

The souls of the alders, the souls of the firs,
        the souls of the red-bellied newts and
the golden-crowned kinglets, the uncountable souls of the grasses,
        making one soul, one bending

at dawn. Where will my soul go
        when it can't walk among them?
When the earth that has shone in our lives turns its back
        and closes its eyes.

I will lie down, then, in the terror and silence,
        in the rot of the forest, in the rot of the wind.
I will lie down in the wreckage of meaning,
        the dust of you filling my mouth.

ROBERT RICE

Cantus for Still Water

1. RIVER

This business of water flowing
always toward some farther-off place—
I'm beginning to think
it's no accident.

If we walked up that road and watched
firs beside it turn to dust,
if we stood stock-still and listened,
the slow breaking-apart of stones
would tell us how it is
with our lives,

and we would come at last to this stream,
surface streaked and riffled,
one of the ocean's dreaming thoughts.

What I'm hoping is
here we are born as the earth.
What I'm hoping:
things indifferent to us
will save us in the end.

Say what you want to,
everything here is scripture—
the way water slides from alder leaves,
the way small waves wash
a streambed rock, the way
the outstretched arm of that conifer
brushes the current,
longing to follow the water downstream.

All I know today: I want to be rain.

2. BRIDGE

You know how it is—
you walk onto a bridge,
look downstream, then up
and up again, and keep
looking upstream
while the inexhaustible river
flows into you, fills you,
promises everything:
bright birds singing,
angels bringing coffee
with cream, songs
that skim gold
from molten lead.
But you, not convinced,
glance across the bridge
to where the grade descends,
and the river
races away.

3. LAKE

Astonishing
how lake becomes river, how
the first faint stir of current
forms, a push of wonder
out of stillness, emerges
from clear, silent water
to dance its descent,
taming the sharp corners surely
in a language we all understand.

It takes no time to be lake
but this river
scouring the banks for cargo
makes me believe it's possible,
my life.
I pick out stones, plans,
drop in hours.
What I mean to have I can.
I only need movement and
something I forget.

So why just now
as I walk the edge content,
almost, does desire lift me
toward the unthinking lake?
It knows only itself.
Wanting it is like waiting
for a lover who doesn't come.

Never mind, the river says,
current's the cure for shadows,
then rounds the corner and falls,
in shock into
indifferent ocean.

In the Great Bend of the Souris River_____

My father, David Whippet, moved a family of eight from Lancaster, in the western Mojave, up onto the high plains of central North Dakota in the summer of 1952. He rented a two-story, six-bedroom house near West-hope. It was shaded by cottonwoods and weeping willows and I lived in it for eleven years before he moved us again, to Sedalia in central Missouri, where he retired in 1975. I never felt the country around Sedalia. I carried the treeless northern prairie close in my mind, the spine-shattering crack of June thunder—tin drums falling from heaven, Mother called it—an image of coyotes evaporating in a draw.

I went east to North Carolina to college the year Father moved us to Missouri. When my parents died, within a year of each other, my brothers and sisters sold the Sedalia house. I took no part of the proceeds. I looked back always to the broad crown of land in Bottineau County that drained away into the Mouse River, a short-grass plain of wheat, oats, and barley, where pasqueflower and blazing star and long-headed coneflower quivered in the summer wind. I came to see it in later years as the impetus behind a life I hadn't managed well.

That first summer in North Dakota, 1952, the air heated up like it did in the desert around Lancaster, but the California heat was dry. This humid Dakota weather staggered us all. I got used to the heat, though the hardest work I ever did was summer haying on those plains. I'd fall asleep at the supper table still itching with chaff. I grew to crave the dark cold of winter, the January weeks at thirty below, the table of bare land still as a sheet of iron. Against that soaking heat and bone-deep cold the other two seasons were slim, as subtle and erotic as sex.

Considering my aspirations at the university in Chapel Hill—I majored in history, then did graduate work in physics—the way my life took shape seemed not to follow. The summary way to state it is that I became an itinerant, a wanderer with an affinity for any kind of work to be done with wood. I moved a lot—back to California from North Carolina, then to Tucson for a while before going to the Gulf Coast, Louisiana—always renting. After that, I worked in Utah for six years, then moved to eastern Nebraska. I considered moving to North Dakota, but that country seemed better as a distant memory. I felt estranged from it.

Over those twenty years of moving around I installed cabinets and counters in people's homes, made fine furniture, and built a few houses. In my notebooks, dozens of them, I wrote meticulous descriptions of more than a hundred kinds of wood, detailing the range of expression of each as I came to know it. I wrote out how these woods responded to various hand tools. In line after neat line I explained the combinations of human desire, material resistance, and mechanical fit that made a built object memorable. I was in my thirties before I saw what I'd been straining after in North Carolina, obscured until then by academic partitioning: the intense microcosm of history that making a house from a set of blueprints becomes; and the restive forces involved in physical labor. It becomes apparent in wiring a house or in routing water through it that more than gravity and the elementary flow of electrons must be taken into account. The house is alive with detour and change. Similarly with squaring its frame. The complex tensions that accumulate in wood grain affect the construction of each house. Nothing solid, I learned, can ever be built without shims.

Aging got me down off roofs by the time I was forty. Pride, I have to think, a desire to publicly acquit myself by choosing a settled and respectable calling, precipitated my first purchase of a house, in Ashland, Nebraska, in 1986. Attached to it was a spacious workshop in which I intended to build cabinets and hardwood tables and chairs for the well-to-do in Omaha and Lincoln. I also found for the first time since a divorce ten years before—and not incidentally, I think—an opportunity for long-term companionship. The money was good. A year into it I felt steady and clear.

It was faith and not nostalgia that eventually sent me up to Bottineau County. The harmonious life I'd found with Doreen, a tall, graceful woman with a gift for design and for the arrangement of things, was disturbed by a single, insistent disaffection. Neither human love nor her praise for what I did could cure it. I had not, since I'd left North Dakota, felt I belonged in any particular place. During the first years in Nebraska I'd reasoned I could settle there permanently if it hadn't been for an entity still missing, like a moon that failed to rise. If I found a place to attach myself in North Dakota, I would muse, I'd stand a chance of bringing all the pieces of myself together in a fit that would last. It did not have to be a life lived in North Dakota, but if I didn't go back and see, I'd forever have that emptiness, the phantom room in a house.

The drive up to Bottineau County from Ashland takes two days. In the fall of 1991 I spent a week crisscrossing farmland there in the hold of the Mouse River, trailing like a lost dog in the big bend the river makes north and east of Minot. Not finding, or knowing, what I wanted, I finally drove up to Cedoux in Saskatchewan, where the river heads in no particular place and where it is known by its French name, the Souris. The river bears east from there, passing near small towns like Yellow Grass and Openshaw before turning south for North Dakota.

That's all the distance I went that first year.

I went back the next spring to the same spot and followed the river southeast to Velva, North Dakota, traveling slowly, like a drift of horses. The river swings back sharply to the northeast there, the bottom of its curve, and picks up the Deep River west of Kramer. Then it runs a long straight reach of bottomland, the Salyer Wildlife Refuge, all the way to the Manitoba border. North of the border the Souris gathers Antler Creek. I parked the car frequently and walked in over private land to find the river in these places. The Souris finally runs out in the Assiniboine like the flare of a trumpet. The Assiniboine joins the Red River near Winnipeg, and from Lake Winnipeg, in a flow too difficult to trace, the diffused memory of the Souris passes down the Nelson and into Hudson Bay.

I needed a sense of the entire lay of the river in those first two years. But it was in the great bend of the Souris in northern North Dakota, the river we called the Mouse when I was a boy, somewhere in that fifty miles of open country between Salyer Refuge in the east and the Upper Souris Refuge to the west, that I believed what I wanted might he found. I rented a motel room in Sherwood and concentrated my search north of State Highway 256, the road running straight east from Sherwood to Westhope. Each day, from one spot or another, I'd hike the few miles from the road up to the Canadian border. Sometimes I'd camp where I thought the border was and the next day walk back to the truck. What I was alert for was a bird's cry, a pattern of purple and yellow flowers in a patch of needlegrass, the glint of a dragonfly—a turn of emotion that would alter my sense of alignment.

In the spring of 1994, walking a dry stretch of upper Cut Bank Creek, I came on the tracks of three or four unshod horses. I followed the short trail out of prairie grass onto fine silt in the river bed, where it then turned abruptly back onto prairie grass and became undetectable. I tested the rim of the hoofprints with my fingertips. I marked the way the horses' hooves had clipped small stones and sent them shooting sideways. In several places the tracks nicked the ground deeply enough to suggest the horses had been carrying riders.

It was hard for me to get away a second time that year. It wasn't until September that I was able to complete and deliver promised work, and when I finally drove north it was with complicating thoughts. Doreen had proposed, and I had enthusiastically accepted. The home we'd made in Ashland suited both of us, and for a while that summer the undertow that had pulled me north went slack. I felt satisfied. It often happens in life, I knew, that while you're searching ardently in one place, the very thing you want turns up in another, and I thought this was what had occurred. But Doreen said I should go on with it. She saw our time spread out still as moonlight on the prairie. She didn't see time being lost to us. She had a deliberateness of movement about her, a steady expression, that led me to consider things slowly.

So that fall—anticipating a familiar motel room and the stark diner in Sherwood—I went back, in a state of wonder at the new arrangement of my life. And I was thinking about the hoofprints. Some of the land north of 256 lies fallow, and Canada's border, like the sight of a distant fence with no gate, turns travelers away here to the west and east toward manned border crossings. The international boundary tends to maintain an outback, a deserted plain on which one traveler might expect to find no trace of another.

I arrived in Sherwood on September 16. With the help of an acquaintance I rented a horse and trailer to let me explore more quickly and extensively along the upper reaches of Cut Bank Creek. On the morning of the seventeenth I parked the truck off the side of the road a few miles east of town and rode north on the mare, a spirited blue roan. I found no fresh horse tracks along the creek bed. Somewhere near the border I turned east. I'd forgotten how much being astride a horse freed the eye. It is the horse, then, that must watch the ground. I'd ridden horses since I was a child, but not recently. I recalled with growing pleasure the way a good horse can measure off a prairie, glide you over its swells.

I was certain I'd walked across parts of this same landscape earlier, but it seemed different to me now, the result of being up on the horse, I thought, and taking in more of a place at a glance than I would on foot. Or it may have been that with the horse under me, traveling seemed less arduous, less distracting. I was watering the mare at a pothole, one of many scattered over these grass plains, when another rider rose up from a swale astride a brown pinto. He did not at first see me. I had a chance to steady myself before our eyes met. The blue roan raised her head from the water but gave no sign of alarm. At her movement the other horse crow-hopped sideways. It took me a moment to separate horse and rider. The pinto bore yellow bars on both forelegs. A trail of red hoofprints ran over its left shoulder, and two feathers spiraled in its mane. The man's dark legs were similarly barred, and there were white dots like hail across his chest. Above a sky-blue neck his chin and mouth were painted black. The upper right half of his face was white. From the left cheek, a bright blue serpentine line rose through his eye and entered his hair. The hair cascaded over his horse's rump, its gleaming black lines spilling to both sides. The man held a simple jaw-loop rein lightly in his left hand. In his right he held out a short bow and an unnocked arrow.

The bold division of his face made its contours hard to read, but the forehead was high, the nose and middle of the face long, his lips full. The adornment of horse and rider blazed against the dun-colored prairie. A halo of intensity surrounded them both, as if they were about to explode. I could read no expression in either face—not fear, not curiosity, not aggression, not even wonder. The man's lips were slightly pursed, suggesting concentration, possibly amusement, as if he had encountered an unexpected test, a stunt meant to throw him.

Of the four of us, only my horse shifted. As she did so, the polished chrome of her bit and the silver conchas on her bridle played sunlight over the other horse and rider. The man's first movement of distraction was to follow the streaks and discs of light running like water across his thighs.

In that moment I remembered enough from a studious childhood to guess the man might be Assiniboin. In the eighteenth century Assiniboin people lived here between the upper Saskatchewan and Missouri Rivers. He could be Cree. He looked half my age.

I turned my reins once around the pommel of the saddle and showed my empty hands, palms out, at my sides.

"My name is Adrian Whippet," I said. "I am only passing through here."

Nothing in his demeanor changed. I'd never seen a human being so alert. He slowly pursed his lips in a more pronounced way, but the trace of amusement was gone. Just then I smelled the other horses, which I turned to see. Another man, his face cut diagonally into triangles of bright red and blue, sat a sorrel mare behind me. He led three horses on a braided rope—a pale dun horse with a black tail and mane carrying pack bags, a black pinto, and a bay with a face stripe. Their flaring nostrils searched the air, their eyes rolled as they took it all in. The second man wore a plain breechclout, like the first. He held no weapon, but studied me as if I were something he was going to hunt.

In a gesture made in response and without thinking, I raised my right arm to point beyond him across the prairie, as though I had something to show or was indicating where we were all headed. I turned the blue roan firmly and started in that direction. It was the direction in which my truck lay and seemed, too, the direction they were traveling. The skin beneath my shirt prickled as I passed before the second man, a chill of sweat. They drew up quickly on each side of me. I was surrounded by the odor of men and horses.

We rode easily together. From time to time they spoke to one another, brief exchanges, unanswered statements. I said nothing. The second man, about the same age as his companion, was leaner. His hair was cut off at the shoulders and raised in a clay-stiffened wall above his forehead. He wore ear pendants of iridescent shell. Wolf tails swung from the heels of his moccasins. I didn't want to stare, but maneuvered my horse in such a way as to fall slightly behind occasionally so I could look more closely at them. From the number of things they carried, skin bundles and parfleches, I guessed they were coming back from a long trip. That would explain the extra horses. Or perhaps they'd been somewhere and stolen the horses.

They, too, tried not to stare, but I sensed them scrutinizing every article of my tack and clothing, every accoutrement. I thought to signal them that we might trade horses, or to demonstrate for them the effect of my sunglasses on the glare coming from the side oats and blue grama grass. But, just as quickly, I let the ideas go. I felt it best to give in to the riding, to carry on with calmness and authority.

Eventually, we stopped glancing at one another and gazed over the country more, studying individual parts of it. In a movement so fast it was finished before I grasped it, the first man shot a large jackrabbit, which he leaned down to snatch from the grass without dismounting. He gutted it with a small sharp tool and spilled the intestines out as we rode along. His movements were as deft as a weaver's, and I felt an unexpected pleasure watching him. He returned my look of admiration with what seemed a self-conscious smile. The harsh afternoon light silvered in a sheen on the horses' necks and flanks, and I heard the flick of their hooves in the cordgrass and bluestem when we crossed damp swales. Hairy seeds of milkweed proceeded so slowly through the air that we passed them by. More often than I, the two men turned to look behind them.

I knew these people no better than two deer I might have stumbled upon, but I was comfortable with them, and the way we fit against the prairie satisfied me. I felt I could ride a very long way like this, absorbed by whatever it was we now shared, a kind of residency. It seemed, because of the absence of fences or the intercession of the horses, or perhaps only as an accident of conducive weather, that we were traveling a seam together. There was nothing to do but ride on, marking the country in unison and feeling the inspiritedness of the afternoon, smelling the leather, the horses, the prairie.

When we came to what I recognized as the intermittently dry bed of Cut Bank Creek, I said the words out loud, "Cut Bank Creek."

The second man said something softly. The first man repeated his words so I could hear, "*Akip atashetwah.*"

I lifted my left hand to suggest, again, our trail. First Man mimicked the gesture perfectly, indicating they meant to go in a different direction from mine, north and west. We regarded each other with savor, pleased and wondering but not puzzled. I laid my reins around the pommel and pulled off the belt my father had given me as a wedding present years ago. I cut two of its seventeen sand-cast silver conchas free with a pocketknife. Dismounting, I handed one to each man. Second Man pulled a thin white object from a bag tied to his saddle frame. When he held it out for me, I recognized it as a large bird's wing bone, drilled with a line of small holes. A flute. I remounted with it as First Man stepped to the ground. He lifted a snowy owl feather he'd taken from his horse's mane and tied it into the blue roan's mane.

We rode away without speaking. The first time I looked back, I couldn't see them. I sat the horse and watched the emptiness where they should have been until dusk laid blue and then purple across the grass.

LOUIS OWENS

Burning the Shelter

In the center of the Glacier Peak Wilderness in northern Washington, a magnificent, fully glaciated white volcano rises over a stunningly beautiful region of the North Cascades. On maps, the mountain is called Glacier Peak. To the Salishan people who have always lived in this part of the Cascades, however, the mountain is *Dakobed,* or the Great Mother, the place of emergence. For more than eighty years, a small, three-sided log shelter stood in a place called White Pass, just below one shoulder of the great mountain, tucked securely into a meadow between thick stands of mountain hemlock and alpine fir.

In the early fall of 1976, while working as a seasonal ranger for the U.S. Forest Service, I drew the task of burning the White Pass shelter. After all those years, the shelter roof had collapsed like a broken bird wing under the weight of winter snow, and the time was right for fire and replanting. It was part of a Forest Service plan to remove all human-made objects from wilderness areas, a plan of which I heartily approved. So I backpacked eleven miles to the pass and set up camp, and for five days, while a bitter early storm sent snow driving horizontally out of the North, I dismantled the shelter and burned the old logs, piling and burning and piling and burning until nothing remained. The antique, hand-forged spikes that had held the shelter together I put into gunny sacks and cached to be packed out later by mule. I spaded up the earth, beaten hard for nearly a century by boot and hoof, and transplanted plugs of vegetation from hidden spots on the nearby ridge.

At the end of those five days, not a trace of the shelter remained, and I felt good, very smug in fact, about returning the White Pass meadow to its "original" state. As I packed up my camp, the snowstorm had subsided to a few flurries and a chill that felt bone-deep with the promise of winter. My season was almost over, and as I started the steep hike down to the trailhead, my mind was on the winter I was going to spend in sunny Arizona.

A half-mile from the pass I saw the two old women. At first they were dark, hunched forms far down on the last long switchback up the snowy ridge. But as we drew closer to one another, I began to feel a growing amazement that, by the time we were face-to-face, had become awe. Almost

Totem pole with beaver and frog, Skidegate. 1928. Graphite on paper by Emily Carr. Royal British Columbia Museum, British Columbia Archives. PDP08933

swallowed up in their baggy wool pants, heavy sweaters, and parkas, silver braids hanging below thick wool caps, they seemed ancient, each weighted with at least seventy years as well as a small backpack. They paused every few steps to lean on their staffs and look out over the North Fork drainage below, a deep, heavily forested river valley that rose on the far side of the glaciers and sawtoothed black granite of the Monte Cristo Range. And they smiled hugely upon seeing me, clearly surprised and delighted to find another person in the mountains at such a time.

We stood and chatted for a moment, and as I did with all backpackers, I reluctantly asked them where they were going. The snow quickened a little, obscuring the view, as they told me that they were going to White Pass.

"Our father built a little house up here," one of them said, "when he worked the Forest Service like you. Way back before we was born, before this century."

"We been coming up here each year since we was little," the other added. "Except last year when Sarah was not well enough."

"A long time ago, this was all our land," the one called Sarah said. "All Indi'n land everywhere you can see. Our people had houses up in the mountains, for gathering berries each year."

As they took turns speaking, the smiles never leaving their faces, I wanted to excuse myself, to edge around these elders and flee to the trailhead and my car, drive back to the district station and keep going south. I wanted to say, "I'm Indian too. Choctaw from Mississippi; Cherokee from Oklahoma"—as if mixed blood could pardon me for what I had done. Instead, I said, "The shelter is gone." Cravenly I added, "It was crushed by snow, so I was sent up to burn it. It's gone now."

I expected outrage, anger, sadness, but instead the sisters continued to smile at me, their smiles changing only slightly. They had a plastic tarp and would stay dry, they said, because a person always had to be prepared in the mountains. They would put up their tarp inside the hemlock grove above the meadow, and the scaly hemlock branches would turn back the snow. They forgave me without saying it—my ignorance and my part in the long pattern of loss which they knew so well.

Hiking out those eleven miles, as the snow of the high country became a drumming rain in the forests below, I had long hours to ponder my encounter with the sisters. Gradually, almost painfully, I began to understand that what I called "wilderness" was an absurdity, nothing more than a figment of the European imagination. Before the European invasion, there was no wilderness in North America; there was only the fertile continent where people lived in a hard-learned balance with the natural world. In embracing a philosophy that saw the White Pass shelter—and all traces of humanity—as a shameful stain upon the "pure" wilderness, I had succumbed to a five-hundred-year-old pattern of deadly thinking that separates us from the natural world. This is not to say that what we call wilderness today does not need careful safeguarding. I believe that White Pass really is better off now that the shelter doesn't serve as a magnet to backpackers and horsepackers who compact the soil, disturb and kill the wildlife, cut down centuries-old trees for firewood, and leave their litter strewn about. And I believe the man who built the shelter would agree. But despite this unfortunate reality, the global environmental crisis that sends species into extinction daily and threatens to destroy all life surely has its roots in the Western pattern of thought that sees humanity and "wilderness" as mutually exclusive.

In old-growth forests in the North Cascades, deep inside the official Wilderness Area, I have come upon faint traces of log shelters built by Suiattle and Upper Skagit people for berry harvesting a century or more ago—just as the sisters said. Those human-made structures were as natural a part of the Cascade ecosystem as the burrows of marmots in the steep scree slopes. Our Native ancestors all over this continent lived within a complex web of relations with the natural world, and in doing so they assumed a responsibility for their world that contemporary Americans cannot even imagine. Unless Americans, and all human beings, can learn to imagine themselves as intimately and inextricably related to every aspect of the world they inhabit, with the extraordinary responsibilities such relationship entails—unless they can learn what the indigenous peoples of the Americas knew and often still know—the earth simply will not survive. A few square miles of something called wilderness will become the sign of failure everywhere.

The Sasquatch at Home

My name is Eden Robinson. My mother is Heiltsuk[1] from Bella Bella, and my father is Haisla from Kitamaat Village, both small reserves on the northwest coast of British Columbia. My maternal grandmother's family was originally from Rivers Inlet. Since both sides of my family are matrilineal, my clan name should have come from my mother's side and I should belong to the Eagle Clan. When I was ten years old, my father's family decided to give my sister and me Beaver Clan names at a Settlement Feast for a Beaver Clan chief who had died a year earlier.

When a chief died, his body was embalmed in a Terrace funeral home and then he was brought back to his house, where he lay for at least three days, attended around the clock by family members, or people hired by his family, to keep him safe from harm as he rested in the living room. Community members paid respects by visiting him in his home and at his memorial. After the funeral itself, the Thank You Supper was held for people who had helped out emotionally, financially, and organizationally. After a year of planning and preparation, the family announced the date of the Settlement Feast and, finally, of the headstone moving. Modern feasts are truncated affairs lasting six hours at the most. Much of the dancing has gone, but the important dirges are sung, names are distributed and redistributed to clan members, and people from the community are gifted according to their status and involvement with the family. In general, headstone moving is considered an affair of the immediate family and close friends. Space in the graveyard is tight, and imposing yourself on the family's grief is considered the height of rudeness.

You aren't supposed to attend a feast or a potlatch without an Indian[2] name, and since we were living in Kitamaat Village, my mother, though annoyed, agreed for the sake of convenience to let us become Beaver Clan. My younger sister and I received our names at the Settlement Feast. Towards the end of the evening, we were told to go and line up with other children receiving names. I mostly remember being embarrassed to stand in front of everyone and not have any idea what I was supposed to do. At the feast, one of my aunts told me that if I wanted to learn more about my name, I should go visit my grandmother, my ma-ma-oo (pronounced *ma-MAH-ew*).

The next day, we went to Ma-ma-oo's house. She told my sister that her name was Sigadum'na'x, which meant Sent Back Chief Lady. A long time ago, a marriage was arranged between a high-ranking lady from up the line and a Haisla chief. They fell deeply in love. Unfortunately, his four other wives became extremely jealous and kept trying to poison her. He couldn't divorce them because they came from powerful families and insulting them in this way would mean, at the very least, nasty feuds. So despite his feelings, he decided to send his love back to her home. He couldn't divorce her without causing her shame, so he made her a chief. I've since learned two other versions of the story behind my sister's name, but I like this one the best.

"Wow," I said when I heard the story. "What does my name mean?"

"Big lady."

"Um, what else does it mean?"

Ma-ma-oo paused. "Biiiiiig lady."

I paused. Names come loaded with rights and histories. Within the Beaver Clan, the name of The Chief of All Haislas (Jasee) is hotly contested and has started many family quarrels. My father is one of the younger sons of a high-ranking family, so my siblings and I receive noble names, but nothing that garners too much prestige and thus requires extensive feasting or that can get me into too much trouble. My name, Wiwltx°, was obtained through marriage and only given to women of noble birth, so it suggests a high rank. I was disappointed in my name, and it had nothing to do with rank: I had story envy. No heartbroken women were standing beside rivers with their long hair unbound as they sang their sadness to the world.

Unfortunately, to change my name I'd have to throw a feast. Putting up a feast is a cross between organizing a large wedding and a small conference. Family politics aside, the minimum cost—if you cheap out and just invite the chiefs and gift them to witness your event—will run you $5,000. But then your name would be marred by your miserliness and people would remember long after you'd died how poorly you'd done things. A real feast starts at $10,000 and goes up very, very quickly.

My aunts also gave my mother a name not long after she'd married my father. My mother had just returned to Bella Bella from residential school in Port Alberni. Meanwhile, in the Village, my father was under pressure from his family to get married. They were worried that he, at age thirty-three, was going to be an embarrassing bachelor forever. Ma-ma-oo was trying to arrange a marriage with someone suitable. My father decided to go fishing instead.

My maternal grandmother lived in a house near the docks in Bella Bella. One day, my mother was looking out the front picture window when she saw my father coming up the gangplank. According to Gran, Mom said, "That's the man I'm going to marry." Mom's version is that she simply asked if Gran knew who he was. They met later that night at a jukebox

Coastal village. 1929?
Graphite on paper by Emily Carr.
Royal British Columbia Museum,
British Columbia Archives.
PDP05698

party held in a house. My father was a hottie and all the girls wanted to dance with him, but he only wanted to dance with my mother. They were getting along so well that they lost track of time. Back then, the air-raid siren left over from a World War II naval base would sound and mark the time when the generator was shut off. The streets went dark. Mom's house was on the other side of the reserve. Dad offered to walk her home.

My father took my mother back to the Village after they were married. Dad's family was upset because Mom was twelve years younger than he was. She was annoyed that they thought she was too young for him, and she expressed her opinion forcefully. My aunts gifted her with an Indian name so that she could attend the feasts in the Village. Mom's new name was Halh.qala.ghum.ne'x, which meant Sea Monster Turning the Other Way. Although it lacks the romance of my sister's name, I like the attitude it suggests and hope to inherit it.

I had been introduced to the concept of "nusa" (the traditional way of teaching Haisla *nuyem,* or protocols) as a child, but had never really understood it until my trip to Graceland with my mother. In 1997, I received £800 for winning the Royal Society of Literature's Winifred Holtby Memorial Prize. In Canadian dollars, it worked out to $2,000 after taxes and currency exchange. One of my co-workers at the time suggested I put it into Registered Retirement Savings Plans or at the very least a Guaranteed Investment Certificate, but I had always wanted a black leather couch. I spent a few weeks searching for just the right one and anxiously awaited its delivery. Once it was in my apartment, it seemed monolithic. And it squeaked. And it felt sticky when the room was hot. I returned it the next day, deciding what I really wanted was a tropical vacation.

I flipped through travel magazines, trying to insert myself into the happy, sunny pictures. Overwhelmed by the choices, I phoned my mother. I asked her where she would go if she could go anywhere in the world.

"Graceland," Mom said.

"Really?"

"I would go in a heartbeat."

I was impressed by her certainty. "Okay."

She laughed, and we chatted a bit longer. I spent the rest of the evening surfing the Internet for cheap flights and a passable hotel. There were some incredible deals on flights, but the cheapest ones had multiple connections. Mom hated flying, especially take-offs and landings, so the fewer of those we could get away with the better. The Days Inn at Graceland promised Presley-inspired decor, a guitar-shaped pool, and a twenty-four-hour Elvis movie channel. The shoulder season rates were great, and it was right beside Graceland, so we wouldn't have to rent a car or grab a cab to get there.

"Hey, how'd you like to spend your birthday in Graceland?" I said.

There was a long silence over the phone. "Are you kidding?"

"I just want to make sure you really want to go, because everything's non-refundable."

Another silence. "You're serious."

"Yeah, we've got a couple of options for flights, but I think our best bet is a connection out of Seattle."

"I don't think I can afford that."

I explained about the Royal Society prize money and the black leather couch and the desire to go somewhere I had never been before.

"That seems like a lot of money," she said.

"Do you want to go to Graceland?"

"Well, yes."

"Then let's go."

Dad wasn't interested in going with us, so it was just Mom and me. Dad had his heart set on driving from Kitamaat to the hundredth anniversary of the Klondike Gold Rush in Dawson City. Mom hates driving vacations, so she said she'd save her money for Graceland, which Dad said sounded like a glorified shopping trip. We drove up to Dawson that July in his denim-blue standard Ford F-150, but that is a story for another time.

Mom hadn't travelled much, except to visit her grandchildren in Ontario and her mother in Vancouver. Three weeks before we were scheduled to leave, her fears about flying were not soothed by the infamous crash of Swissair 111 near Peggy's Cove in Nova Scotia and the near-constant media coverage of the wreckage and grieving relatives. At that point, a series of hurricanes marched across the Gulf States, causing widespread damage and flooding. I had a shaky grasp of American geography, so trying to convince Mom that our plane would not be blown out of the sky was difficult.

"It's a sign," Mom said.

"It's not a sign."

"We aren't meant to go."

"The tickets are non-refundable."

And then our airline pilots went on strike, which was probably why the tickets had been dirt cheap. Another airline offered to carry its rival's passengers, but things were still iffy when Mom flew into the Vancouver airport to meet up with me. From her pale complexion and bug-eyed expression, I knew the only things that could have gotten her on that plane were her grandchildren or Graceland.

We landed in Memphis at night. The cab ride to the hotel was quiet. We were both exhausted. I think I was expecting a longer ride because the blue billboard announcing our arrival at Graceland seemed to appear abruptly. After dragging our luggage to our room, I asked if she wanted to look around or just pass out.

"I'm going to the gates," Mom said.

We passed an Elvis-themed strip mall called Graceland Plaza. We peered in at the closed stores and then crossed the street. The manor was lit by

Nootka. 1929?
Graphite on paper by Emily Carr.
Royal British Columbia Museum,
British Columbia Archives.
PDP05694

floodlights. It seemed smaller than I'd been expecting. A stone wall surrounding it was covered in graffiti left there by fans, who were invited by a sign to use the black Sharpies provided to leave a note or signature. We took pictures of each other, and then other tourists took pictures of us, looking shell-shocked. In the morning, we went straight to the ticket counter and bought the Platinum Tour, which included all four Elvis museums and the manor.

Mom wanted to go straight to the manor. We were given audio headsets, which would guide us through the rooms. I put my headphones on. Mom left hers hanging around her neck, ignoring the flow of traffic and irritated glances as she slowly made her way through the entrance. I turned my Walkman on and began the tour. Halfway through the first room, I realized Mom wasn't with me. I found her staring at a white bedroom with purple furniture. I was about to explain the headphones to her when I realized she was trembling.

"This is his mother's room," she said.

We spent a week in Memphis, and I got the immersion course in Elvis. But there, at that moment, while Mom was telling me stories about Elvis and his mother, I was glad we were at Graceland together. You should not go there without an Elvis fan. It's like Christmas without kids—you lose that sense of wonder. The manor wasn't that impressive if you just looked at it as a house.

More importantly, as we walked slowly through the house and she touched the walls, I could see everything had a story, a history for her. In each story was everything she valued and loved and wanted me to remember and carry with me.

This is nusa.

NOTES

1. The Heiltsuk Nation's main reserve is Waglisla, BC, which is more commonly referred to as Bella Bella, the name given it by Spanish explorers. Kitamaat Village is known by its residents simply as the Village and was originally a winter camp and then a Methodist mission. It is now the main reserve for the Haisla Nation. The reserve is also referred to as C'imotsa, or Snag Beach, because of all the stumps and logs that decorate the waterfront.
2. *Indian, aboriginal, First Nations,* and *Native Canadian* are used interchangeably in the context of this essay and most of my work.

EVE JOSEPH

Three Poems

SIWASH ROCK

Sing to me, she said, sing me the name
of the man turned to stone. Again
and again remind me of the hero—
and what it is I need to know
about currents and tides in this burial place.

What of the mask and the moon's blue face?
Where do you go when you go far away?
Here where the river meets up with the sea, oh
sing to me, Papa, the story of water.

Am I not your beautiful daughter?
Sing me to sleep, sing me awake,
teach me to see the shape of the old
in the haze of the city and all of your ghosts—
is it true that we're made of rubies and clay?
Stay with me, Papa—
                    sing me oh sing me
                            the very first names.

CANOE BUILDER

Porch lights have come on all down the street. In front of one of the
houses a white cat sleeps on a pillow in a dugout hollowed by fire. If
you could look back, you'd see an old man tending that fire. You'd
hear the river talking to the stones, the grass shrugging off the wind.
The smell of red cedar would put you to sleep. You'd see a dog tied to
the clothesline with a long leash and a colossal log drying in an old
shed. The old man has nothing to do with magic but that doesn't stop

the carved bear from rocking or the feast dish from dancing. He offers you bread and jam at his table with the blue-and-white plastic tablecloth. He gives you a new name. It's late. You haven't stayed up like this for a long time. It's a kind of visit. He didn't come to you; you had to go to him. The dead, you realize, are preoccupied with winter. The river will freeze. All of us will need a sturdy boat, a few provisions. Each time he pokes the fire it bites down hard: when you look up you can't tell the stars from sparks.

STYAWAT: WIND THAT BLOWS THE CLOUDS AWAY

for Leigh

All summer you watched the clouds.
Shapes shifted: swans turned into fish,
winged horses plunged through white drifts.

Shadows moved across the ground.
Impossible to know fact from myth—
All summer you watched the clouds.
Shapes shifted: swans transformed into fish.

Your grandfather remembers a time when salmon
walked out of the river as men. Your small face lifts.
You are the wind that brings the sun, he whispers.
All summer you watched the clouds,
shapes shifted, men turned into fish,
winged horses plunged through white drifts.

Ancient Songs of Y-Ail-Mihth

William K'HHalserten Sepass (circa 1840–1943) was chief of the Skowkale First Nations people and a hereditary chief of the Chilliwack Tribe. As a keeper of the tribal knowledge, he had been taught the Coast Salish tradition of storytelling by memorizing ancient songs. Recited in Halq'eméylem, the native Coast Salish language, the songs were part of an epic cycle traditionally recited at special gatherings, especially during the sun ceremonies held in Chilliwack every four years in precontact time. The songs are creation stories and legends of X̱á:ls, the Great Transformer, who "walked this earth in the distant past to put things right." Chief Sepass was seventy years old when he began to preserve the songs of Y-Ail-Mihth for his people by working with Sophia White Street, the daughter of one of the first missionaries sent out to the Pacific coast by the Wesleyan Methodist Church. Mrs. Street was fluent in both English and Halq'eméylem, having been raised by Stó:lō nannies. Between 1911 and 1915, Chief Sepass recited the songs to her, and they translated the work into English. The songs were published in 1963 and again in 1974 by Sophia's daughter, Eloise Street. In 2009, Longhouse Publishing issued a commemorative edition of Sepass Poems: Ancient Songs of Y-Ail-Mihth, *which included a "missing" sixteenth poem. The Longhouse publication marks the first time the poems appear under the copyright of the Sepass family—through his grandson, Gerald Sepass. Chief Sepass' people in the Fraser Valley continue to cherish these works, and he remains an honored ancestral figure. The following are two of the poems in the cycle.*

THE BEGINNING OF THE WORLD

Long, long ago,
Before anything was,
Saving only the heavens,
From the seat of his golden throne
The Sun God looked out on the Moon Goddess
And found her beautiful.

Hour after hour,
With hopeless love,
He watched the spot where, at evening,
She would sometimes come out to wander
Through her silver garden
In the cool of the dusk.

Far he cast his gaze across the heavens
Until the time came, one day,
When she returned his look of love
And she, too, sat lonely,
Turning eyes of wistful longing
Toward her distant lover.

Then their thoughts of love and longing,
Seeking each other,
Met halfway,
Mingled,
Hung suspended in space . . .
Thus: the beginning of the world.

Sat they long in loneliness
The great void of eternal space
Closing in upon them.
Despair hung in their hearts.
Gone was the splendor of the golden throne;
Gone was the beauty of the silver garden;
Their souls burned with a white flame of longing.

Up leaped the Sun God,
Chanting his love song,
The words of his love thoughts:

> "My heart wings its way to you,
> O daughter of the Moon!
> My heart wings its way to you
> Where you stand
> In your silver garden;
> Your white face turned toward me.
>
> You will receive a gift,
> O daughter of the Moon!
> A gift of my great love
> For you only;
> You will receive a gift of my love
> This day, ere the dusk falls."

He seized his knife,
And with swift slashes,
Tore a strip of bark
From a great tree.
Still he chanted his songs
Of love and longing,
As he wrote on the birch bark
In the speech of springtime,
The language of lovers.

Then,
From his place at the gate of the Sun,
He, the Sun God,
Raised his arm high
And cast his message
Far into the sky.
Swift it flew,
Following an unerring course
Toward the distant garden
Where sat the Moon Goddess.

> But what of the message?
> Alas! It wavers in its flight;
> Drops;
> Falls on the embryo world;
> Thus: the land.

Far across the heavens,
In her silver garden,
The Moon Goddess wept bitterly.
A tear was borne by the wind;
Fell on the half-formed world;
Thus: the water.

There from the love thoughts,
Longings and love words
Sprang beautiful trees and flowers.
Little streams gurgled through the forests;
Leaping waterfalls foamed;
Great rivers flowed to the sea;

Fish abounded;
Buffalo roamed the plains;
And through the wood paths
Sped all the wild things
Of a new world.

The Sun God left the seat of his golden throne;
Swung wide the gate of the Sun!
A ringing shout cleft the heavens!
The Moon Goddess,
From her silver garden,
Heard the cry;
Stood,
And answered.

He of the Sun,
She of the Moon,
Stood they
With arms outstretched
A moment,
Silent,
Then, in the first shadow of evenfall;
They leaped into space;
Came to rest
On the new world of their love;
Thus: the first man and woman.

X̱PÁ:Y, THE CEDAR & THE FLOOD

There was one good man.
To him X̱á:ls said:
"You shall be a tree,
A good tree;
You shall be X̱pá:y, the cedar;
You shall be houses, beds, ropes;
You shall be baskets and blankets;
You shall be a strong boat
In the flood that I shall send
To show this Syewá:l
That there is One other than he
In Swáyél, the earth."

So X̱pá:y, the cedar,
Gave his stem and his branches,
Gave his roots and his peeled bark,
And soon a boat floated upon the waters
Wherein sat the children of X̱pá:y
And waited for what would come.

Rain fell, floods came.
Shxwexwó:s, the thunder, rolled loud over the mountains;
Skw'elkw'elxel, the tornado, snapped the groaning trees.
Syewá:l died,
Not knowing whence death came.

But the boat,
Which was the body and life of X̲pá:y,
Sailed smoothly in the tumult,
Saw the clouds beat before the wind;
Saw Syó:qwem, the sun,
And Kwósel, the stars in the night sky;
Saw the anger of X̲á:ls
And the death of Syewá:l,
And the end of the flood.
There waited Smá:lt, the snow-white peak,

With birds and beast crouched, chilled and fearful,
Listening to the long-drawn wail of Swókwel, the loon,
Upon the waste of waters.

Then X̲á:ls looked out from Syó:qwem, the sun,
Looked down upon the snow peak . . .
And suddenly
The boat was gone,
But X̲pá:y, with his children around him,
Stood on the mountain,
Kind trees to shelter the small things
Until the earth was green again.

> X̲á:ls stepped out of Syó:qwem, the sun.
> And stood within the sky.
>
> "Syewá:l," he cried,
> "You who lie in the mud.
> Grow up to man again
> Out of the mud.
> Be a wish hidden in the mud,
> Be a Wish and a Will
> To crawl out, climb out, rise up,
> To be a man again upon Swáyél, the earth.

"Many lives will pass
In the mud,
In the water,
In the forest,
In Sóyéx̱el, the wide sky;
Fish, bird, beast you will be
Before you stand upright.
Syewá:l again,
Lord of Swáyél, the earth,
And friend of X̱á:ls."

And X̱á:ls slept.

The Salmon of the Heart

SPECKLED DREAM

I went to the sea
for myself.
She fed me
health,
new legs.
Perhaps a speckled dream
to wrestle in the night.

Years ago, working as a boat puller on a troller in southeast Alaska, something happened that is an image for the beginning and end of this essay. We were fishing the Fairweather Grounds off Lituya. The skipper called me to bring the landing net to his side of the boat. He was working a big king on the kill line[1] and gave me instruction on how to approach the salmon with the net. It was the biggest king I had ever seen, perhaps a hundred pounder. As I brought the net behind and under the salmon, it began to swim away—not fast, but steady, like a draft animal pulling a heavy load. The moment had the inexorable quality of awakening: as the kill line went taut, the salmon and I were in the same world—the hundred-pound test leader snapped, and the fish flashed out of sight. I recall this story to remind me that the salmon is *free* and that these musings are only lines and hooks that hold it momentarily.

As I turn forty and enter the second half of life, it occurs to me how the salmon is like the life of the soul. Salmon is born in a rivulet, a creek, the headwaters of some greater river. He runs to the sea for a mysterious sojourn; his flesh reddens. Mature, he awakens once again to his birthplace and returns there to spawn and die. Loving and dying in the home ground resound in us. We all want a meaningful death in a familiar locale. Salmon embodies this for us, our own loving deaths—at home in the world. Salmon dwells in two places at once—in our hearts and in the world. He is essentially the same being, the sacred salmon, salmon of the heart.

The Leaper

> The doctor was explaining how sperm moves, like salmon, and how the uterus
> gives them hold, creates "current" so they know which way to swim. I thought,
> *Jesus, salmon!* and knew I was one once. It was as real as this: I could remember
> the slow torture of rotting while still alive in a graveled mountain stream.
> Humped up, masked in red and green, dressed for dancing, I was Death's own
> delight, her hands caressing me . . . and this is the part I can't remember:
> whether she laughed or wept as we rolled in love.

Introduction is a word that at root means being led into the circle. Here is
one last introduction to salmon. Not long ago, a friend and I were sitting
by Admiralty Inlet talking. I mentioned an idea to create a sculpted "rainbow" of salmon of all species. One end of the rainbow would rise out of
Puget Sound, and the other would end in a well in an alder grove on the
shore. My friend responded to the idea by saying, "The salmon is the soul
in the body of the world." Indeed the salmon is at least the soul of this
biome, this green house. He is the tutelary spirit that swims in and around
us, secret silver mystery, salmon of the heart, tree-born soul[2] of our world.

This essay depends in part on the notion that language—like salmon—
bridges subject and object worlds, inner and outer. Language is the path, the
game trail, the river, the reverie between them. The language-bridge shim-
mers there, revealing and nourishing the interdependence of what it joins.
Each word *bears* and *locates* our meetings with the world. A word is a
clipped breath, a bit of spirit—*inspire, expire*—wherein we hear the weather.
Our "tongues" taste the world we eat. At root, language is sacramental. The
study of etymology reveals that language is trying to contain, remember,
and express the religious event at the core of our mundane awareness.[3]

The heart of language is not merely communication but consecration,
each word the skin of a myth. A telling example of this is our word *resource*.

In current usage, *resource* means raw material or potential energy. We
have resource planning, resource development, and resource allocation. In
our day, *resource* denotes an energized plastic something we practice our
clumsy cleverness on. But beneath current usage of the word lies deeper,
religious information. Etymology reveals that *resource* derives from *surge*
and *re*. *Re* means back, as in *return, refund. Surge* is a Latin-rooted word
whose cognates include regal, resurrection, light, and rule. *Surge* is a contraction of the Latin word *subregere*, to rule or direct from below. In its root
sense, its heart sense, *resource* is a recurring directed energy sent by powers
hidden from view. A *resource* surges back, sent by a hidden power. What
the word knows in its heart is that *resources* are *sacred powers, deities.* A
resource is the unseen river. The roots of the word tell us that the powers,
the deities, can be attended, are venerable. *Resources* require our prayer
and poise, not our machinations. The spear light above the numinous

salmon, not estuarine fish factories where cannibal clones—hungry ghosts of our cleverness, homeless seagoing spam—return to a managed hatchery for "processing." Part of this essay's intent is to re-awaken the religious sense nascent in language; to coax words and their objects back into the sacred realm where the *resource* is what we listen to and for—where our "tongues" are tasting sacramental food, and our speech is "soul food."

Mircea Eliade said in his work *The Sacred and the Profane,* "To settle in a territory is, in the last analysis, equivalent to consecrating it." We are nowhere near consecrating this place. We have destroyed the original human vision of this place, and now we are busy pillaging the *resources* that inspired that vision. Our culture here is prophylactic and profane, a kind of *battle armor* rather than careful turning and re-turning of the soil that the etymology of *culture* reveals. We see the world through the glass of a speeding machine whose servants we are. The locale, the *resource,* is just another roadkill to quarrel over. This essay cannot stop the machine or consecrate the landscape; no one person can do that. But we can roll down a window, the *wind-eye,* and look into the local vision, let it see us, re-awaken our longing for connection, witness the vanity of our speed. I want to praise the sacred salmon, the salmon of the heart, shuttle of Gaia's loom, swift silver thread . . .

I once swam down the Duckabush River in a wetsuit and mask. It was during the dog salmon run, and there were a lot of fish in the river. The current ran both ways that day. I came to a deep pool where a river eddy had piled a perfect pyramid of golden alder leaves. Farther on, resting in the shallows by a large submerged snag, I was musing on what I'd seen when I noticed a shape move behind the snag. It was a large dog salmon, splotchy gray and yellow, vaguely striped, probably a male, spawned out but alive in his eyes. We were a foot apart. I looked into his eye. He saw me but did not move. I was just another river shadow, an aspect of his dying, a guest at his wedding, another fellow at the feast. He was the eye of the *resource,* the subterranean sometime King, fish-eyed inscrutable god, alder-born elder, tutor.

The salmon of the heart is not *cuisine;* it is soul food. We are subsistence fishing in the craft of language. Everyone knows when there is a bite. Imagine what follows as hooks or cut herring, "hoochies" or knots in a net, eddies in the home stream; imagine the salmon in your heart, spawning, dying.

An Etymological Glossary of Salmon Terms

A *term* is in its roots a terminus, a boundary, a moment looking at the other side; a *glossary* is a collection of glosses, terms hard to ken; *etymology* is the story of the truth in words.

Alevin. From Old French *alever,* to rear, from Latin *ad-levare,* to raise; literally: a reared one.

Anadromous. From Greek *ana,* up, and *dromos,* running. The Indo-European root is *der,* whence thread, treadle, trade, tramp, trap. (Salmon is the one who runs up.)

Fry. Originates in the Indo-European root *bhrei,* to cut, break, crumble. Hence friction, debris, fray, and fry. (Fry are the raveling ends of a mysterious rope.)

Milt. Salmon sperm, from Proto-Indo-European root *mel,* soft, with various derivatives referring to soft or softened materials; hence melt, mulch, bland, schmaltz, and smelt (metals). (Alchemical salmon, gold in the sea, mulching the soil, melting in the rivers.)

Net. From the Indo-European root *nedh,* to bind or knot. Cognates include node, nexus, dénouement, and connection.

Parr. A young salmon. When runs decline, the parrs sometimes spawn early. Though the origin is unknown, I propose Latin *parere,* to produce a child. The Indo-European root is *per,* to procure, produce, prepare. *Oxford English Dictionary* suggests a Scottish origin.

Poach. From Middle French *pocher,* to thrust, hence to encroach upon, trespass. Probably akin to Middle Dutch *pocken,* to boast, talk, big talk, bluff. A cognate of poach is poker, the bluffing game. (A poacher pokes the resource; dangerous game.)

Redd. Nest of salmon eggs; to put in order, to ready or arrange. Partridge, in *Origins,* has *redd* as salmon spawn from red, the color, in addition to *redd,* from dialect English: to tidy, arrange, as above. The two senses seem mixed in the salmon redd, the bed of gravel heaped over the fertile eggs. It's interesting to note that redd may be related to ride and road. (Redds like grave mounds, tumuli beneath the torrent, resurrection of the resource, cradle and the grave.)

Religion. From Latin *re,* back, and *ligare,* to bind. Religion binds us back. Religion is the tie that binds. Cognates include rely, ally, obligation, ligament, lien. (Our connection to salmon is religious. He binds us to a sacred world, sews us into a sacred web.)

River. From Latin *ripa,* a riverbank. Cognates are arrive, derive, rivalry. Deep in the root of this word is the Indo-European *ri,* flow, which is akin to Greek *rhein* (flow), whence Rhea, the mother of the gods. (Much of salmon's power derives from its connection to rivers, to the flow, mother of gods—silver shuttle in *Gaia's loom.*)

Roe. Salmon ovum. "Hard roe" are eggs; "soft roe" are sperm, milt.

Salmon. Uncertain, but probably from Latin *salmo,* from Gaullic *salmo,* "the leaping fish." Folk etymology derives salmon from *salire,* to leap, with the cognates resilient, exultant, exile, sally, and somersault.

Smolt. A young salmon entering the sea. Akin to smelt. Ultimately akin to Indo-European *mel,* soft.

Spawn. From Old French *espandre,* to shed, from Latin *expandere,* to stretch, to spread out. Spawn probably akin to *patere,* to lie open; cognates are petal and patent.

Troll. From Old French *troller,* to walk about, to wander. Probably akin to German *stroloh,* vagabond, and English *stroll.* And French *trollerie,* aimless wandering of dogs. (Little boats bobbing on the great sea, hoboes.)

Tutelary. Ultimate origin unknown but derived from Latin *tueri,* to guard, to watch. Cognates are tutor, tuition, intuition. (Salmon is a tutelary spirit of this place. He teaches and guards our health.)

Weir. From Old Frisian and Old Saxon, *wearian,* to defend, protect, hence to hinder others. The root sense is to warn. Cognates are guarantee, warrant, garret, and warn. (Indian weirs always had a hole to let salmon through. The weir warned both ways; the resource's guarantee.)

Well. From Indo-European *wel,* to turn, roll, with derivatives referring to curved, enclosing objects. (The well rolls . . . the well wells.)

Scientists guess that Atlantic salmon migrated across the Arctic Ocean during a warm period between ice ages, and then became isolated when renewed glaciation blocked the water passage above the American or Asian land masses. Through specialization, these colonizing salmonids separated into six species, taking advantage of somewhat different niches in the North Pacific environment. The Pacific salmon developed one characteristic that separates them from the Atlantic parent stock and adds greatly to their mystique—all six species return to the river only once, dying shortly after they spawn.

All salmonids prefer cold, oxygen-rich waters. They range between about forty and seventy degrees north latitude. There is considerable overlap in the individual species' ranges. Only the chum and pink salmon inhabit the rivers of Siberia and northern Alaska that empty into the Arctic Ocean, and only the Chinook travel as far south as Monterey Bay, but in the middle of their range all species are represented. The exception is the cherry or *masu* salmon, which is found only on the Asian side of the Pacific, primarily in Japan.[4]

Nine years ago I read "Totem Salmon,"an essay by Freeman House. It changed my life and is the inspiration for much of this essay. His description of salmon's life cycle and behavior establishes a background to salmon's appeal to our imaginations. The following, a portion of "Salmon Mind," is a kind of "photo," a documentary of the resource, the god's dance.

There are seven varieties of salmon which range and feed in the North Pacific. At the northern extreme of their range they frequent and feed in the Bering Sea, but at the southern extreme are rarely found south of forty-one degrees. These are their names:

Onchorynchus chavica. Called King, Chinook, Tyee, Spring, Quinnat Northern Hokkaido to the Sacramento River.
O. kisutch. Called Coho, Silver Monterey Bay to the Kamchatka Peninsula.
O. nerka. Called Sockeye, Red, Blueback, Nerka Fraser River to the Kurile Islands.
O. gorbucha. Called Pink, Humpbacked, Humpie Klamath River to Korea.
O. keta. Called Chum, Dog, Keta Puget Sound to Korea.
O. masu. Called Cherry, Masu Amur River to the Pusan River of Korea.
Salmo gairdneri. Called Steelhead Trout Klamath River to the Stikine in Alaska.

Salmon eggs are deposited in more or less evenly graded gravel with enough cold water running over them to maintain an even temperature but not enough to disturb the eggs. The eggs are a brilliant translucent orange-red, about the size of buckshot. Sockeyes will spawn in lakes rather than streams. A single female will deposit up to a thousand eggs in a single "redd" or nest.

After a gestation period of 50 days to three months, the "alevins" hatch out with yolk sacs still attached. The babies nestle in the gravel for several weeks until the yolk sac is gone and they have gained an inch in size. At this point, they emerge from the gravel as "fry" quick and light-shy. It is at this stage of development that life is most perilous, the small fish being vulnerable to hungry larger salmon, other fish, water birds, and snakes.

The fry feed at dawn and dusk and into the night on planktonic crustacea and nymphs, growing fastest in the summer when insects are most available. Most salmon remain in lakes and streams for two years, though pinks and dogs begin their journey to the sea in the first year, as fry.

The migration to salt water is an epic event involving millions of smolt (as the little salmon are called at this stage). On the Yukon River, this journey can be as long as 1,800 miles, on the Amur 700–800. The fish travel in schools, at night to avoid predators, following the guidance of a single larger smolt who seems to make decisions for schools at obstructions, rapids, etc. Out of two million eggs, perhaps 20,000 fish have survived to make the migration.

On the way downstream, the smolt can be killed by (1) natural predators; (2) irrigation ditches which confuse and trap the fish; (3) undissolved human sewage; (4) turbine intakes at dams which act as meat grinders; (5) nitrogen-rich water on the downstream side of dams; (6) wastes from pulp mills; (7) wastes from chemical plants; and (8) warm or oxygen-depleted water created by industrial flow-through.

Now the smolt will spend three to five months in estuaries and bays, gradually acclimatizing to salt water. They begin by feeding on zooplankton. As they grow larger and develop stronger teeth they will eat crustaceans such as shrimp (which some biologists believe colors their flesh), euphasids, amphipods, copepods, pteropods, and squid.

It is at this point in the consideration of salmon that biologists begin to slide into weary human-centered metaphors for the talents and strengths of the fish. We are talking about the great ocean migrations of the salmon, wherein they range and feed for thousands of miles in the North Pacific, grow to maturity, and navigate unerringly back to the stream of their birth on a time schedule which can be predicted to within a few days.

In general, North American salmon make this circular journey in a counter-clockwise direction while Asian salmon move clockwise. Often the great schools' paths will mingle, sharing the search for food that has brought them halfway across the Pacific. Pinks make the circuit once and race home to spawn; sockeyes once each year for three or four years. The enormous schools travel at a general rate of ten miles per day until the spawning urge takes them and they increase their speed to thirty miles per day. The fish are nearly always found in the top ten meters of water during the migrations.

No one really understands the mechanisms that guide the fish through the trackless ocean and back to a specific spot at a specific time. Evidence would seem to indicate that the circuits are printed on the genes of the individual fish. It is probable that neither a consciousness common to a school nor memorized information guides them. There is, however, plenty of room for speculation. This evidence is in as of 1968:

- The migration is in a circular motion, rather than to and fro, eliminating the possibility of the fish backtracking on themselves.
- Salmon find their ways to the spawning grounds as individuals, not in schools.
- Arrival of the fish at the spawning grounds is less variable than the seasonal changes in the weather, making the use of temperature gradients as guidance cues unlikely.
- The nearly constant overcast skies in the North Pacific makes celestial navigation unlikely (but not impossible).
- Migration routes tend to be across open water, even in areas where it would be easy to follow the coast, so that the use of physical landmarks is eliminated.
- The fish swim actively downstream in and across the currents of the Pacific. The currents have subtle differences in salinity, but in order to use these differences as cues, the salmon would have to group up near the edges of the streams, which they do not do.
- Seawater is an electrical conductor moving through the planet's magnetic field, thus the ocean currents generate small amounts of electrical potential. Some fish are able to detect such small amounts of voltage and there is reasonable speculation on the part of Dr. William Royce et al. that salmon may have similar receptors and use the electricity as a navigational cue.

Salmon always find their way back to the stream or lake where they were born and spawn there again, generation after generation. As they approach fresh water, they have reached the peak of their physical and instinctual genius. Fat and shining and leaping, schools will swarm restlessly at the mouths of rivers and streams, waiting for optimal conditions of run-off. They feed voraciously now, generally on herring, for they will not feed again once they enter fresh water. This is the time to take salmon for meat. The flavor and texture of the flesh is at its very best and, eaten fresh, the strength of the fish will stay with the eater.

It is likely that the salmon use their keen sense of smell to identify their home estuary and to choose the right forks as they push upstream. Biologists have run experiments on the fish at this stage of their journey, plugging the salmons' nostrils. Without a sense of smell the spawning run tends to move in a random manner and the fish get lost.

The trip upstream is an enormous effort. Even in the absence of human improvements on the rivers, cataracts, rapids, and waterfalls must be overcome. In spite of obstacles, the fish travel between thirty and ninety miles a day until they have reached the spawning ground. The salmon now undergo striking physiological changes. Humpback salmon will grow the hump for which they are named. Dog salmon grow long, sharp teeth and the upper mandible grows out and extends down over the lower. The body of the sockeye salmon will turn flesh-blood red, and its head an olive green. In general, the fish turn dark and bruised; the organism begins to consume itself. Drawing its last strength from ocean-gained food, the flesh turns soft.

Now the salmon perform the breathtaking dance for which their entire lives have been in preparation. As they reach their spawning home, the fish pair male and female. A sort of courtship ensues, the male swimming back and forth over the female as she prepares the nest, rubbing and nudging her, then darting out to drive off other males. The female builds the nest with her tail, scooping out silt and smaller stones to a depth of several inches and in an area twice the length of the fish. Finally all that is left in the nest is a silt-free aggregate of stones. The crevasses and fissures between the stones will provide shelter for the eggs. (Spawning females move thousands of pounds of silt, sand, and clay downstream to the sea, thereby keeping streams and rivers in channel and eliminating the need for dredging and other artificial river "remedies.")

The nest completed, the female assumes a rigid position over the center of it and the male approaches, curving his body up against hers. The eggs and clouds of milt are deposited simultaneously. The sperm, which stays alive in the water for seconds only, must enter the egg through a single tiny pore or micropyle, which itself closes over in a matter of minutes. In situations where the current is extremely fast, two males will sometimes serve a single female to ensure fertilization. The nest is covered and the process is repeated for a day or a week, until the eggs are all deposited. (Males fight each other for dominance, females fight each other for territory.)

A single female will deposit from 2,000 to 5,000 eggs, but only a small percentage of these are destined to hatch. The rest are eaten by fish or birds, attacked by fungi, or washed downstream.

Now the fish, already decomposing, begin to die, and within days all have finished their migration. Their bodies are thrown up on the banks of streams and rivers, providing feast for bear and eagle.[5]

A fish like our Pacific steelhead, which does not die after spawning but returns to the sea and may spawn again, the Atlantic salmon was once much more extensive than it is today, with huge runs on all the major rivers of northern Europe. Runs extended as far south as Portugal and as far north as subarctic Norway and Iceland. The fish were once so plentiful that nobility would not eat them because they were a staple of their serfs' diet. Today only Iceland, Scotland, Norway, and Ireland have decent salmon fisheries. England is trying with varied success to coax salmon back into its polluted waterways. The fish is essentially extinct in the rest of Europe, except for a small single-river run in Normandy, which is being poached into extinction despite official efforts to save it.

Compared to its European cousin, the wild Pacific salmon is in relatively good shape. But it is by no means a healthy resource. Logging has blocked streams, even whole rivers at times. Soil failures, siltation, and slope failures caused by clear-cutting have destroyed spawning habitat.

Overfishing has depleted breeding stocks, and dams have exterminated whole races of salmon. The most recent threats to the wild Pacific salmon are genetic contamination and competition from aquaculture clones, which threaten to contaminate and/or starve out a gene pool adapted to the essential climatic and geologic variables of this locale. Cloned salmon are genetically adapted to the economic and technically determined environs of state and corporate aquaculture centers. Hatchery fish are fundamentally different from wild fish. Hatchery fish are bred for their ability to survive the crowded, *single-feed* hatchery environment. (Wild salmon survive life in the ocean at twice the rate of hatchery clones, since they are better adapted to natural conditions.) Aquaculturists brag about the differences. They are breeding salmon to work for corporate interests, efficient production, and high profit—in short, they are being bred as anadromous Herefords. Soon there may be salmon with corporate names: *Ore-Aqua* silvers, *Anadromous* kings, *Weyerhauser* dogs (all real names of aquaculture corporations).

Corporate fish biologists often use the buffalo–cattle analogy when discussing[6] wild and hatchery salmon. The plains were cleared of wild herbivores so the cattle industry could expand. Corporations interested in aquaculture argue that we needn't worry about habitat or spawning grounds, because they can grow all their "herds" of fish at the river mouths, with technology and money. That means that watershed health would no longer be essential to salmon livelihood, and thus watersheds could be indiscriminately developed. This may be part of the reason why timber companies are investing in salmon aquaculture. Perhaps they figure if they can keep salmon on the industrial consumer's dinner plate, the "consumers" won't yell so loudly when logging devastates wild salmon habitat.

An interesting aspect of the wild-versus-hatchery salmon issue is the controversy over carrying capacity. Some biologists have begun to argue that there is a limited carrying capacity for salmon in the ocean (common sense versus the profiteers' logic again). They predict that heavy releases of cloned salmon may further reduce the food of wild salmon. (Russia and Japan also have extensive hatchery programs which may affect the food supply.) What the aquaculturists are creating is an "economy" that is exploitive, and hence unstable, in place of one that has been highly productive, self-regulated, and self-maintained for millennia. (I recall Odum's remark that solar energy technologies were doomed to inefficiency because trees had already maximized the use of solar energy.) Wild salmon are a much more productive resource than phony resources produced by corporate aquaculture. The drawback of wild salmon, from the corporate viewpoint, is that they cannot be manipulated to serve a market economy. Wild salmon have too many connections, too many harmonies. They are the thread of a story that is destroyed when taken out of its context. Hatchery fish are comic-book versions of epics, the Muzak version of a

Cannery, Port Renfrew. 1929.
Graphite on paper by Emily Carr.
Royal British Columbia Museum,
British Columbia Archives.
PDP08804

complex traditional tune. Of course, corporate and state aquaculturists pay lip service to wild salmon stocks as gene-pool reserves. But the entire thrust of modern aquaculture is to "co-operate" with the industrial, not the ecological, economy. Consciously or unconsciously, they are working to eliminate the wild salmon, the salmon of the heart. Fishermen of various sorts—trollers, gillnetters, sportsmen—know the difference between wild and domesticated salmon. Their word for hatchery fish is *rag*. (Washington State is beginning to pay attention to the voices of fishermen, and to the importance of maintaining wild runs through habitat restoration and protection.)

The decline of the wild Pacific salmon—especially the far-swimming Chinook and the estuary-loving dog—is tragic because it means the whole ecosystem is in decline. The salmon is the crown of the Northwest forest biome, the *soul* of our ecosystem. It is, with cedar, the paradigmatic expression of this place. If the forests and their waters are healthy, if the sea is clear and uncrowded, then wild salmon thrive.

The salmon is a kind of current between forest and sea.[7] One study shows that salmon may accumulate trace minerals and marine carbon that—passed naturally through the forest food chain—provide nutrients for green plants, which are unavailable to them through local geologic and hydrologic processes. In other words, the trees nurture salmon, and salmon nurture trees (alchemical salmon: turning sea into soil, salmon eyes in the treetops). The salmon is the archetypal resource—meaningful energy directed by unseen powers. It is the *incarnation* of the forest–sea connection, silver needles sewing the ties that bind, religious fish . . . The salmon travels in our hearts as well, swims in our blood, feeds and eats the dreaming tree of truth. The deep resonance between the salmon of the heart and the salmon of the world is the *note* of our dwelling here.

WELL

An old Bavarian farmer told me
if I was unlucky
and could not take my water
from a stream,
I might keep a trout in my well
and the water would stay clean.

The salmon is a powerful symbol of the interdependence of the outer world but it is, as an image, also a manifestation of our inner health. Indeed the resolution of the two images, salmon of the forest and salmon of the heart, may be the inception of a healing myth. Jung associated *fish* with the nourishing influence of the unconscious (salmon comes from the sea to feed the *locale*). The alchemical stone, symbol of the immortal self, is said to appear like fish eyes. (The salmon knows the way home through the chaos of waters. Von Uexkell, a German ethnologist, experimented with salmonids to determine their inner time and discovered they see twice as much per second as we do. Their world is hence much "slower" than ours.)[8]

I once saw a rain cloak made of an enormous king salmon. The head was made into a kind of cap and the body draped over the shoulders. It was worn in the river drizzle while spearing salmon. I imagine it moving the wearer into salmon time, making the swift salmon walk. I imagine it decoding the rain. In Babylonian mythology there was a figure, Oannes, who came from the sea dressed as a fish to teach the people wisdom. Fish are symbols of wisdom throughout the world. What we fail to realize in our culture of alienated, self-conscious rationalism is that fish—salmon in our case—are literal *embodiments* of the wisdom of the *locale*, the resource. The salmon are the wisdom of the Northwest biome. They are the old souls, worshipful children of the land. *Psychology without ecology is lonely* and vice versa. The salmon is not merely a projection, a symbol of some inner process; it is rather the embodiment of the soul that nourishes us all.

We love salmon; it is the Northwest *food.* But to the original peoples of the Pacific Northwest, salmon were not merely food. To them, salmon were people who lived in houses far away under the sea. Each year they visited the human people because the Indian peoples always treated them as honored guests. When the salmon people traveled, they donned their salmon disguises and left them behind, perhaps in the way we leave flowers or food behind when visiting friends. To the Indians, the salmon were a resource in the deep sense: great, generous beings whose gifts gave life. The salmon were energy: not "raw" energy, but intelligent, perceptive energy. The Indians understood that the salmon's gift involved them in an ethical system that resounded in every corner of their locale. The Aboriginal landscape was a democracy of spirits where everyone listened, careful not to offend the *resource* they were a part of.

The salmon was to the Indians what oil is to us. And while oil is a nonrenewable resource—a "non-renourishable resource," and hence perhaps not a true *resource* at all—the salmon was a true *resource* to whom great heed was paid by Aboriginal peoples. In Fraser River Salish mythology, the wife of Swanset, the creator spirit, was a sockeye salmon. In Western terms we might say, "The organizing principle of the world was married to the salmon." Human life was bound to the salmon. Swanset lived at his wife's village and ate with them. In the evening when Swanset's wife and her brothers and sisters went to the river to bathe, his wife's mother would come up from the riverside, carrying a fish in her arms as if it were a child. She cooked it and, laying it on a layer of Indian consumption[9] plant, summoned Swanset and his wife to eat. Swanset's wife scrupulously washed her hands before she sat down, and warned Swanset to do likewise. Her parents admonished him not to break the salmon bones but to lay them carefully on one side. When Swanset and his wife had eaten and washed their hands again, the mother-in-law gathered up all the bones and carried them to the riverside. When she returned from the river, a young boy followed, skipping and dancing gaily in circles around her. This happened at each meal. The salmon people loved to see the skipping boy; he was a joy to them.

Swanset was careless once and lost a bone. The boy appeared that evening limping after the grandmother. This made the salmon people sad and after much effort the bone was found and returned to the water, whereupon the boy was made whole, and the people were glad again. This is the Native understanding of the salmon. When the salmon *bones* are respected, they experience life as a young boy dancing around an old woman. The wife of the human imagination (Swanset) was the salmon, their harmony symbolized in the young boy and old woman. Food tells a story—food has eyes, fish eyes. "Is this our body?"

One ritual common to all Native American peoples who ate salmon was the first salmon-welcoming ceremony. As mentioned above, Indian peoples believed that "salmon is a person living a life very similar to the people who catch him. The salmon has a chief who leads them [his people] up the streams during the run. In performing the ceremony for the [fish] actually caught first, they [Indian people] believe that they are also honoring the chief of the salmon."[10]

In the Indigenous view, the salmon is endowed with a conscious spirit. It can present itself in abundance or not appear at all. This belief required special treatment for all living things, and hence many taboos evolved to ensure safe relations with the non-human world. Below I list some Northwest taboos and customs associated with salmon.[11]

1. The Klallam, like most tribes that use salmon extensively, have a certain veneration for the fish and mark its coming in the spring with a ceremony. The first fish is handled with great care. After being cut along the two sides, the parts are laid together again and it is hung with the head up. The first fish is boiled into a soup and all the people of the village partake of it except the host. The cooking is done by the host's wife.

2. The Klallam of Beecher Bay share the British Columbian custom of performing the ceremony for the sockeye salmon, which is considered the most important variety. When the first sockeye is caught, the little children sprinkle their hair with down, paint their faces, and put on white blankets. From the canoe, they carry the fish on their arms as though they were carrying an infant. A woman cuts it with a mussel-shell knife, after which the fish is boiled and given only to the children to eat. The sockeye is just like a person, they say; that is why they must be careful. This ceremony is an example of acculturation, as the procedure is identical

with that of the Vancouver Island people and not at all like that of the other Klallam.

3. When a salmon with a crooked mouth is caught, it is regarded as an omen of a dreadful occurrence. To forestall misfortune, the people boil the fish and let all the children of the village eat some of it. Then the backbone is taken to the end of the village and set upon a pole facing the water. The other bones are thrown into the water. Another informant speaking of the same ritual reports that this special treatment is limited to the dog salmon only. A dog salmon with a crooked lower jaw is called *suxqwxtaiyuk*. Such a fish is boiled, the backbone is removed, and the fish is spread open with cross pieces of ironwood (oceanspray) and roasted. It is eaten only by young people, who very carefully save every bone. When they are through eating, they all go to the water with the salmon bones, dive under the water, and release the bones. The fish is treated this way because it is considered the leader of the salmon: it must be shown respect so that the run will not cease.

4. When a boy catches his first salmon, his grandmother—or if she is dead, some other woman past her climacteric—cleans the salmon, boils it, and eats it. Only old people are permitted to eat of the fish. The bones are thrown into the water.

5. Children are always admonished not to play with salmon that are lying on the ground before being cleaned. If they tamper with the eyes or make fun of the fish, they will get sick and behave like the salmon when it is dying. A girl of about ten was swimming in the Dungeness River and made fun of an old salmon. Soon after, she became ill. Her eyes began to look like salmon eyes, and her actions were just like the movements of fish as they swim. Her people asked her if she had played with a salmon, and she admitted that she had. The shaman could do nothing for her, and she soon died.

6. It is the common belief that the old salmon come back to lead the young ones up the river. Some young men who had just been initiated into the secrets of adult society doubted this. They found a very old salmon dying on the bank of the river. The boys removed strips from their ceremonial headdress and tied them to the fins and tail of the fish. Then they pushed him into the river, saying, "If you are the one who leads the young salmon back, we will see you again next year." The next salmon season, the young men went to the place where they had marked the old fish with the strips of their headdress. They found it and then became ill. The shaman could not help them. When they were dying, they acted like dying salmon.

7. Each season new poles are made for drying the salmon. It is believed the salmon play on these poles while they are drying and

new poles make them happy. The fish are always treated as if they are alive.

8. Bones of salmon are burned or thrown into water.
9. Hearts of salmon are burned to keep them away from dogs.
10. Care is taken not to break bones.
11. Eyes are eaten.
12. People close to death, in puberty, or near birth are prohibited from eating salmon.
13. Children are rubbed from throat to belly with the fat of the season's first salmon.
14. It was believed that twins were salmon people and had the power to call salmon and increase runs.
15. People of Twana Fjord (Hood Canal) prohibited garbage dumping and boat bailing when salmon were running.

To the original Northwest people, salmon were a *resource* in the sense that the roots of our language define *resource:* that which is resurgent and regal. Salmon are an aspect of the ordering power of creation and must be respected. Salmon have a fateful connection to death, birth, and puberty because they are a manifestation of the power of the other side. All biological systems are dependent on death—the detritus pathways—for health. We are nourished on death, supported by it, the way the dead heart of a tree holds it up in the light. Death is the sinew of the soul. There is a Nootkan tradition wherein the chief swims upriver, towing skeletons of various fish, to entice the living fish back into the river. That salmon were eternal and moved between both worlds was believed worldwide. Maybe salmon are a manifestation of the spirit world's migration through ours— radiant beings leaving us their warmth, their cloaks, the *blossom* of their souls. It is no wonder that Northwest Indian peoples saw twins as "salmon born" and ascribed to them the power to increase and predict runs. Twins are the literal expression of nature's ambivalence, the revelatory power of coincidence. Twins seem more "fated" than other children. People close to the power of the other side—children, widows, menstruating women, new fathers and mothers—had restricted relations with salmon. It was believed they were closer to and hence more vulnerable to the *resource.*

Researching this essay, I discovered that "flash" in our phrase "flash of inspiration" is etymologically grounded not in lightning but in the flash-splash of a fish. Ideas do not flash like lightning but rise like trout to caddisflies. Deep in our speech is the notion that fish are prescient witnesses to the cosmos. They are quick, as in quickened, quicksand, or that tender flesh beneath your fingernail.

Each year the silver salmon return to the little creek that runs through the forest south of my home. I marvel at their speed and freshness, and how they sense my presence long before I see them. My witness is always of them as disappearing, flashing shadows. It is hard to imagine anyone hunting them with a spear. On the other side of life, the eternal salmon were daily witnesses to the living. They played in the drying racks while gear was mended, berries gathered. We fail to realize how intimate Native Americans, especially Native women, were with the salmon. To dry salmon properly the women had to knead the flesh to break the fibers and allow air to enter. But the fish were "alive," *conscious* until eaten. The Aboriginal world was so particularly animate that the individual crows that Klallam women shooed away from the drying racks had names. Contrast our worldview—in which resources are believed to be inanimate, soulless, "dead," because they are non-human—with the *Native* (Indian, Ainu, Irish, Finn, et cetera) view, in which everything is alive. Even the strips of meat in the alder smoke can play, and know joy.[12] This is not sentimentality or naïveté on the Natives' part. It is the deep recognition of a *resource*'s true nature. The bright light of our *objectivity* (an ironic, revealing word) has eliminated the shadows, the shades. Even after contact with white people gave them unlimited access to blade steel, the Natives continued to clean and dress the first salmon with their old mussel knives, out of respect. In contrast, it is as if we are overly enamored with the sharpness of our knives, in love with cutting. Our science, our knowing, lacks religion, reverence. We can cut the world apart, but we forget to call it home, and we are left alone with arid technical skills and their attendant bad dreams.

The Native peoples of the Northwest believed that orphans and others who have not fared well socially will get the best spirit guides, because they will make the greatest effort to receive them. Our pride and greed have orphaned us from the Earth inside and out. The tragedy is that we don't know it. We are proud of our isolation; we call it progress. The spirits are offended by our pride and avoid us, amplifying our loneliness until it becomes our *secret reason for self-destruction.*

The salmon were sacred to many peoples of the Pacific Rim. The indigenous people of Japan, the Ainu, have a belief system similar to that of Northwest coastal people. In the Ainu world, everything is a *kamui,* a spirit of natural phenomena. In their world the *kamui* are Ainu, but when they come to this world, they disguise themselves as salmon, bear, deer, et cetera. They bring their disguises as gifts to the Ainu. The *kamui* are not ghosts but eternal spirits. Some researchers report that the Ainu believe that those who lived well went to the *kamui* homeland when they died. Because the Ainu experience the *kamui* as eternal *people* in the beings around them, the Ainu world is a humane place, and righteous human behavior—care, politeness, cleanliness—assure them that the *kamui* will reside in their locales and enliven their world. To the Ainu, life depends on good relations with the *resource* world, not upon owning it. The Ainu and the Indians of the Northwest know that *resources* can't be owned, in the same way that Christians know they cannot own the Holy Ghost.

The Ainu believe that the hearth is an eye of the *kamui*, which watches and welcomes all game that enter through the hunting window. As game enter through the hunting window, the fire reports its treatment back to the appropriate *kamui* community. Fire is the appropriate witness for the *resource,* flickering warm light rising from the broken limbs of trees. (The leaves of the cottonwood trees are the *food* of the salmon *kamui*.)[13] The mythic images circle and knot together into a reality that is a story, a parable, where legendary incidents are facts, not data.

For the Ainu, river systems are families: major rivers are parents, and the tributaries are children. One can address the whole family by speaking to a single member. One can address an entire watershed—its *being*—by invoking the main river's *kamui*.

The Ainu cook the first dog salmon and offer it to the fire spirit so that it will report the people's kind treatment of the fish. The bones are offered to the river spirit along with other offerings so that all spirits involved in the salmon's arrival are acknowledged. The Ainu also have a send-off ritual, in which they bid the salmon spirits farewell as they journey in their boats back to the *kamui* homeland. These rituals are described in more detail in Hitoshi Watanabe's *The Ainu Ecosystem,* a thorough explication of Ainu cosmology.

It seems to me that modern ecologists have yet to find language that communicates with the compactness and imagery of Native peoples, whose myths not only *explain* the workings of ecosystem ethics, but also *locate* us in the story, *instruct* us.

RIVER SONG

I lay cold
and sleek
in that swift river.

The sun sang small
faint rainbows round
all there was to see.

I lay still like a fish
letting my body dream.
Waiting I lay watching
my quick dogs stalking
earnest on the shore.

I lay bright and dumb
as a stone
and while the river sang
I listened to my heart.

He sounded strong and far away.
He sounded like a man digging slowly
in a half-finished well.

As I mentioned above, European peoples have a long association with salmon. In fact, if philologists are right, salmon have been with us from the beginning. Calvin Watkins, in a fascinating essay in the *American Heritage Dictionary*, "Indo-European and the Indo-Europeans," notes that we can tell much about the homeland of our linguistic ancestors from the roots of our language. In the Indo-European homeland there were, among others, wasp, bee, bear, wolf, mouse, eagle, thrush, sparrow, crane, eel, and salmon. The Indo-European root word for *salmon* is *laks,* whence our word *lox.* (Our word *salmon* is from Latin *salire,* to leap.) Some interesting etymological coincidences constellate around *laks;* and while my thoughts are speculative, I offer them in hope that someone more skilled will comment on them. *Laks* is the root word for *salmon.* The root for *lake* is *laku.* From this, we have Greek *lakkos* (pond), Latin *lacus* (pond, lake), *lagoon, loch, lake.* It seems possible that *laks* and *laku* are related. Salmon could be "laks," the lake dweller. It is interesting that *laku* also gives us Latin *lacuna,* originally a pool or cistern; Celtic myth has the salmon of wisdom living in a well. Last, there is the old English dialectic "to lake," to play or sport, from Old Norse *leig,* to leap or tremble. It is a thin etymological line, but salmon may have been with us always, animating that word. (How sad that the animals are leaving our language as they leave our lives.) In any case, the salmon was a sacred fish to our ancestors, who saw him in lakes, coming and going, a mysterious being. The sacredness survives in various ways. The aboriginal Finns found fire in the bowels of the salmon, the salmon's flesh being a form of fire. To the Norwegians, a happy person is a "glad Laks," a glad salmon. Until Christian times, the Celtic peoples venerated the salmon as the fish of wisdom, and numerous folktales continue to bear witness to its sacredness.

HUNTER'S SONG

Striking,
stricken.
An eagle
with a fish too big to lift.
I answer from my place.

In Celtic mythology, the sacred well of inspiration and wisdom was surrounded by hazel trees, whose blossoms or fruit fell into the well and were eaten by the sacred salmon, whose bellies turned purple from the color of the fruit. The salmon ate the fruit of the tree of wisdom and hence knew all. Again, the flash of inspiration is more like the splash of a fish than a bolt from the blue.

The Welsh hero Mabon was once captured by a fiend. Gwryhr, his wife, asked the creatures to help her find him. She asked ouzel, who sent her to owl, who sent her to eagle, who, though he flew highest and saw farthest, could not find him. The eagle told Gwryhr this story: "I once tried to capture a large salmon, but he drew me into the deep and I was barely able to escape.[14] I sent my kindred to attack him, but he sent messengers and we made peace. I took fifty fish spears from his back. He will know where your husband is if anyone does." Eagle took Gwryhr to salmon, who located her husband. In Celtic cosmology, the salmon is the wisest of all the creatures.

In the ancient Irish cosmology, the wife of Dagda, the good god, was driven by curiosity to approach the well of Boann, with its hazels and salmon. All the creatures of the cosmos, even the gods, were forbidden access to this well of wisdom. Only the salmon were permitted to eat of the well fruit. The Irish called them the salmon of knowledge. As Dagda's wife approached the well, it rose up in anger and rolled away to the sea, freeing the salmon and creating the river Boyne. The gods may be powerful, but they are not wise. Only salmon are privileged to wisdom.

The Irish hero Finn happened upon an old man fishing by a deep pool in the Boyne. This old man was Finn the Seer; he had been fishing seven years for the salmon of knowledge. It was prophesied that a man named Finn would obtain its wisdom. Finn the Seer caught the salmon the moment before young Finn arrived. He gave the salmon to Finn to cook, warning him not to eat any of the fish but to only cook it and return it. The old man planned to eat it all and gain its wisdom. When Finn returned with the cooked salmon, the seer asked him if he had eaten any part of the fish. Finn answered, "No, but while I was cooking it, a blister rose on its skin. I put my thumb on it, but it burned me and I put my thumb in my mouth to cool."

"It is enough," said Finn the Seer. "Eat the fish yourself. You must be the Finn of the prophecy." Thereafter Finn had only to put his thumb in his mouth to gain knowledge of where he was at any moment. It seems that the salmon of knowledge is available to the innocent and the lucky.

The Irish folktale "Country under the Waves" is a charming story about a peasant family's fate, the well of wisdom, and its tutelary animal, the salmon. (*Charm* is etymologically akin to *cirm,* Old English for clamor, cry, and to Latin *carmen,* song. Originally, *charm* meant a magic spell that was sung.) In the story, there is a widow who has three sons and a daughter. One of the sons is a dunce, and the mother despairs thinking of the time when she can no longer care for him. She consults a witch, who advises her to visit the undersea country of the hazel-ringed well of wisdom and the salmon. The witch instructs her to send her eldest son to obtain the hazel fruit on All Hallows' Eve, when there is an "opening" in the world through which he can pass into the country under the waves.[15] The eldest son undertakes the journey at the proper time and passes into the country, where he meets the sea people. They offer to help him, and he accepts their hospitality. But when he offends them with his bragging ways, the sea people decide he is not worthy of the fruit of wisdom. They drug his food, and he falls asleep at the well. As the berries fall and the waters and salmon rise to eat them, he turns to stone. A similar fate befalls the second brother, who searches for the well and its fruit the next year. He is lazy and selfish, so he is drugged and turns to stone near the well. The daughter then pleads with her mother to let her go on the quest for the well fruit. The mother refuses, saying she could not bear the loss of her daughter. But on the next All Hallows' Eve, the daughter steals away to the country under the waves. She too meets the sea people, and she impresses them with her ready wit and good manners. They guide her to the well, where she catches the fruit before it falls to the rising salmon. Enlightened when she touches the well fruit, she lifts the curse from her brothers and returns home with them to cure their foolish brother. Evidently the wisdom of the salmon is *properly* won by a feminine spirit and by following the subtle path of right relations, rather than by force.

Following salmon is a winding path. The image is knotted in us like a nerve. But in our pose of modernity we do not know this. We water-ski on the clear, dark waters of Creation. But it is time to let salmon home again to our brook hearts, our well hearts. "Old quartz nose," embodiment of wisdom, silver shadow, far-ranging flash of the sea, tree ghost, silver needle sewing our world together, mending the coat we wear, shuttle of dreams . . . sacred salmon, moon-bright tutor who teaches death is the door to love. If salmon disappear, the splashing and flashing in the well will frighten us and we will become superstitious about the Earth and our dreams. We need salmon to remind us that we are not alone.

Finally, I want to offer an Estonian folk song, "The Wonder Maiden from Fish." Estonians are a Finno-Ugric people who have lived in the same location for perhaps eight thousand years. They have maintained their language and traditions despite crusading Germans, imperialistic Swedes, and totalitarian Russians. It was the women of Estonia who kept the folklore alive. They were the singers; songs were passed from songstress to songstress— charms smoothed and polished like sacred stones. My mother-in-law, Silva Peek, a Finno-Ugric philologist who clarified the folklore text and the German translation of that song, says it is probably part of an Estonian folk song tradition wherein a fish turns into a maiden. The song and its many levels of meaning deserve longer treatment; still, it speaks for itself quite well. For me it is a kind of bell tone of the salmon of the heart, a shape to hold these disparate yet connected notes. It rings true.

Silva explained that "The Wonder Maiden from Fish" is a kind of "nonsense" song: in the original Estonian, the lines are joined by alliteration and rhyme rather than by consciously chosen meaning. The song's shape and form are therefore worked by the unconscious wisdom of the people. This is precisely its *charm*. I hear the salmon singing through the wonder maiden, its wisdom and desire gliding bare beneath the surface of her song,[16] resurgent—the *resource* singing through human voice.

THE WONDER MAIDEN FROM FISH

The spruce stands high in Kurland,
The alder, free and affable in Westernland,
The birch in Harrien beside the cow path:
Together their roots run,
Together the tops fall.
From below the roots a river flows,
Three kinds of fish therein:
One is whitefish, the black-sided one,
The other is pike, the gray-backed,
The third is salmon, the wide-blazed one.
I took the fish into my hand;
Carried the fish home myself.
I began cooking the fish
With the help of Father's well-stocked woodpile,
With the help of Mother's broad shavings.
The fish began to speak, saying:
I wasn't brought up to be brutalized
Nor brought up to be roughed up.
Why, I was brought up to sing,
To sing to rhyme.
I sing; why wouldn't I?
I sing turf out of the sea,
  Tilth out of sea bottom,
  Fish from sea shores,
  Malt from sea sand.
I sing the meaning of some other tongue
Helper of teeth.

NOTES

1. A rubber line to which a leader is attached while playing the fish. (Normally a gaff is used by fishermen who are trolling. An exceptionally large salmon calls for a net.)
2. Trees provide detritus, organic energy forms, to feed caddisflies and other aquatic larvae that in turn feed salmon fry. In salmon-spawning areas, the upper reaches of rivers, the major energy source is forest detritus. Trees also shade the home creeks, maintaining cool water temperatures vital to salmon. The forest is mother to the salmon.
3. My bet is that very few "modern" words will last, precisely because our age has lost the religious instinct. It is not "language" but human intelligence that has created most "new" words.
4. Johnson, Philip. "Salmon Ranching." *Oceans* 15:1 (1982).

5. House, Freeman. "Totem Salmon." *Truck 18, Biogeography Workbook (1)* (1978).

6. Much of what follows is from Philip Johnson's article, "Salmon Ranching."

7. Probably because dams have destroyed so many runs, a Nisqually spokesman once made the Thurberesque remark that he saw salmon leaping out of all the lightbulbs.

8. Is salmon "time" a key to the fish's uncanny navigational abilities?

9. So named because of its curative properties.

10. Gunther, Erna. *Further Analysis of the First Salmon Ceremony.* Seattle: The University of Washington Press, 1928.

11. Gunther, Erna. *Klallam Folk Tales.* Seattle: The University of Washington Press, 1925.

12. Can an industrially canned salmon dance?

13. Intuitive knowledge of the detritus pathways?

14. Most salmon fishers have seen eagles swimming in the sea, unable to lift off with their catch.

15. Another example of pagan cosmology: resourceful, submerged, persistent beneath the Christian overlay.

16. I have quoted Silva's translation nearly verbatim, changing only a few words for rhythmic reasons.

Two Poems

KEROUAC CREEK WORK TUNE

After three days of summer rain,
I'm back splitting cedar
      in the hills.
The horse skid trail
       is muddy
        and rain clouds dapple
          the peaks.

But work goes well,
      the saw and truck run fine;
      cedar splits
         into fifty
       sturdy rails,
     and by evening
—truck loaded, tools packed away—

the moon and stars
    jingle in the sky
      like wages.

THROUGH SWORD FERN, THROUGH NETTLE

New spring snow on Mount Townsend,
on Buckhorn, on Constance.

On my way to work
near hamlet Quilcene,
a cloud of smoke
from a logging show
whips over the car.

It's Burn Day in the county
and that cloud—that
wood-smoke smell—
lifts me back
to slash-choked hills
above the Strait

where Finn and I,
with canisters
of gas & diesel
(in a cork-boot dance
with fire),
drip-torched
a hundred clearcut acres.

And further back: night burning—

fir and cedar snags
(colossal Roman candles)
spewed sparks and fire
across the heavens—

for the Forest Service,
circa 1970, at Bon Jon Pass.

*

From here on Alan Polson's land
above the Big Quil River—

digging with pulaski
(axe & mattock in one head)
fresh trail
through sword fern, nettle,
elderberry, around spruce roots,
and huge moss-bearing maples—

I hear 'cross valley
the Jake-brake whine
of log trucks
descending Walker Mountain,
the river's steady spring-melt movement,
and wrens singing to each other
in the trees.

*

And I recall jumping
into a helicopter (where's the door?)
far up this very watershed;
dynamite caps, boxed and
balanced on my knees,
earmarked for the crew
at Marmot Pass.

A clear and sunny morning.
My first trail-building job,
and soon, my first grown beard!

What views from that Hornet chopper!
What mountain wilds below!

The night before, at the bunkhouse barn,
I wrote postcards to three girls:
to one I'd lost but still held hope for,
to one I had, but might be losing,
and to one too young, perhaps,
but awfully hip for sweet sixteen.

All the postcards read the same:

I'm off to the high old mountains
to work on Forest Service trails.
If I don't return, remember:
I loved you unto my dying breath.

Sincerely,
Mike

P.S. I'll be back in ten days.

Two Poems

ALL THE WILD WINDS OF THE WORLD
GO HOWLING THROUGH YOU

as you write one more poem of longing
and send it shivering into the next world
because, inside you, it no longer has a home.

What do you expect—
to sit under the cedar trees all day
and come away the wiser?

Your boy on the winter beach, knee-deep in foam,
laughing and stumbling towards his father's arms,
like the rest of us, perhaps, longing for home.

THE SEX LIFE OF SAND

A poem found in The Guardian *July 2007*

The first rule of this world is to grab
hold of something. Beneath the beach
lies a largely unexplored microscopic
ecosystem populated by sand-lickers,
sticky-toed worms and four-legged water
bears. Scientists estimate that in a few
square metres of beach there might be millions.

They have puffed-up bodies
and stubby limbs, and use tiny claws
to hold on. Some are covered
with suction cups that secrete a cement
to bind them to grains of sand. Others

use spikes that produce sticky glue.
They live on or in between the grains,
to them the size of boulders—grains
often covered in bacteria
that are eaten by invisible (to the naked
eye) shrimp-like creatures with waving legs
or by larger ones that look like
flying carpets with mouths, which propel
themselves on bellyfuls of hair
and vacuum up bacteria in their giant
maws. Still other worms eat the sand grains
whole and let their digestive systems
clean them off. Out the back end,
eventually, comes a trail of clean sand.

Life in this environment is short
so these organisms must be ready
for reproduction a few days after birth.
Some have both male and female organs
and can switch back and forth.

Less than a quarter of these microscopic
creatures have been identified; finding
names is a regular problem. They get
named after mothers-in-law and old
girlfriends. It is considered bad form
to name one after yourself.

In the Shadow of Red Cedar

In the shadow of red cedar, along a stream colored by salmon, in a place where plants draw food from the air and small creatures living on dew never touch the forest floor, it is difficult to imagine a time when the coastal temperate rain forests of North America did not exist. Today, these immense and mysterious forests, which in scale and wonder dwarf anything to be found in the tropics, extend in a vast arc from northern California 2,000 miles north and west to the Copper River and the Gulf of Alaska. Home to myriad species of plants and animals, a constellation of life unique on Earth, they spread between sea and mountain peak, reaching across and defying national boundaries as they envelop all who live within their influence in an unrivaled frontier of the spirit.

It is a world anchored in the south by giant sequoias, the most massive of living beings, and coast redwoods that soar 300 feet above the fog banks of Mendocino. In the north, two trees flourish: western hemlock, with its delicate foliage and finely furrowed bark; and Sitka spruce, most majestic of all, a stunningly beautiful species with blue-green needles that are salt tolerant and capable of extracting minerals and nutrients from sea spray. In between, along the silent reaches of the midcoast of British Columbia, behind a protective veil of Sitka spruce, rise enormous stands of Douglas fir. Intermingled with hemlock and fir, growing wherever the land is moist and the rains abundant, is perhaps the most important denizen of the Pacific slope, the western red cedar, the tree that made possible the florescence of the great and ancient cultures of the coast.

To walk through these forests in the depths of winter, when the rain turns to mist and settles softly on the moss, is to step back in time. Two hundred million years ago vast coniferous forests formed a mantle across the entire planet. Dinosaurs evolved long supple necks to browse high among their branches. Then evolution took a great leap, and flowers were born. What made them remarkable was a mechanism of pollination and fertilization that changed the course of life on Earth. In the more primitive conifers, the plant must produce the basic food for the seed with no certainty that it will be fertilized. In the flowering plants, by contrast, fertilization itself sparks the creation of the seed's food reserves. In other words, unlike the conifers,

South Bay. 1928. Graphite on paper by Emily Carr. Royal British Columbia Museum, British Columbia Archives. PDP08742

the flowering plants make no investment without the assurance that a viable seed will be produced. As a result of this and other evolutionary advances, the flowering plants came to dominate the Earth in an astonishingly short time. Most conifers went extinct, and those that survived retreated to the margins of the world, where a small number of species maintained a foothold by adapting to particularly harsh conditions. Today, at a conservative estimate, there are over 250,000 species of flowering plants. The conifers have been reduced to a mere 700 species, and in the tropics, the hotbed of evolution, they have been almost completely displaced.

On all the Earth, there is only one region of any size and significance where, because of particular climatic conditions, the conifers retain their former glory. Along the northwest coast of North America the summers are hot and dry, the winters cold and wet. Plants need water and light to create food. Here in the summer there is ample light for photosynthesis but not enough water for most deciduous trees, except in low-lying areas where broad-leafed species such as red alder, cottonwood, and vine maple flourish. In the winter, when both water and light are sufficient, the low temperatures cause the flowering plants to lose their leaves and become dormant. The evergreen conifers, by contrast, are able to grow throughout the long winters, and since they use water more efficiently than broad-leafed plants, they also thrive during the dry summer months. The result is an ecosystem so fertile and so productive that the biomass in the richest sites is easily four times as great as that of any comparable area of the tropics.

Indeed it is the scale and abundance of the coastal rain forests that overwhelms the visitor. White pine, the tallest tree of the eastern deciduous forests, barely reaches 200 feet; in the coastal rain forests there are thirteen species that grow higher, with the redwoods reaching nearly 400 feet, taller than a twenty-five-story building. Red cedars can be 20 feet or more across at the base. The footprint of a Douglas fir would crush a small cabin. The trunk of a western hemlock, a miracle of biological engineering, stores thousands of gallons of water and supports branches festooned with as many as 70 million needles, all capturing the light of the sun. Spread out on the ground, the needles of a single tree would create a photosynthetic surface ten times the size of a football field.

These giant trees delight, but the real wonder of the forest lies in the details, in the astonishingly complex relationships: a pileated woodpecker living in the hollow of a snag, tiny seabirds laying their eggs among the roots of an ancient cedar, marbled murrelets nesting in a depression in the moss in the fork of a canopy tree, rufous hummingbirds returning each spring, their migrations timed to coincide with the flowering of salmonberries. In forest streams dwell frogs with tails and lungless salamanders that live by absorbing oxygen through their skin. Strange amphibians, they lay their eggs not in water but on land, in moist debris and fallen logs.

Invertebrate life is remarkably diverse. The first survey to explore systematically the forest canopy in the Carmanah Valley of Vancouver Island yielded 15,000 species, a third of the invertebrates known to exist in all of Canada. Among the survey's collections were 500 species previously unknown to science. Life is equally rich and abundant on the forest floor. There are 12 species of slugs, slimy herbivores that in some areas account for as much as 70 percent of the animal biomass. A square meter of soil may support 2,000 earthworms, 40,000 insects, 120,000 mites, 120,000,000 nematodes, and millions upon millions of protozoa and bacteria, all alive, moving through the earth, feeding, digesting, reproducing, and dying.

None of these creatures, of course, lives in isolation. In nature, no event stands alone. Every biological process, each chemical reaction, leads to the unfolding of other possibilities for life. Tracking these strands through an ecosystem is as complex as untangling the distant threads of memory from a myth. For years, even as industrial logging created clearcuts the size of small nations, the coastal rain forests were among the least studied ecosystems on the planet. Only within the last decade or two have biologists begun to understand and chart the dynamic forces and complex ecological relationships that allow these magnificent forests to exist.

One begins with wind and rain, the open expanse of the Pacific, and the steep escarpment of mountains that makes possible the constant cycling of water between land and sea. Autumn rains last until those of spring, and months pass without a sign of the sun. Sometimes the rain falls as mist, and moisture is raked from the air by the canopy of the forest. At other times the storms are torrential, and daily precipitation is measured in inches. The rains draw nutrients from the soil, carrying vital food into rivers and streams that fall away to the sea and support the greatest coastal marine diversity on Earth. In the estuaries and tidal flats of British Columbia, in shallows that merge with the wetlands, are 600 types of seaweed, 70 species of sea stars. Farther offshore, vast underwater kelp forests shelter hundreds of forms of life, which in turn support a food chain that reaches into the sky to nourish dozens of species of seabirds.

The land provides for life in the sea, but the sea in turn nurtures the land. Birds deposit excrement in the moss, yielding tons of nitrogen and phosphorus that are washed into the soil by winter rains. Salmon return by the millions to their native streams, providing food for eagles and ravens, grizzly and black bears, killer whales, river otters, and more than twenty other mammals of the sea and forest. Their journey complete, the sockeye and coho, chinooks, chums, and pinks drift downstream in death and are slowly absorbed back into the nutrient cycle of life. In the end there is no separation between forest and ocean, between the creatures of the land and those of the sea. Every living thing on the rain coast ultimately responds to the same ecological rhythm. All are interdependent.

The plants that dwell on land nevertheless face particular challenges, especially that of securing nutrients from thin soils leached by rain throughout much of the year. The tangle of ecological adaptations that has evolved in response is nothing short of miraculous. As much as a fifth of the biomass in the foliage of an old-growth Douglas fir, for example, is an epiphytic lichen, *Lobaria oregana,* which fixes nitrogen directly from the air and passes it into the ecosystem. The needles of Sitka spruce absorb phosphorus, calcium, and magnesium, and their high rate of transpiration allows moisture to be released to the canopy, allowing the lichens to flourish.

On the forest floor thick mats of sphagnum and other mosses filter rainwater and protect the mycelia of hundreds of species of fungi; these elements form one of the richest mushroom floras on Earth. Mycelia are the vegetative phase of a fungus, small hairlike filaments that spread through the organic layer at the surface of the soil, absorbing food and precipitating decay. A mushroom is simply the fruiting structure, the reproductive body. As the mycelia grow, they constantly encounter tree roots. If the species combination is the right one, a remarkable biological event unfolds. Fungus and tree come together to form mycorrhizae, a symbiotic partnership that allows both to benefit. The tree provides the fungus with sugars created from sunlight. The mycelia in turn enhance the tree's ability to absorb nutrients and water from the soil. They also produce growth-regulating chemicals that promote the production of new roots and enhance the immune system. Without this union, no tree could thrive. Western hemlocks are so dependent on mycorrhizal fungi that their roots barely pierce the surface of the earth, even as their trunks soar into the canopy.

The story only gets better. All life requires nitrogen for the creation of proteins. Nitrates, a basic source, are virtually absent from the acidic, heavily leached soils of the rain forest. The mycorrhizae, however, contain not only nitrogen-fixing bacteria that produce this vital raw material but also a yeast culture that promotes the growth of both the bacteria and the fungus. There are scores of different mycorrhizae—the roots of a single Douglas fir may have as many as forty types—and, like any form of life, the fungus must compete, reproduce, and find a means to disperse its spore. The fruiting body in many cases is an underground mushroom or a truffle. When mature, it emits a pungent odor that seeps through the soil to attract rodents, flying squirrels, and red-backed voles, delicate creatures that live exclusively on a refined diet of truffles. As the voles move about the forest, they scatter droppings, neat little bundles of feces that contain yeast culture, fungal spores, and nitrogen-fixing bacteria—in short, all that is required to inoculate roots and prompt the creation of new mycorrhizae.

Fungi bring life to the forest both by their ability to draw nutrients to the living and by their capacity to transform the dead. In old-growth forests 20 percent of the biomass—as much as 600 tons per hectare—is retained in fallen debris and snags. There is as much nutrition on the ground as there is within it. The moss on the forest floor is so dense that virtually all seedlings sprout from the surface of rotting stumps and logs, which may take several hundred years to decay.

When a tree falls in the forest, it is immediately attacked by fungi and a multitude of insects. The wood provides a solid diet of carbohydrates. To secure proteins and other nutrients, the fungi deploy natural antibiotics to kill nitrogen-fixing bacteria. Chemical attractants emitted by the fungi draw in other prey, such as nematode worms, which are dispatched with exploding poison sacs and an astonishing arsenal of microscopic weapons. The assault on the log comes from many quarters. Certain insects, incapable of digesting wood directly, exploit fungi to do the work. Ambrosia beetles, for example, deposit fungal spores in tunnels bored into the wood. After the spores germinate, the tiny insects cultivate the mushrooms on miniature farms that flourish in the dark.

In time other creatures appear: mites and termites, carpenter ants that chew long galleries in the wood and establish captive colonies of aphids that produce honeydew from the sap of plants. Eventually, as the log progresses through various stages of decay, other scavengers join the fray, including those that consume white cellulose, turning wood blood-red and reducing the heartwood to dust. An inch of soil may take a thousand years to accumulate. Organic debris may persist for centuries. Dead trees are the life of the forest, but their potential is realized only slowly and with great patience.

This observation leads to perhaps the most extraordinary mystery of all. Lush and astonishingly prolific, the coastal temperate rain forests are richer in their capacity to produce the raw material of life than any other terrestrial ecosystem on Earth. The generation of this immense natural wealth is made possible by a vast array of biological interactions so complex and sophisticated as to suggest an evolutionary lineage drifting back to the dawn of time. Yet all evidence indicates that these forests emerged only within the last few thousand years. In aspect and species composition they may invoke the great coniferous forests of the distant geologic past, but as a discrete and evolving ecosystem the coastal temperate rain forests are still wet with the innocence of birth.

Some twenty thousand years ago, what is today British Columbia was a place of turmoil and ice. The land was young, unstable, given to explosive eruptions that burst over the shore. A glacial sheet more than 6,000 feet deep covered the interior of the province, forging mountains and grinding away valleys as it moved over the land, determining for all time the fate of rivers. On the coast, giant tongues of ice carved deep fjords beneath the sea. The sea levels fell by 300 feet, and the sheer weight of ice depressed the shoreline to some 750 feet below its current level. Fourteen thousand years ago, an instant in geologic time, the ice began to melt and the glaciers retreated for the last time. The ocean invaded the shore, inundating coastal valleys and islands. But the land, freed at last of the weight of eons, literally sprang up. Within a mere thousand years, the water drained back into the sea, and the coastline became established more or less as it is today.

Only in the wake of these staggering geological events did the forests come into being. At first the land was dry and cold, an open landscape of aspen and lodgepole pine. Around ten thousand years ago, even as the first humans appeared on the coast, the air became more moist and Douglas fir slowly began to displace the pine. Sitka spruce flourished, though hemlock and red cedar remained rare. Gradually the climate became warmer, with long seasons without frost. As more and more rain fell, endless banks of clouds sheltered the trees from the radiant sun. Western hemlock and red cedar expanded their hold on the south coast, working their way north at the expense of both fir and Sitka spruce.

For the first people of the rain coast, this ecological transition became an image from the dawn of time, a memory of an era when Raven slipped from the shadow of cedar to steal sunlight and cast the moon and stars into the heavens. Mythology enshrined natural history, for it was the diffusion of red cedar that allowed the great cultures of the Pacific Northwest to emerge. The nomadic hunters and gatherers who for centuries had drifted with the seas along the western shores of North America were highly adaptive, capable of taking advantage of every new opportunity for life. Although humans had inhabited the coast for at least five thousand years, specialized tools first appear in the archaeological record around 3000 B.C., roughly the period when red cedar came into its present dominance in the forests. Over the next millennium, a dramatic shift in technology and culture occurred. Large cedar structures were in use a thousand years before the Christian era. A highly distinct art form developed by 500 B.C. Stone mauls and wooden wedges, obsidian blades and shells honed to a razor's edge allowed the highly durable wood to be worked into an astonishing array of objects, which in turn expanded the potential of the environment.

Though in time some 500 plants would be used on the coast, red cedar was from the beginning the tree of life. Its soft and pliant inner bark provided cordage and the fiber that was woven into clothing. Steamed, the wood could be bent into boxes that allowed for the efficient storage of food, especially salmon, berries, and eulachon oil. Cedar provided wood for armor and weapons of war, hewn planks for housing, dugout canoes for transportation, fishing, and hunting whales and seals. It also provided the template upon which dreams could be brought into daylight, families celebrated, and mythological time remembered in the form of crests, memories of the dead displayed for generations of the living.

With cedar as the material foundation of culture, and salmon and other marine resources providing the mainstay of the diet, the seafarers forged the most complex civilization ever to emerge without benefit of agriculture. Although living in permanent settlements, in a stratified world of commoners, slaves, shamans, and noble elite, the people remained foragers, nomads of the open seas, hunters whose lives depended on their relationship with the wild. Unlike so many who had succumbed to the cult of the seed, the nations of the coast believed in the power of animals, accepted the existence of magic, acknowledged the potency of the spirit. The physical world presented but one face of reality. Behind it existed an inner world of meaning, a place reached through transformation, a passage familiar to shamans and recalled by all during the great winter dances and ritual celebrations.

Living from nature, and lacking the technology to dominate it, the people watched the Earth for signs. The flight of eagles helped fishermen track salmon. Sandhill cranes heralded the onset of herring runs. The flowering of certain plants brought families to the shore to gather clams, but if ravens and crows abandoned the beach, so did the people, for it was a sure indication that the shellfish were toxic. Between humans and animals there was a constant dialogue, expressed in physical action, in gesture and repartee, but also in myths and stories that resonated with magical and mystical ideas. The Tlingit addressed plants as spirits, offering prayers before harvesting a tree. Nuu-chah-nulth ceremonies sought protection for the hunter and beseeched whales to give freely of their lives. When raging currents threatened Haida war parties, paddlers scattered swan feathers upon the water to calm the sea. Encounters with grizzly bears brought power to the Gitxsan. The Kwagiulth dispatched initiates into the forest to seek Huxwhukw and the Crooked Beak of Heaven, cannibal spirits living at the north end of the world.

Though neither sentimental nor weakened by nostalgia, these indigenous cultures forged through time and ritual a traditional mystique of the earth that was based not only on deep attachment to the land but also on far more subtle intuition—the idea that the land was breathed into being by human consciousness. Mountains, rivers, and forests were not perceived as inanimate, as mere props on a stage upon which the human drama unfolds. For these societies, the land was alive, a dynamic force to be embraced and transformed by the human imagination. Whether this was true in some absolute sense is not the point. Rather, the significance lies in the manner in which the conviction played out in the day-to-day lives of the people. A child raised to revere the forest as the domain of the spirits will be a fundamentally different person from a child brought up to believe that a forest exists to be cut.

I was fifteen when I first learned that all of these ancient forests, from California to Alaska, were dying. This startling information was presented to my high school biology class in a documentary film sponsored by Weyerhaeuser and featuring as host and narrator the actor Eddie Albert, famous for his role as the husband of Eva Gabor in the television hit *Green Acres*. It was difficult news to swallow. The script called for Mr. Arnold to make his pronouncement while walking along a trail in a verdant grove of hemlocks and cedars. The trees were massive, ten feet or more across at the base, and all were draped in lichens that fused with the dense and lush moss of the forest floor. Mist hung in the air. From fallen logs sprouted wisps of red huckleberry and salal. A stream ran through the frame, and on either bank grew dense thickets of sword ferns and salmonberry.

"True, it looks healthy," Arnold cautioned, "but don't let it fool you. This forest is dying."

Our teacher, a flaccid individual with a brilliant shock of red hair, explained the scientific foundation for Arnold's astonishing assertion. Science had shown that the annual increment of cellulose in a young tree plantation was greater than that of an ancient forest. The old growth was, by definition, a forest in decline. The trees were overmature. To see evidence of decadence, one had only to look at the deadfall, tons of rotting timber wasted on the forest floor. The goal of proper management was to replace these inefficient stands with fresh and productive new forests. A regime of carefully monitored clearcut logging would eliminate the old growth, the debris would be burned, and the land sown with a uniform plantation comprised of only the most up-to-date conifer seedlings. In short, modern forestry would clean up the mess inherited from nature.

Even as a teenager, sitting in a classroom overlooking the forested slopes of Vancouver Island, I had the sense that somebody was playing with a short deck. Industrial logging on a massive scale had been underway in British Columbia since the end of the Second World War. The rotation cycle—the rate at which forests were to be cut across the province, and thus the foundation of sustained-yield forestry—was based on the assumption that all of the old growth would be cut and replaced with tree farms. The intrinsic value of the ancient forests had no place in the calculus of forest planning. The science of forestry provided the rationale for eradication. The obvious beneficiaries of such ideas and policies were the large timber concerns, including the sponsor of the film we had been obliged to watch.

Some years later, soon after graduating from university, I experienced firsthand the actual practice of modern forestry. Working for one of the largest timber companies in British Columbia, I spent a long winter in a logging camp near the west coast of Haida Gwaii, or the Queen Charlottes as the islands were then commonly known. Hired as a forestry engineer, I worked as a surveyor, which meant that I spent most of my time in the primary forest, far ahead of the fallers and loggers, laying out roads and falling boundaries, determining the pattern in which the trees would come down. In the depth of winter our small crew moved through stands of red cedar, hemlock, and Sitka spruce, trees as tall as cathedrals.

Inevitably there was, at least for me, an almost surreal quality to life in our remote camp, where men lived away from their families and earned a wage cutting down in minutes trees that had taken centuries to grow. The constant grinding of machinery, the disintegration of the forest into burnt slash and mud, the wind and sleet that froze on the rigging and whipped across the frozen bay, etched patterns into the lives of the men. Still, no one in our camp had any illusions about what we were doing. All talk of sustained yield and overmature timber, decadent and normal forests we left to government bureaucrats and company foresters. We used to laugh at the little yellow signs stuck on the sides of roads that only we would ever travel, announcing that twenty acres had been replanted, as if it mattered in a clearcut that stretched to the horizon.

With haunting regularity, winter gales swept through the islands, and along the face of the forest exposed by the clearcut, it was not unusual to encounter acres of timber brought down by the wind. The result was a nightmare of overlapping trunks and roots, thousands of tons of wood weighted down with immense pressure and ready to explode with the first cut of a saw. Salvaging blowdown was dreaded work, dangerous and sometimes deadly. To mitigate the hazard and avoid the loss of fiber, government foresters permitted us to expand our cutblocks with wind-firm boundaries as the goal. As a result, openings grew to encompass entire valleys, with the edge of the clearcut reaching to the ridge line of distant mountains. If a slope was deemed too steep to be logged, it was only because machinery could not get to it. Trees left standing by the edge of lakes or along streams inevitably blew over in the next storm. So these too were cut. My immediate boss used to joke about getting rid of the forest so that we could see something. Once, when questioned about the wisdom of logging across a salmon stream, he replied, "Hell, that's no creek, just a draw with a little bit of water in it."

Everyone knew, of course, that the ancient forests would never come back, at least not in any meaningful time frame. The tangle of halfhearted trees that grew up in the slash no more resembled the forest they had displaced than a wheat field resembles a wild prairie meadow. But nobody was worried about what we were doing. It was work, and living on the edge of that immense forest, people simply believed that it would go on forever.

If anyone in the government had a broader perspective, we never heard about it. Our camp was nineteen miles by water across an inlet from a back road that ran forty miles to the nearest forestry office. The government had cut back on overtime pay, and what with the statutory coffee and lunch breaks, the forestry employees had no way of traveling to our camp and back in less than seven and a half hours. So they rarely came. The bureaucracy within the company was not much better. The mills down south often complained that our camp was sending them inferior grades of Douglas fir, which was surprising since the species does not grow on the islands of Haida Gwaii.

There were, of course, vague murmurs of ecological concern that filtered through to our camp. One morning in the cookhouse I ran into a friend of mine, a rock blaster named Archie whose voice had been dusted by a lifetime of cigarettes and the dirt from a dozen mine explosions. He was reading an old newspaper, and the headline said something about Greenpeace.

"Sons of bitches don't know a damn thing about pollution," Archie said. He then proceeded to tell me about working conditions in the hardrock uranium mines of the Northwest Territories shortly after the Second World War. Concerned about the impact of radioactivity, the companies used to put the workers, including Archie, into large sealed chambers and release a gas with particles of aluminum suspended in it. The idea was that the aluminum would coat the lungs, and at the end of the shift the men would gag it up, together with any radioactive dust.

"Now that," growled Archie, "was environmental pollution."

In truth, it is difficult to know how much life in the midst of such destruction actually affected the men working in the forest. Some clearly believed blindly in the process and were hardened by that faith. Others were so transient, moving from camp to camp, sometimes on a monthly basis, that they never registered the full measure of the impact of any one logging show. Some just didn't care. Because the entire industry was so itinerant, no one ever developed a sense of belonging to a place. There was no attachment to the land, nor could there be, given what we were doing. In the slash of the clearcut, there was little room for sentiment.

Talk for the most part was of wages and survival. Logging is among the most perilous of occupations. Were a government office of five hundred employees to suffer the injury rate typical of a west coast logging camp, the office workers would see someone carried out on a stretcher virtually every day. Six or seven times a year there would be a death. In the year I worked in the woods I heard of a faller killed by a snag that pierced his hard hat and exited his groin. Another returned to camp covered in blood; his saw had kicked back and ripped a trench in his face. In a neighboring camp, a trigger-happy rigging slinger blew in the main line before the chokermen were clear of the bight. The logs hung up, nose-dived into the ground, and then, torn by the force of the yarder's two-thousand horsepower, swung about like a giant scythe. One man was crushed beneath a hundred tons of spruce. Another miraculously escaped unscathed, losing only his hard hat. The third and youngest was struck in the back of the head. No one was able to find his face.

The fallers were a breed apart, the elite of the camp, rough-cut individuals willing to risk their lives in exchange for the highest industrial wages in the province. They loved the solitude of the forest, even when its silence was broken by the whine of their saws. In their massive hands these formidable machines could appear almost toylike. But each weighed nearly thirty pounds, packed the power of an outboard motor, and at full throttle drove a hundred feet of sharpened steel chain around a four-foot bar every second. Such a tool cuts through a three-foot log in a minute, a leg in the wink of an eye. In time the vibration affects the circulation in the hands. Several old fallers in camp could get to sleep at night only by tying their hands above their heads to reduce the pain. Others had nightmares of trees that twisted and split as they fell, or hollow snags that collapsed and exploded. One spoke of a friend who never returned from a shift. Buried by blowdown, his body was not found until the setting was logged.

It was impossible not to admire these men, but it was equally difficult to ignore the consequences of what we were doing. Week by week, month by month, the edge of the clearcut spread, consuming the forest and leaving in its wake a torn and desolate landscape, pounded by winter rains that carried away the thin soil in dark torrents to the sea. What ultimately happened to the land was irrelevant. It was simply abandoned to nature. In the nine months I spent in the camp I never saw a tree planted, let alone evidence of a sustained program of modern silviculture. I cannot recall a single decision that was influenced in any way by an ecological concern. The priority and focus of every aspect of the logging operation was the extraction of timber. Roads were built as cheaply and efficiently as possible and, with the exception of mainline corridors, expected to last only long enough to access the wood. Streams clogged by riprap, mountainsides etched with erosion and scarred by landslides, clearcuts piled high with wood, wasted and abandoned—these were the norm, the inevitable result not just of an economic imperative but of a way of thinking that viewed the forest as but a resource to be exploited. As surely as a miner rips coal from the earth, we were cutting away the rain forest. It was a one-time deal, and we all knew it.

Like all the others in camp, I was there to make money. On weekends, when our survey crew was down, I picked up overtime pay by working in the slash as a chokerman, wrapping the cables around the fallen logs so the yarder could drag them to the landing where they were loaded onto the trucks. Setting beads was the most miserable job in a logging show, the bottom rung of the camp hierarchy.

One Saturday I was working in a setting high up on the mountain that rose above the camp. It had been raining all day, and the winds were blowing from the southeast, dragging clouds across the bay and up the slope, where they hung up in the tops of the giant hemlocks and cedars that rose above the clearcut. We were working the edge of the opening, but the landing was unusually close by. It took no time at all for the main line to haul the logs in and for the haulback to fling the chokers back to us. We had been highballing all day, and both my partner and I were a mess of mud, grease, and tree sap. He was a young Nisga'a from New Aiyansh on the Nass River, but that's all I knew about him.

Late in the afternoon something got fouled up on the landing, and the yarder shut down. Suddenly it was quiet, and you could hear the wind that had been driving sleet into our faces all day. My partner and I abandoned the slash for the shelter of the forest. We found a dry spot out of the wind, in a hollow at the base of an enormous cedar, and waited for the yarder to start up. We didn't speak. He kept staring off into the forest. All hunched up with the cold, we looked the same—orange hard hats, green-black rain gear, rubber cork boots. We shared a cigarette. I was watching his face as he smoked. It struck me as strange that here we were, huddled in the forest in silence, two young men from totally different worlds. I tried to imagine what it might have been like had we met but a century before, I perhaps a trader, he a shadow in the wet woods. His people had made a home in the forest for thousands of years. I thought of what this country must have been like when my own grandfather arrived. I saw in the forest around us a world that my own children might never know, that Nisga'a children would never know. I turned to my partner. The whistle blew on the landing.

"What the hell are we doing?" I asked.

"Working," he said. I watched him as he stepped back into the clearcut, and then I followed. We finished the shift and, in the falling darkness, rode to camp together in the back of the company crummy. That was the last I saw of him.

Twenty years have passed since I left that camp, and much has changed in the forest industry. I've often wondered what became of that Nisga'a youth. It is a good bet that he is no longer working as a logger. Native workers rarely get promoted beyond the landing, and what's more, over the last two decades a third of all logging jobs have been lost. Industry blames environmentalists, but the truth lies elsewhere. All the conservation initiatives have not cost the unions more than a few hundred jobs, if that. In many sectors of the forest economy, new regulations have in fact enhanced employment by mandating, for example, labor-intensive restorative efforts on cutover lands. Jobs have been sacrificed on a massive scale because industry, in an intensely competitive global marketplace, has consistently chosen efficiency and profit over employment.

In the last thirty years, the volume of timber logged has increased three-fold, but the number of jobs generated per unit of wood has been cut in half. Modern mills consume wood at twice the rate but use half the labor to produce the same volume. In many camps, grapple yarders have eliminated rigging crews; two men now do the work of six. Automation, together with dwindling timber supplies, has put almost thirty thousand people out of work in British Columbia alone, and their jobs will not be replaced. Over fifty years ago exclusive timber rights to the most productive lands in British Columbia were granted to private companies on the condition that they would provide employment to the people of the province. This social contract, the foundation of a tenure system that ultimately locked up 94 percent of the commercially viable provincial forests in timber supply, has been broken and betrayed.

Still we keep cutting. In Oregon and Washington only 10 percent of the original coastal rain forest remains. In California only 4 percent of the redwoods have been set aside. In British Columbia, roughly 60 percent has been logged, largely since 1950. In the two decades since I stood in the forest with that Nisga'a youth, over half of all timber ever extracted from the public forests of British Columbia has been taken. At current rates of harvest, about 1.5 square miles of old growth per day, the next twenty years will see the destruction of every unprotected valley of ancient rain forest in the province.

In truth, no one really knows what will happen to these lands once they are logged. Forests are extraordinarily complex ecosystems. Biologists have yet to identify all of the species, let alone understand the relationships among them. Although we speak with unbridled confidence of our ability to reproduce the ecological conditions of a forest and to grow wood indefinitely, there is no place on Earth that is currently cutting a fourth generation of timber on an industrial scale. The more imprecise a science, the more dogmatically its proponents cling to their ability to anticipate and predict phenomena.

Forestry as traditionally practiced in the Pacific Northwest is less a science than an ideology, a set of ideas reflecting not empirical truths, but the social needs and aspirations of a closed group of professionals with a vested interest in validating its practices and existence. The very language of the discipline is disingenuous, as if conceived to mislead. The "annual allowable cut" is not a limit never to be exceeded but a quota to be met. The "fall down effect," the planned decline in timber production as the old growth is depleted, is promoted as if it were a natural phenomenon, when it is in fact a stunning admission that the forests have been drastically overcut every year since modern forestry was implemented in the 1940s. "Multiple-use forestry"—which implies that the forests are managed for a variety of purposes, including recreation, tourism, and wildlife—begins with a clearcut. Old growth is "harvested," though it was never planted and no one expects it to grow back. Ancient forests are "decadent" and "overmature," when by any ecological definition they are in their richest and most biologically diverse state.

The most misleading of these terms is "sustained yield," for it has led the public to believe that the trees are growing back as fast as they are being cut. But they are not. In British Columbia alone there are 8.7 million acres of insufficiently restocked lands. We continue to cut at a rate of 650,000 acres per year. Every year 2.5 million logging-truck loads roll down the highways of the province. Lined up bumper to bumper, they would encircle the Earth twice. In practice, sustained-yield forestry remains an untested hypothesis:

after three generations we are still cutting into our biological capital, the irreplaceable old-growth forests. As a scientific concept, sustained yield loses all relevance when applied to an ecological situation the basic parameters of which remain unknown. At best, sustained yield is a theoretical possibility; at worst, a semantic sleight-of-hand, intended only to deceive.

Anyone who has flown over Vancouver Island, or seen the endless clearcuts of the interior of the province, grows wary of the rhetoric and empty promises of the forest industry. Fishermen and women become skeptical when they learn that logging has driven 142 salmon stocks to extinction and left 624 others on the brink. Timber for British Columbia mills now comes from Manitoba. Truck drivers from Quesnel, a pulp-and-paper town in the center of the province, haul loads hundreds of miles south from the Yukon. Just one of the clearcuts southeast of Prince George covers 500 square kilometers, five times the area of the city of Toronto. This, after sixty years of official commitment to sustained-yield forestry. The lament of the old-time foresters—that if only the public understood, it would appreciate what we do—falls flat. The public understands but does not like what it sees.

Fortunately, this orthodoxy is being challenged. Many in the Pacific Northwest, including the best and brightest of professional foresters, recognize the need to move beyond, to an era in which resource decisions are truly based on ecological imperatives, in which the goal of economic sustainability is transformed from a cliché into an article of faith. To make this transition will not be easy, and it will involve much more than tinkering with the edges of an industry that generates $15.9 billion a year in the province of British Columbia alone. Dispatching delegations to Europe to reassure customers, or devising new regulations that if implemented may mitigate some of the worst ecological impacts, will neither restore the public's confidence and trust nor address the underlying challenge of transforming the economy.

Any worker who has wielded a saw or ripped logs from a setting knows that in the end it all comes down to production. The enormous wealth generated over the last fifty years has been possible only because we have been willing to indulge egregious practices in the woods that have little to do with the actual promise of forestry. Spreading clearcuts ever deeper into the hinterland is a policy of the past, crude and anachronistic, certain to lead to a dramatic decline in the forestry sector and to bitterness and disappointment in the communities that rely upon the forests for both spiritual and material well-being. Revitalizing cutover lands with vibrant tree plantations, implementing intensive silviculture to increase yields, establishing the finest model of forest management on a finite land base— these are initiatives that will both allow communities to prosper and enable them to fulfill a moral obligation to leave to the future as healthy an environment as the one they inherited.

There is no better place to pursue a new way of thinking than in the temperate rain forests of the coast. At the moment, less than 6 percent has been protected; the remainder is slated to be logged. If anything, this ratio should be reversed. These forests are as rare and endangered as any natural feature on the face of the Earth, as biologically significant as any terrestrial ecosystem that has ever existed. If, knowing this, we still allow them to be cut down, what will it say about us as a people? What will be the legacy of our times?

The truth is that in an increasingly complex and fragmented world, we need these ancient forests, alive and intact. For the children of the Nisga'a and other Native groups, they are an image of the beginning of time, when Raven emerged from the darkness and young boys went in search of mysteries at the far reaches of the world. For my own two daughters, they echo with a shallower history but one that is nevertheless rich in the struggles of their great-grandparents, men and women who traveled halfway around the world to live in this place. Today, all peoples in this land are drawn together by a single thread of destiny. We live at the edge of the clearcut; our hands will determine the fate of these forests. If we do nothing, they will be lost within our lifetimes, and we will be left to explain our inaction. If we preserve these ancient forests, they will stand for all generations and for all time as symbols of the geography of hope. They are called old growth not because they are frail but because they shelter all of our history and embrace all of our dreams.

(1998)

Fresh Horses

Out of alleys rumpled kings emerge
rolling cigarettes cadged from butts one-handed
and hitching up their pants with the other
wheezing, gasping, coughing
spilling onto the street on a morning
gray as campfire smoke—the remnants
of last night or yesterday slung on their lips
in drool or a snarl, shaking like a dog shitting razor blades
for another hit, another fix. A drink, an eye-opener
is how they call it

one by one the assemblage of pain
emerges from the holes and shadows
where they've hunkered in or hunkered down
and the street becomes a loose parade
marching back and forth between
a smoke and the feral early-morning dealers
slinging someone else's product for enough to start the trip themselves
wheelmen push their carts along behind
the dumpster divers scratching for scraps
you'll eat anything when you're starved enough
you can even nudge the rats aside
if there's enough for both of you
broken women with wild eyes
and skimpy dresses swiped off Army & Navy racks
slink in and ply what remains of their charm
and wiles for a taste, a hit, a drag, a smile even
if it might mean twenty dollars later
when everyone's looped and stranger things
have happened than a furious hump in the alley
between friends and a good ten rock
passersby have learned to walk the line
that exists two feet away from the edge of the curb
where you can't be grabbed or sprung upon

or where it takes a good determined lurch to reach you
so that there's an open lane of concrete
between worlds like a land claim where
they've learned to stick to their side of the deal

there's cowboys and Indians, space cadets and hippies
sidewalk commandos and bikers without bikes
and someone's college sweetheart holding hands
with a rancher's son who dreams of horses
out beyond the derricks of Alberta grazing
with only the wind for company and the sun
shining down upon it all resplendent
as memories when they vanish in the wash
of this life, the tide of it beyond
all knowing

he dreams of horses
the roll of them beneath his butt and thighs
and the land swept by in the push and punch
of hooves and snorted breath across
the hardpan prairie and how it feels sometimes
to run them hard as far as they can go
before climbing on a fresh one
and kicking it to a gallop that pulls the foothills
closer

"We need fresh horses," he mumbles to her
but she can only squeeze his hand and squint
into the near distance
On a morning hard as stone

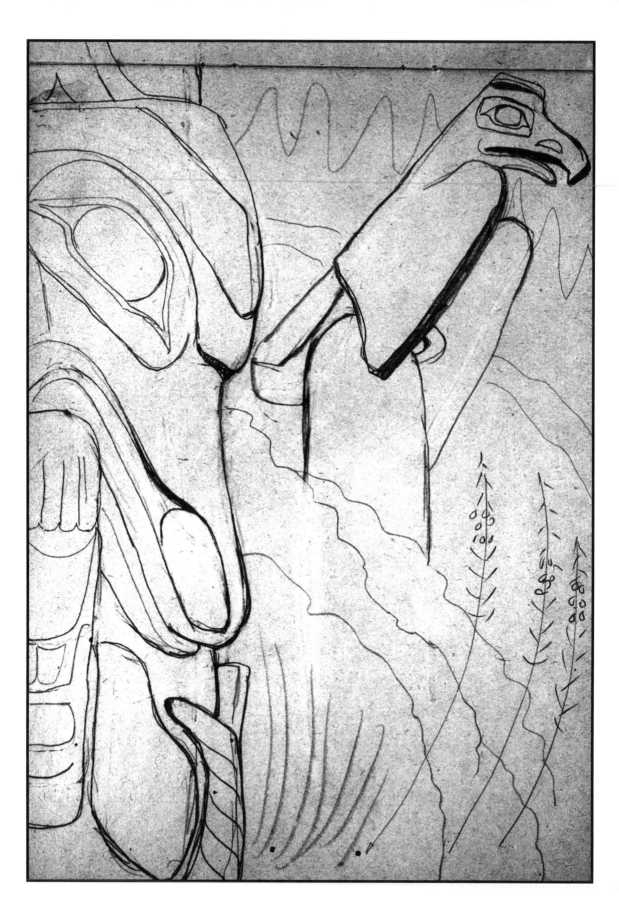

Writers for Clayoquot

The following talk was given by Charles Lillard to support the mass protests against corporate, large-scale logging around Clayoquot Sound, on the west coast of Victoria Island, British Columbia. Protests had been mounting since the 1980s. In 1993, over ten thousand people—members of the Nuu-chah-nulth First Nation, environmentalists, and others—converged to resist the clear-cut logging of lush, old-growth forests, which they regarded as "multinational corporate vandalism." More than five thousand loggers and their supporters mounted a counter protest. Over nine hundred activists were arrested, and the majority were found guilty of criminal intent.

Totem poles, Maude Island. 1928. Graphite on paper by Emily Carr. Royal British Columbia Museum, British Columbia Archives. PDP08732

Some years ago a friend and I were up behind Bamfield. Prospecting. One moment we were in thick timber, moving up a ridge, the next we were nose-to-nose with a clear-cut. My partner let out a long whistle, then said, "From here it looks we're winning the war." I didn't need to ask what war.

Once—once upon a time so recent some of us can remember its shape—an ancient forest of terrible beauty ran for 2,000 miles along the coast from Afognak Island, Alaska, to Big Sur, California. This forest did not welcome intruders. Peoples out of Asia moved through it, leery of its darknesses and clinging heat, attuned as they were to open skies and tundra. After them came a riverine people, downriver from the interior, to be welcomed by salmon and eulachon. The land did not welcome them. No matter, these river people were used to living along the shoreline—in fact, preferred it—so the land lay quiet.

It was different when the first Europeans arrived in the sixteenth century. For the next two hundred years this wilderness fought Europeans, step by step, every inch of the way. Fog and wind led ships off course; rain and tides protected the snug harbours and safe passages; mountains and forests stood, solid as a wall; and forest fires half the length of the wilderness beat the people back. Until 1778, no one broke through to lay a finger on the coast.

That was the year Captain James Cook cut timber for masts and spars at Nootka Sound. Keep the date in mind: 1778.

By 1500 B.C. the lowlands of China had been deforested; 2,300 years later, the ancient forests of Japan were gone. It took a thousand years for the deforestation of Mediterranean shores. At the time of the conquest of Gaul—call it present-day France—the country was 80 percent forest. The last ancient forests of Britain were cut for military purposes at the time of the Spanish Armada—400 years ago.

Our war—and what else are we to call it—has been more successful. Stateside it was all over by 1945. Today 90 percent of the ancient forest in the U.S. is gone; 60 percent here in Canada. But even these dates and facts are misleading. Cook landed here two centuries ago, but the war didn't start then. It didn't start until the 1830s and 1840s, when pioneers broke through into the forest. It started when the first steam equipment came into use, about 1890, but did not really get underway until the teens and twenties of the twentieth century.

War. There is no other way to describe it. In one century we leveled our portion of the ancient forest. If this sounds like a long time, think again. You and I are only some 40 human lifespans away from Christ, 66 away from Moses, 400 away from the arrival of man in the New World. Put differently: there are Douglas-fir in the Clayoquot that are only two lifespans away from Christ, three from Moses. These trees are 1,500 lifespans away from the Pleistocene—1.5 million years ago.

Here's another perspective. Ed Bearder was a beachcomber in Alaska. One unhappy camper. He'd started logging in Northern California about the time of World War I. Through the Depression and the war years, he'd worked his way up the coast and had ended up logging in the Charlottes. After that he'd worked in Alaska. But by the time I met him, all this was behind him. He hated loggers and logging.

What caused this change of heart? I asked him once, and he said, "I was falling Sitka spruce at Windy Point—120 feet without a knot. Sometimes 150 feet, clear, sweet wood, and it was all going to a pulp mill. Pulp mill."

Sometime in the summer of 1966, Bearder moved to Long Island, just north of the Queen Charlottes: a rugged, weather-beaten island we'd beachcombed earlier. "The fuckers won't log it in our lifetime" were almost his last words to me.

Now to flip backwards for a moment. When he was born, the term "Douglas-fir" had only been in general use for 25 years. He was six when "Sitka spruce" first appeared in print. And when "clear-cut" was first used in Canada in 1922, he was a young man. By my reckoning, he could have been 89 when the past he hated caught up with him.

In 1990 I met a woods boss in Oregon. Days earlier he'd had a phone call from Alaska, offering him management of a logging camp for one of the Southeastern Alaska Indian bands. There were two conditions: "Don't hire any Indians. Clear-cut the island." What island, I asked. Long Island, he said.

Is it any wonder then that the long, narrow west coast wilderness has been called "one of the greatest battlegrounds for existence on Earth"?

From the look of it, man is the winner in this war. Just saying this brings to mind a *New Yorker* cartoon from the height of the Cold War. A man comes out of his bomb shelter to a world flat as a plate and steaming like fresh roadkill, and turns to the door behind him to yell, "Come on out, Martha, our side won."

Today we can fly from Sitka to Seattle and see almost nothing of the ancient forest. Not long ago, a forester looking down on some of this wrote, "I think of the unconscionable act of crucifixion, for surely we are crucifying the Earth that sustains us, and all I can say is, 'Mother Earth, forgive us, for we know not what we do.'"

That was then. Today we know what we're doing. That's why we're here.

Stopping By

I

Whose woods these are I do not know.
I bought them from a man who said
he owned them, but I only have to be here
long enough to take a breath
and then it's clear he did not own them,
nor do I.
        What is it possible to own?
The woman who says to me in the darkness,
I'm your woman, you're my man,
is speaking, I'm sure, of belonging
rather than owning. There is only so much
owning you can do, I guess, before it turns
against you. Yet we marry one another
every day, that woman and I.
It's what we do; it's who we are.
You know, it's taken us our lives
to get this clear. You know, it's what
our lives were for.
         Suppose we married
forests, rivers, mountains, valleys,
grasslands, hills. Suppose we married
rocks and creeks and trees. Suppose
we married them over and over, every day.
Suppose we also did this knowing
they will change, and so will we,
and we will die, and so will they.
Suppose we married the world itself
in spite of the fact, or because of the fact,
that whatever is real is always barely
coming into view or going away.

You might remember what it says
in Snyder's poem. *The land belongs
to itself,* it says. *No self in self;
no self in things.* How else could anywhere
ever be home?

                And is that what the land
understands that we don't?
No self in self or in anything else?
Which is to say, no self at all?
Suppose the land just understands
that it belongs. That's all. It just
belongs. Could it belong to us?
I do not think it does or ever
has. Could we belong to it?
I do not think the land will ever
buy us, and I do not think we ought
to sell ourselves or ought to be
for sale. But if we gave ourselves away,
do you suppose the land would take us?
Another way to put that might just be,
Do we belong? I want, of course,
to say we do. Except I know,
the way things are, it isn't true.
The way we are, we don't belong.
We're passing by or passing through.
That's how things are this afternoon,
here in the woods I do not own,
here in the world I understood
a good deal better before I was born
than I do now. Another way
to put that might just be,
we never learn.

I I

                That poem I lifted
a few words from—Snyder's poem—
is called *What Happened Here Before.*
It takes its name from where we are.
Wherever we let the land belong
is called What Happened Here Before,
because what happened here before
is that the land learned how to be
what it became. That is to say,

it learned how to learn, day after day,
to belong where it is. That is the story
of each place that is a place and every
thing that is a thing. It is the only way
a being can become what being is.
It is the story of the riverbeds, the gravels,
bedrocks, mosses, Douglas-firs,
the northern toads and black-tailed deer.

What-is consists of what is happening
right now and what has happened here
before. It wasn't always how it is.
It wasn't always even here.
No self in self; no self in things;
no self in others either. Just
the shape of what has happened here
before, which keeps on shifting, changing,
singing. Not forever. For a time
you cannot measure in the way
you measure time. That is the thing
that singing does. It carries whatever there is
around and over the edge of time.
That might just be how what has happened here
before can keep on being. And it has,
it does, it is.
           The land, as you see,
is a tissue of scars—collisions and slippages,
floods and eruptions, fires and slides—
and the dying, the dead, the unborn, and the living
are jumbled together, eating each other.
A tissue of scars and a tissue of wounds—
and yet it keeps singing itself into being
and into belonging. That's how it is
that the granite and limestone and basalt belong,
the redcedar and shore pine and alder and hemlock
belong, and the tree frogs and redlegs,
foot-long slugs and sideband snails,
squirrels and black bears, flickers and sapsuckers,
pilpeckers, downies and hairies,
and the five young ravens playing grab-ass
on the porch rail yesterday at noon.
They all belong. Because they do,
these woods are theirs.

III

Whose woods these are I said I didn't
know. I don't, it's true. I am trying
to learn, but the learning is slow. I do not
know—but my hunch is that they do.

I said they could sing, and they do.
We've all heard it. You might, in that case,
think they would tell us. They do, I suppose,
in their polyglot language. But there are no words,
only grammars and things, in the thousands of tongues
spoken at once by the forest. The sounds
go way below and way above
what our ears can keep track of.
And some of the phrases take millions of years
to unfold; some make barely a nick
in a tenth of a second. The forest can sing,
and it does, but we might as well say
it is playing the chamberless orchestra
it has built of itself: stone, wood,
bone, horn, water, leaf,
feather, hoof, shell, tooth,
spilling its seed on the ground
and its truth in the air. There are grammars
and things—that is, living things, beings—
not words, in its tongues—just as there are no words
in the fingers and palms of a drummer.

You can say things with things
that you can't say with words. But even
with words, I can try to say this:
these trees and tree frogs, slugs and flickers
really live here. They belong; they don't
belong to. They're the ones who are
these woods, and they're the ones whose woods
these are. I know a few scraps of the grammar
and bits of the list, which is never the same,
season to season and hour to hour.
I work at the names, and some I remember,
but still there are many I learn and forget,
and a million more I've never heard.

The forest consists of the beings who live
and have died in the forest, some coming and going,
some staying, and many long gone but still feeding
the ones who are living and singing here now.
No self in self; no self in things;
no self in parts or wholes. There is no
self, but there is recursion, reflection,
rebirth, and return. That the forest belongs
to itself means the forest belongs.

These woods and I are only partly
married because one of us
gives everything away and one
does not. That's how it is this afternoon,
here in the woods I do not own,
here in the world I just might once
have understood but soon lost track of
in the aftermath of birth. But in
the aftermath of love, we start to learn.

The Mountain Poems of Stonehouse

Bill Porter has been translating for thirty years under the name Red Pine. He was born in California and now lives in Washington State. Much of his interest is in classical Chinese poetry in the tradition of rivers-and-mountains (shan-shui) *poetry.*

In 1983, he self-published The Mountain Poems of Stonehouse, *a collection of nearly two hundred poems by Shih-wu, the fourteenth-century (1272–1352) poet known as Stonehouse. Porter says, "He was one of the exceptional Zen students who became a poet. Stonehouse had a genius for poetry that is unique. I've always said that he was the greatest of all the Chinese Buddhist poets. And although he was a hermit, he was a Zen teacher, too, and he taught individuals through his poetry." On one of Porter's many trips to China, he attempted to visit the place where Stonehouse had lived as a hermit. He succeeded with the help of a military officer who*

> *got out his machete and personally led me through the undergrowth to an old farmhouse made of rocks on the mountain. He said, "This is where those poems were written. When we moved here it used to be a little Buddhist temple." There was a farmer living there who confirmed that this was where Stonehouse lived. The spring was still flowing right behind the hut, the only spring on the mountain.*

Like the rivers-and-mountains poets, Porter lives frugally, to the south of the Olympic Mountain Range.

#99

a clean patch of ground after a rain
an ancient pine half-covered with moss
such things appear before our eyes
but what we do with them isn't the same

#41

the ancients entered mountains in search of the Way
their daily practice revolved around their bodies
tying heavy stones to their belts to hull rice
shouldering hoes in the rain to plant pines
moving mud and rocks it goes without saying
carrying firewood and water they stayed busy
the slackers who put on a robe to get food
don't come to join an old zen monk

#87

Eight or nine pines behind his hut
two or three mounds of taro in front
a mountain recluse doesn't have many interests
all he talks about are his provisions

#54

Sunrise in the east sunset in the west
the bell at dusk the rooster at dawn
the flux of yin and yang have turned my head to snow
over the years I've emptied a hundred crocks of pickles
I plant pines for beams where I find room
I spit out peach pits and make a peach-tree trail
this is for all the bow-wary birds in the world
head for the mountains and choose any tree

Walking Ts'yl-os, Mt. Tatlow_____

The blue mountains are constantly walking.　　　　　　Master Dōgen

In 1986, Don Brooks and I climbed to the top of Mount Tatlow as it was then called, a monumental, snowy eminence of 10,058 feet overlooking Nemaiah Valley to the north. Tatlow largely stands alone. The peaks behind it are lower, less massive, less imposing, but even from as far away as the Chilcotin Highway west of Riske Creek, eighty miles to the northeast, Mount Tatlow stands dominant in the blue distance if the air is clear. Long stretches of gravel road in from Lee's Corner on the way to Nemaiah look to have been sighted exactly on the peak, perhaps a hint as to the route's history as a foot, horse, and wagon trail through lodgepole pines without end.

Mount Tatlow has since reverted to its old name of *Tsoloss* or *Ts'yl-os* and, acknowledged as a living entity once again, the mountain has a considerable aura of mythos and power about it, or should I say "him." Most of the mainly aboriginal residents of Nemaiah are careful to use restraint and appropriate decorum in referring to Ts'yl-os. Visitors might be wise to do the same. Like creatures of the wild, the great mountain does not like people to point or stare at him, so they say, and there is talk of consequences for those who do. What I am unsure of still is whether it is right to even refer to him by name. Am I being too direct, too presumptuous now in the telling of this story?

R. G. Tatlow, on the other hand, Vancouver financier and finance minister in Premier McBride's conservative government in the early years of the twentieth century, had a short-lived impact on the world—significantly less than Ts'yl-os did. I suspect the honourable minister's concern for protocol would be more likely limited to the appropriate use of titles. Staring and pointing would have probably been construed as simply an outcome of inferior upbringing, something to be expected in the colonies.

Stories too have energies and intentions of their own. I can tell you that after the usual wait for inclinations of story to emerge, due to the percolations and perambulations of time and mind and I presume spirit, this story of our dogged walk up the flanks of mighty Ts'yl-os fairly elbowed its way into my awareness. The story has been many years in the steeping. Finally, I had little choice but to sit down at the keyboard and begin. Ts'yl-os, a mountain being of limited patience it seems, had had enough of waiting and was prodding the story into action.

Ts'yl-os and his wife, Eniyud, were given to arguing and mean spiritedness, so the tales from distant myth-time go. Eniyud, obviously overwrought at one point, thrust the baby onto his lap, left the two oldest kids for him to keep an eye on, swept up the rest of the children, and moved on over by Tatlayoko Lake, where as Niut Mountain she sits, their jagged offspring lined up behind her. They look severe and moody even now. Ts'yl-os, his ex-consort, Eniyud, and their progeny eventually turned to rock. You can see the two quite large, older children tucked in behind Ts'yl-os and the infant now, but mind your manners; be sure not to be careless or off-handed, and please do not point. Even the youngest child looks rough and tough.

The reputation of Ts'yl-os does perplex me, though. I can understand that the fracas and the responsibility of child-rearing might leave him in a bad mood. He has a powerful influence over the climate, so they say. The local weather is frequently blustery and changeable: dangerous winds come up suddenly from out of the peaks and ridges to the south and southwest and blow down the long lakes, Taseko, Tatlayoko, and especially Chilko. There is a story of a Tsilhqot'in man up on a mountain, sighting invaders on a raft, Kwakwaka'wakw—Kwakiutls from the coast— as they moved down Chilko Lake, and calling on a great wind to destroy them. Ts'yl-os stands on the edge of the Chilcotin plateau, and with the heightening of each summer day, the warming Interior air rises. Cold winds from off the shining glaciers and snow fields beyond the lakes in the heart of the Coast Mountains rush in to fill the void. Nemaiah Valley below Ts'yl-os is often windy, and exposed trees grow slowly with a gnarled list to leeward.

But, and I say this with as much respect as I can muster, the stories that come down to us say this massive mountain eminence is unduly touchy, perhaps even pushy, certainly hard to get along with. All mountains have their moods, but Ts'yl-os stands out—though I have heard that to offend anywhere near Eniyud when she is in an off mood brings on a wrath with a stormy, some might say mean, edge that is unparalleled. I remind myself that these are mountain gods we are talking about here, a world I know little of, so these years I back away with deference, eyes and mind averted, mutter a quick acknowledgment—not too intense, not too dismissive— and carry on.

Perhaps the issue is simply that, however mighty, Ts'yl-os is a wild being in a wild, subtle, and sensitive world, and like all denizens of the wild, and like "wild" itself, he requires an appropriately respectful approach, a light touch. Perhaps a point or stare is simply too aggressive and causes even a mountain to flinch, to withdraw, like small birds circling imperceptibly to the back of the bush the moment you focus your binoculars on them. Maybe Ts'yl-os is the mountain equivalent of a wolverine or grizzly bear and simply needs to be left alone.

In 1984, before Don and I made our slow way up Ts'yl-os, we drove south, off the long and dusty Nemaiah road, to the mouth of the Tchaikazan (Tsichessaan) River Valley at the top end of Taseko Lake. From there we walked up the river flowing in its customarily uproarious manner out of a mass of glaciers in the southwest, most notably Monmouth and Tchaikazan. The 1:50,000 topo map of the headwaters of the Tchaikazan and the Lord River further east in the heart of the Coast Range—a desolate and unexpectedly lifeless and spooky place that Don and I ventured into laboriously by canoe in 1990—is mainly alpine white. The map differentiates a bluish white for glaciers and thin, brown contour lines on white for peaks, treeless rock, tundra, and sub-alpine terrain; forest green is minimal. The Tchaikazan trip was our first foray into that wild and chilly region.

We walked as far as Goetz's Cabin, below Spectrum Pass, where we camped for a few days. The river was high and muddy after half a summer of snow and ice melt, and the water was backed onto the trail in places. There were few sandbars visible, and where the trail followed them we had to cut into the bush. We came upon clean-edged, long-clawed grizzly tracks in damp earth in several places, notably the trail beneath our feet. The weather was mostly overcast and rainy; the hanging glaciers on the southwest side of the valley were half-hidden in cloud, and we had to work to stay warm. The next day we climbed up onto the pass to look down into Dorothy Lake and the Yohetta route on the far side, and to see if we could spot upper Chilko Lake. On the way up, we spied a mule deer and her fawn sneaking along a gully below. A small herd of bucks bunched up on the snowfields above us, escaping the bugs, and a cluster of mountain goats in a hurry, not their typical pace, retreated across the sloped open tundra below RCAF Peak. They obviously knew what it was to be hunted by two-leggeds and were taking no chances. On the way back down, we found at the edge of the drop-off, goat wool hanging in strands on the stunted alpine fir trees, like faded Tibetan prayer flags waving in the wind. This was where the goat herd had been feeding and shedding early in the season, when the snow line was still low. Don collected wool samples for his two young daughters.

When we reached the valley bottom, I stopped to kneel in moss and splash water on my face at the edge of the little creek chuckling its way down beside us. Something in that cold, clear, wet moment has stayed with me, pungent to this day. Goetz's Cabin is situated at a big bend in the valley where the Tchaikazan is especially wide and braided. At the end of each day, if the rain wasn't too bad, I would meditate, hunkered into my Gore-Tex coat, on a rock out in a dry meadow in front of the cabin. A doe would come out of the buckbrush across the river to feed in the late afternoon, her fawn hidden, scentless, and curled into itself, back in the scrub timber. She glanced over occasionally, and I wondered if she was using the proximity of the cabin for cover.

We drank hot, over-proof rums in the evenings. In those days we carried fresh limes, nutmeg or cinnamon, brown sugar, and butter squeezed from a plastic tube. Once, years before in the Rainbow Mountains, Don and I stood at dusk outside our campsite with half-consumed drinks in hand and slightly crooked smiles, watching a big bull caribou with a full antler rack trot by us in the gloom. We had been route-finding by compass bearings across rolling alpine tundra that day, a gloriously free way to travel. On an old rock slide on the far side of a gentle pass, the route coalesced briefly into a tidy, unexpectedly level trail, the rock slabs worn and shifted most elegantly into position by generations of wear from those big caribou hooves.

One rainy day, we walked up the river to the snout of Tchaikazan Glacier, crossing the outlets of the several small glaciers on our side of the valley, Friendly and Miserable Glaciers among them. Each creek was steep and on a rampage, and we had a tough job crossing them. We passed the Alpine Club base campsite looking weather-beaten already, and made our way up the mile or so of barren, outwash plain and lateral moraines to the ice front; most of the plain was still without plant life, the glacier having retreated recently. The ice was twenty feet thick or more at its margin, and propped up in a newly stacked rock pile just in front was an ice ax with a helmet hanging off it. This was a monument to a young climber who, while roping up farther up the glacier, backed onto a snow-covered crevice and fell to his death.

Of course, the day warmed, the rain and melt water increased, and on the way back we found, not to our surprise, that the glacial side creeks had risen sharply. We were wading in white water—ice only minutes before— that reached the tops of our thighs. Don carried a small ax in his big pack, and we cut ourselves a solid fir pole for a third leg to reduce the chances of a quick tumble into oblivion. That short, sub-alpine, krummholz brush was as impenetrable as any up-coast salal jungle, and the pole we cut was almost as dense, hard, and old as the boulders we were clambering over; the ax, filed sharp, bounced when we trimmed the wood.

Goetz had recently bought the cabin from Johnny Blatchford, an old-time guide-outfitter from down at Tsuniah Lake off Chilko, and had boarded the window from bears, and removed the doorknob, somewhat inhospitably we thought, from people like us. Goetz was originally from overseas and apparently did not fully appreciate the old Chilcotin values of an open cabin in bad weather or the free use of traditional trails in wild places. On a cold, wet, late afternoon a day or two earlier, we split a piece of kindling to fit the slot where the shaft of the missing door handle had been, turned it to release the latch and open the door, and proceeded to spend a pleasantly warm evening inside. Before we left, we re-boarded, wrote a grateful note, locked up, and departed the valley.

On the way out, we picked up our stash of cold beer from a side-creek pool near the car, a time-honored, nourishing end-of-trail ritual. Camping that night at Big Lake on the edge of the Chilcotin Plateau, away from the mountains, we saw not a drop of rain had fallen out there; the ground was dust. Later, I awoke to a juvenile coyote's howl next to a corner of our tent, then a low, measured, adult answering howl from farther off. In my half-consciousness, I heard the conversation, the tone of it clearly. Junior had yipped in his high-pitched, coyote-pup voice, "Wow, Mum, lookit what I found here!" Mother had answered in a slow, low-pitched howl, the archetypal call of all worried mothers, "Watch it, son. It's a pair of those dangerous and tricky two-leggeds I've warned you about. Get out of there fast if you know what's good for you."

In the morning, the story was all there to read in the campsite dust. Junior's footprints a few feet away, coming and going, and Mum's much larger tracks, including her butt-end markings where she'd sat, waiting for him, a hundred feet off by a brushed-in bend in the track. I knew there must be a den close by. I have a memory of a bright, sharp-edged moon that night, low and large in the sky above Ts'yl-os, and long, pointed tree shadows on the ground.

For decades, I have dipped in a passing way into the world of trickster and the ephemeral, difficult-to-define nature of myth-mind. I have long held the conviction that Trickster Coyote, in all his many incarnations around the world—Raven, of course, and Mink, Blue Jay, Br'er Rabbit, Spider, Praying Mantis, Reynard the Fox, and all the rest of that pantheon out of the land of myth—in his persistent self-absorption and his oblivious isolation, is too much like our modern, linear conception of ego to be an accident. He is a foxy, creative, destructive, irresponsible, horny, greedy, often funny fool, like ego, and every bit as deceiving, especially of himself.

Coyote has the unfailing way of outsmarting himself, then picking up, and unlike Humpty Dumpty—but just like ego—putting himself back together again, even after the most debilitating of disasters. In his many escapades, Coyote has lost more body parts than a regiment of Crimean War veterans, and amazingly, he seems always to get them reattached and back in working order in time for his next scheme or impulse. No matter what, Coyote insists on being heard and seen and on taking part—often for me in that hazy crack in consciousness at the first light of day or those last crepuscular moments before nightfall.

But Coyote is more than just a cunning, wily, bumbling, and fantastically and usually canny creative fool. He comes down to us from the times of the animal-gods, those olden-day myth-times when animals informed us and helped us to become human. Coyote and his ilk appear to have been an essential, near-eternal presence in older times, a persistent reminder to us still—if we choose to look—that we are part of the animal world. Beneath the modern, civilized masks we wear, our wild, shadowy, animal nature persists. Just below the surface we manifest traces of our evolution from our older, more primal selves to the self-reflective, ego-based creatures we have become. Above all else, trickster/coyote reawakens the wildness in us that we share with him. Karl Kerenyi writes that trickster exhibits "his true nature as . . . *the spirit of disorder, the enemy of boundaries.*"

In "The Incredible Survival of Coyote," an essay in *The Old Ways,* Gary Snyder says, "Coyote Old Man. Not that he's 'old' now, in white-man times, but that he's always been old. Not the oldness of history, but the oldness of 'once upon a time'—outside history; in Dream Time, which surrounds us. And out of 'Dream Time' comes the healing."

Snyder concludes, "We slip those masks a bit to the side, and see there Coyote/Man, the Trickster; Bear/Man, King of the Mountains; Deer/Mother, Queen of Compassion. In turn those Type-Beings, Mind-created, Earth-created, are again masks. The Shining One peeks out from behind a boulder and is gone—is always there."

Two years later Don and I walked slowly up the slopes of Mount Tatlow, or Ts'yl-os, unaware of who or what we were dealing with. We had minor pretensions to actual climbing then, and the top of Tatlow was steep snow. The upper end of Nemaiah Valley sits close to 4,000 feet; so we had over 6,000 feet of climbing to reach the peak—not a major deal for the congenitally rugged, but plenty for us. We would each carry an extra five to ten pounds of climbing gear in case we needed it.

We followed the long road in from Lee's Corner, parked our vehicle in some thick brush, laced up our boots, and circled about to be sure of the right route. Then we started the slow plod up the hill. At first the route followed a grown-in Cat trail, originally a firebreak but later used for access to summer cattle range and for hunting by the Purjue Brothers and their descendants. A younger Purjue had, as part of his business as a guide, a hunting cabin up on Tsoloss ridge, though it had been recently burned out. It was a warm August afternoon. We passed a couple of happy horses—domestic stock, friendly and recently set loose—slowly grazing their way up the hillside into high country. That evening, we found the remains of the Purjue cabin a short distance up the creek from our campsite, the grass already growing green and tall over charred wood, rusted chimney pipe, tin cans, and stove bits. Here, the question of possible First Nations "land-claims" issues intrudes, inescapably. Did the cabin just burn, or did it *get* burnt? Or did Ts'yl-os simply find the shack offensive, an eyesore and blight, and any handy means of removing it from his person would do?

We ate our evening meal by the campfire. A pair of great horned owls began their *"Who's awake me too—who's awake me too"* calls, back and forth, echoing across the wet-meadow, swamp birch creek bottom below us. That old, "high lonesome" feeling was starting to set in. Alpenglow lit up the mountain; it just stood there, a great, glowing, silent mass above us.

In the morning we hoisted our packs, carried on across Tsoloss creek at a place where the gully wasn't too steep, and caught up to those two horses again in sub-alpine brush, soopolallie, and false mountain azaleas. They were even more easy going than before and were definitely working their way toward the expanse of open alpine on the east side of the mountain, perhaps to join wild relatives up there. We had heard there were wild horses up on Tatlow, mostly on those mid-elevation slopes at the headwaters of Elkin Creek.

We headed south, then veered right at the divide and picked a route across a long, boulder-strewn side hill to the southwest, aiming at ponds at the base of some distinctively shaped snowfields we had spotted while driving in. Our packs were heavy, and the mossy boulder field was slippery and hazardous.

We camped at 6,500 feet, behind scrubby alpine firs next to a narrow, snow-fed tarn. The area had been grazed by cattle in past years, and old, desiccated dung was banked under the trees. The trees had obviously served as a windbreak and cud-chewing stop for passing stock. It was warm up on the mountain that evening, and the view north and northeast across the wide Chilcotin was vast and blue, with just the rolling plateau, a few bright lakes below us reflecting sky here and there, and shades of deepening, dusty, smoky reds over the far northwestern mountains. Night lowered its blanket across the land, and a single light flashed once only somewhere to the northeast, evoking for me lonely memories of solitary navigation lights flashing in the dark on boat voyages home in my youth along Johnstone Straits off Vancouver Island. Always those lights had reminded me of Mathew Arnold's "Dover Beach" and the lines we studied in school: "the light/Gleams and is gone; . . . /The Sea of Faith/Was once, too, at the full, . . . /[and now] ignorant armies clash by night."

Early next day we began our final walk up Tatlow's great, rounded shoulder, above the snowbanks. It was a long, grinding, monotonous walk, but for the startling blue of the clear sky and the incredible views in all directions. While I walked, I found myself meditating on some opening lines of the Mountains and Rivers Sutra by Master Dōgen, Soto Zen Buddhist teacher of the thirteenth century. Or was it the verses that fixed on me? I had first heard them through Gary Snyder:

> The blue mountains are constantly walking. The stone woman gives birth to a child in the night. . . . He who doubts that the mountains walk does not yet understand his own walking.

As I trudged and mulled, the smaller peaks southeast and south of Tatlow that I now believe to be the older offspring of Eniyud and Ts'yl-os were elevating and lowering themselves according to the undulations of the ridge, up and down, slowly up and down. The skyline was sharper than a knife edge honed fine: rock and snow on blue. I tried to intuit how the mountains could possibly be "walking." I could see that the two tooth-shaped humps of rock moved as much or more than I did, up and down and sideways, seemingly of their own volition, like great whales surfacing and sinking. To the degree that I was not looking at myself, the mountains moved.

I have always been mesmerized by skylines honed to infinity. There is never a line so fine, so sharp as the one between the sky and a mountain ridge in thin, clear, high-altitude air, particularly when the ridge is long and the sky has turned that deep, high-country ultramarine blue of early dusk, say, or when there has been a cleansing rain or quick summer snowfall.

There is a saying from Haida Gwaii: The world is as sharp as the edge of a knife. It seems to be about the hard-edged dangers of existence and the constant need for being fully aware in life. These years I hear the saying as a keen observation on the acute differences in the intrinsic nature and meaning of all things.

I have wondered sometimes if—to Haida, Nuu-chah-nulth, and other coast peoples immersed in sea space—this observation might also refer to that fine, far-off line where the blue-grey North Pacific Ocean meets the blue-grey sky, an edge so fine that those two great spaces sometimes merge into one.

As Master Dōgen says in the Mountains and Rivers Sutra,

> The blue mountains are neither sentient nor insentient; the self is neither sentient nor insentient. Therefore we can have no doubts about these blue mountains walking.

For myself, I am maybe sure about one thing. The knowing here is about intrinsic truth: the intrinsic truth of blue mountains, of every sentient and insentient body in existence, including that busy, doughty Bewick's wren I observe in our Victoria backyard. It is a resident there and, with its partner, lives an active, purposeful life in the shrubs and trees along our fence lines. The female of the couple nests occasionally in the bow of our upside-down canoe in springtime. Sometimes, in one of those clear moments of grace that most of us have experienced, I know the bird to be Bewick's wren, inimitably, absolutely, nothing less: the Buddha-nature of wren, a glimpse—a quick sense of the Buddha-nature of all beings upon this earth, animate or otherwise.

We are all walking, constantly it seems—Bewick's wrens, the blue mountains—like the ages passing. The other day, I remarked on Dōgen's amazing opening sentences to my partner, Marne, then said, "I don't get that second line: 'The stone woman gives birth to a child in the night.' What on earth does he mean?"

"That's easy," she said, busy but forbearing as always. "Stone woman is

Eniyud, giving birth to all those kids." Perhaps it takes a mother: these intuitions are simple when you begin at the beginning.

Don and I worked our way to the top by early afternoon and stopped for lunch. The pitch got steeper, and we had to kick or dig toe holes in the hard snow. We only reached the first, lower peak. There were several hundred feet of steep snow cornices and the icy, near-vertical mother of all drop-offs, an incredibly long way down—most of the mountain—between us and the primary peak of the mountain. Extremely steep places make me queasy. There was no way I would attempt to go over there, not with those overhanging cornices. I was perfectly happy where I was, nestled in a snow hole, eating my bread and cheese up there in an infinity of snow and sky.

It was an exceptionally warm, calm day. Ts'yl-os stood alone, dozing I would think. We sat and munched and looked out at the big wide world around us, while small flocks of twittering birds flew by overhead. What else could they be doing up there at over 10,000 feet but having fun? Perhaps they were drawn skyward to the light—the same reason I walk in these wild places and write: to get as close as I can to light. I believe those birds, looking down at us, were astounded to spot a new, arresting addition to Ts'yl-os's wind-blown exterior. This is how legends begin.

On our last night, down on Tsoloss Ridge, the horned owls were still hooting to each other in the cool evening air. We listened. The mountain watched. The following, fresh morning, after we swabbed the late-August dew off the tent and packed up, we stood looking up at the great sunshiny mountain, an extended pause before hoisting our near-depleted packs to shoulder and heading back down the hill. As we scanned, we spotted movement up above the tree line on the northern slope. Wild horses were feeding in low brush, about two dozen of them—sorrels, bays, blacks, greys, roans, coyote duns—their bodies glistening, their tails and manes twitching in the morning sun. The shadows were still long. The horses were on a fast graze, moving west, across the mountainside, feeding and moving, being horses. They had a deep, restless energy. The animals keep on informing us, just as in the old myth-time days, if we show up and pay close attention. They haven't stopped. Nothing has changed.

Coyote, in all his forms—natural, mythic, tricky—has always been here. The blue mountains still constantly move. Is there anything anywhere that is not wild?

READINGS

Aitken, Robert. "Gandhi, Dōgen, and Deep Ecology." In *The Mind of Clover*. San Francisco: North Point Press, 1984.

Bringhurst, Robert. *A Story as Sharp as a Knife.* Vancouver: Douglas & McIntyre, 1999.

Dōgen, Eihei. "The Mountains and Rivers Sutra." In *The Mountain Spirit,* ed. Michael Tobias and Harold Drasdo. Woodstock, NY: Overlook Press, 1979.

Duff, Wilson. "The World is as Sharp as a Knife: Meaning in Northwest Coast Art." In *The World Is as Sharp as a Knife,* ed. Donald Abbott. Victoria: BC Provincial Museum, 1981.

Glavin, Terry. *Nemiah: The Unconquered Country.* Vancouver: New Star, 1992.

Harris, Bob. "Tchaikazan-Yohetta." In *BC Outdoors,* 1983.

———. "Tsoloss Ridge: South of Nemaia Valley." In *BC Outdoors,* Oct. 1975.

Kerenyi, Karl. "The Trickster in Relation to Greek Mythology." In *The Trickster.* New York: Schocken, 1972.

Lopez, Barry. *Giving Birth to Thunder, Sleeping with His Daughter.* New York: Avon, 1977.

Radin, Paul. *The Trickster.* New York: Schocken, 1956.

Ricker, Karl. "Mt. Tatlow: An Access Trick." *Canadian Alpine Journal,* Vol. 66 (1983).

———. "Tchaikazan Valley Earth Science Notes." *Canadian Alpine Journal,* Vol. 59 (1976).

Snyder, Gary. "Blue Mountains Constantly Walking." In *The Practice of the Wild.* San Francisco: North Point, 1990.

———."The Incredible Survival of Coyote." In *The Old Ways.* San Francisco: City Lights, 1977.

Tatla Lake School Heritage Project. *Hoofprints in History,* Vol. 3. Tatla Lake, BC: Tatla Lake Elementary Junior Secondary School, 1988.

Teit, James. *Traditions of the Thompson River Indians of British Columbia.* Boston: Houghton, Mifflin, 1898; reprint New York: Krauss, 1969.

Wyborn, M. and G. Barford. Tchaikazan Valley ACC Vancouver Section Camp 1–14 Aug. 1982. *Canadian Alpine Journal,* Vol. 66 (1983).

JUDITH ROCHE

Salmon Suite

This series by Seattle poet Judith Roche depicts the five species of salmon found in the Northwest. The poems were written as part of the "Salmon in the City" project of the 2001 Seattle Arts Commission, whose aim was to raise public awareness that in 1999, Puget Sound's chinook salmon were added to the list of "regionally threatened" species under the U.S. Endangered Species Act. A printed version of the poems was designed by Barbara Longo and is displayed at the Hiram Chittenden Locks in Seattle's historic Ballard district, the gateway to the Seattle watershed. Constructed by the U.S. Army Corps of Engineers in 1917, the Locks include a fish ladder for migrating salmon. Visitors to the installation can press a button at the fish-viewing windows and hear "Salmon Suite" being read aloud.

STEELHEAD

Steelhead   January to May

Deep waders have found a vein
  to the heart of cold,
    the resplendence of river,
the grandeur of muscle
  and elegant economy of spirit.

They leave lives unattended,
  wives in childbed
    husbands in beery bars,
to step into swift waters.

They're there for the fight.
Wild winter-run spawners, Steelhead
are trout on steroids, river's darlings,
  the prize at the end of every sea-slung

rainbow, not stay-at-homes
like their cousins, but heroes
on the romance of the journey.
        Deep waders understand this

at pre-lingual level. There are
many kinds of love in life.

Railbird, Copper Demon, Queen of the Waters,
Parmacheene Belle, Grizzly King,
Silver Doctor, Wet Spider, Princess,
        spoon and spinner.

The Samish, Stillagamish, Cowlitz,
Chehalis, Hoh, Humptulips, Nisqually,
Quinault, Skagit, Skykomish,
        Toutle, Washougal.

Flyline and cast,
        weight and diameter,
silk to monofilament. If spirit
is the fusion of thought and feeling

connecting one being to another,
and *kairos* a moment when everything
can change. Of the many,
        this is one kind of love.

SMOLT

Smolt   Mid-April to late July
                Smolt travel backwards until they reach salt water.

Being young, I don't know
        where I go.
I face my lake
        and float
                backward into my future.
Trembling on the edge
        of what I can't yet see,
                green-shadowed
I go with water's flow and trust strange
                rapture singing in my blood,
        ride the river like a knife's edge.

Breathe and float
    oxygen and insect,
        cut and rise,
I've seen where I've been
    so, rehearse my return
tracing it in latticed strands
    recorded in starry lace
        fabric of night.
Current pulls me down
    to spill over smolt slide,
slip the snap of gray bird's beak,

turn to face ocean opening flat and wide
    beyond imagining   no horizon,
    taste first fingers of bitter brine,
      flick silver and learn salt.
Because my throat itches
    I swallow what awaits me.
Begin young, I've cut my heart
    on the dream
      of the high seas.

CELESTIAL NAVIGATION

Sockeye   June to August (October)

I remember, I remember
the hollowed nest in stream of stars
the size of my eyes, I remember
the swell of water, shape
of light, celestial order to mirror
the song of river, the constellations
glitter into place to make the map—
    Scorpio, Virgo, Libra, Canis Major—
Sirius, the brightest, Orion, my own
clean cold water over stones, the whir
of the earth spinning through starry sky,
drag of tide waters lifting
the estuary, sweet taste of reeds
and rushes, edged sedge grass
in dance with wind and water flow,
in silver pool pulsing scent,
deep home loam, the river
where I was born.

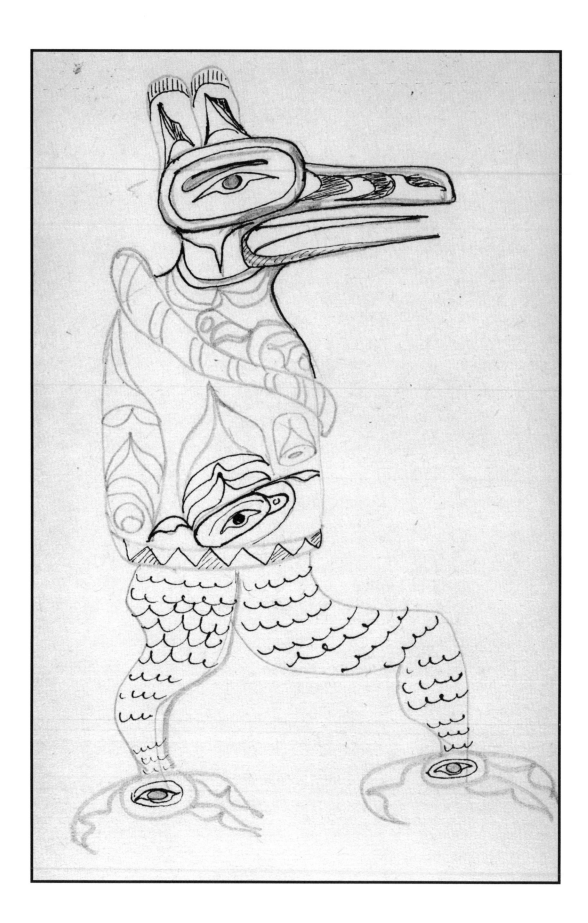

THE RIVER DANCE

Fish and bird creature. 1927. Graphite on paper by Emily Carr. Royal British Columbia Museum, British Columbia Archives. PDP08855

Chinook/Sockeye   August to September (October)

Aflame with the crimson color of marriage, the salmon
Seek their lovers.
For the salmon, the act
Spinning out life
Is an act of death
For the salmon
Life lives in death.
The salmon bets its life on love.
        from "Salmon Coming Home in Search of Sacred Bliss"
        by Mieko Chikappu; translated from the Ainu by
        Jane Corddry Langill with Rie Taki and Judith Roche

Choose the site for depth and current
        water flow and roll.
Turn, push and burrow gravel,
        deepen the redd.
Settle in to test the depth.
Busy while the males fight
        to get to me,
                the prize,
        my hope chest full of posterity.

I choose the reddest one—

Aflame with the crimson color of marriage,

torn and tattered but flushing
        deep burgundy slash-mark pattern.

I pass back and forth over him
        caressing his back and sides
                while the others drift away,
                all their fire fading to dull gray.

Crouching together we hover
        pulsing along the thin dark stripes,
                our lateral lines, sensing
                        every quiver,
throbbing our ancient dance of love and risk.

Spinning out our lives
        we love each other to death.

GHOST SALMON

Coho/Chinook/Sockeye   September to October (November)

The salmon die
Ahh, so tenderly.
    from "Salmon Coming Home in Search of Sacred Bliss"
    by Mieko Chikappu; translated from the Ainu by
    Jane Corddry Langill with Rie Taki and Judith Roche

Everything draws down toward autumn
and the way light is broken in splintered color
        we are broken to feed the multitudes
                take, eat, this is my body
                        this is my blood
eagle and osprey
        raven and bear,
                stonefly and gull
                        tear my flesh.
My silt settles and salts the stream
        cedar and fern,
                algae and fungi,
                        amoeba and protozoa
                                suck a rich soup.
My body emptied of eggs,
        milky milt settled,
completing
        the circle,
                eelgrass and catkin,
                        cougar and lynx,
creating life from the dead,

Food for the stream,
        I feed all comers.

Chief Dan George, Sacred Ecology, and Sustainable Environmental Design

I was born a thousand years ago, born in the culture of bows and arrows . . . born in an age when people loved the things of nature and spoke to it as though it has a soul.　　　　　　　　　　　　　Chief Dan George

In 1971, when I was a twenty-one-year-old undergraduate student in philosophy, I heard Chief Dan George speak on Native spirituality in Edmonton, Alberta. He was already a respected actor in the U.S. Having played a significant role the previous year in the hit movie *Little Big Man*—based on the novel by Thomas Berger and directed by Arthur Penn—he was nominated for Golden Globe and Academy Awards and won New York Film Critics' Circle and National Society of Film Critics' Awards. Dan George had had no training as an actor, but he was a true chief: from 1951 to 1963, he was the elected leader of the Tsleil-Waututh Nation, a Coast Salish band in North Vancouver. He was a man of great dignity and wisdom. The authenticity of his spirit and his character is what moved people who saw him in film, on TV, or on the stage.

Before he was famous in Hollywood, Canadians already knew Chief Dan George well. Almost by chance, he was cast by the CBC in a 1960s television series called *Caribou Country,* and he stunned audiences with his portrayal of David Joe in George Ryga's play *The Ecstasy of Rita Joe.* In 1967 he became a national figure when he delivered "Lament for Confederation"—accompanied by the drumming and chanting of his family—to a crowd of over thirty thousand at the Empire Stadium during Vancouver's celebration of Canada's Centennial. In this famous speech he said, "Today, when you celebrate your hundred years, oh Canada, I am sad for all the Indian people throughout the land." He asked, "Shall I thank you for the reserves that are left to me of my beautiful forests? For the canned fish of my rivers? For the loss of my pride and authority, even among my own people?"

Chief Dan George later gained more success as an actor, but he was cherished foremost as a spokesman for First Nations people, speaking out against injustices done to them and against the environmental degradation of their land.

When I heard him speak in 1971, I had been studying Asian wisdom traditions in the writings of Alan Watts and Krishnamurti. His talk addressed the large questions of humanity's relationship to nature and reminded me of what I was studying. Krishnamurti, for example, taught that nature was a vital part of our being: if we hurt nature, we hurt ourselves. Chief Dan George spoke of our being part of Mother Earth, of the interdependence of everything, and of the need to be caring and respectful always. This was before the Norwegian philosopher Arne Næss coined the term "deep ecology" and before Greenpeace brought environmental activism to the high seas of Alaska's Aleutian Islands and then to the rest of the world.

Chief Dan George was the first Native person I had ever met. He wore a tweed jacket, blue jeans, and pointy black shoes. His long silver hair framed a weathered face. He was then in his seventies, and had been a longshoreman and laborer into his forties. His appearance was at once fragile and powerful. A passionate storyteller, he described where he had grown up in North Vancouver: on land surrounded by mountains and the misty rain forests near the water's edge. The Chief joked about being an "old Indian," explained how living in that environment defined who he was—a member of the Tsleil-Waututh, or People of the Inlet—and described intimate relationships with the land, sea, and animals. He said that human beings did not own nature and that we should take from Mother Earth only what we need, sharing it; that we should connect to the land where we live, instead of trying to escape to a remote, pristine wilderness; and that we need to return to the land with a spiritual perspective, one that recognizes the soul of a place. Listening to him speak, it was clear to me that he was someone who lived by the stories he told.

Later, as a graduate student in environmental design, I was influenced by the new interdisciplinary strategies pioneered at the University of California–Berkeley in the late sixties and introduced to us at the University of Calgary. They emphasized a holistic view of planning that integrated environmental studies and architectural design. To those of us in Western Canada who had been inspired by Chief Dan George, these unconventional approaches to architecture complemented his wisdom, and we found a mantra in the title of E. F. Schumacher's book *Small Is Beautiful.* After receiving my graduate degree, I interned with Jack Long, Canada's earliest environmental architect. The creator of the country's first commercial building "green roof"—at Rogers Pass in the Rockies in 1977—Long headed the Solar Research Shelter. At this working studio, I and others experimented under his direction with renewable energy from the sun, the wind, and other sources. Not surprisingly, when I began my own architectural and planning practice in British Columbia, I founded it on ecologically sound, community-based ideals. Since then, I've seen the approach that Chief Dan George advocated continue to influence communities and leaders, despite resistance from corporate interests, government agencies, and regulators.

Many of us non-Natives have had homesteading grandparents who had direct connections to the land and relied on it for sustenance. However, today, we live mostly indoors, in climate-controlled buildings that keep us isolated from nature but have an enormous impact on the environment. These structures are situated across vast tracts of land, without regard for how they alter the flow of rain to the water table, disturb wildlife habitat, and consume materials and fuel in their construction and maintenance. According to the Rocky Mountain Institute, "America's 120 million buildings consume a prodigious amount of energy: 42 percent of the nation's primary energy, 72 percent of its electricity, and 34 percent of its directly used natural gas." The design, construction, and maintenance of residential housing and office buildings consume the majority of the world's natural resources and contribute most of the waste in our landfills. Almost 50 percent of all greenhouse gas emissions are traceable to these human-made environments.

What mainstream media analysis consistently overlooks is that of all the world's building stock, single- and multi-family residential housing contributes most to the global ecological crisis. What are our options? Successful, sustainable design compels us to rediscover the ecological interconnectedness First Nations people have with their environments. This means we need building projects, particularly housing, that benefit directly from the sun's and earth's passive energy. Examples include low-technology applications, such as passive-solar and earth-tubes for heating, the incorporation of natural ventilation—in plain English, more windows that open—and more effective use of natural daylight, rather than energy-intensive mechanical systems.

In Canada, we've seen First Nations communities take the lead with such demonstration projects as the ground-breaking Seabird Island First Nations Sustainable Community. Located in rural Agassiz, British Columbia, this was the first on-reserve housing project regarded as environmentally sensitive. From the beginning, in 2002, my company was involved in the design and planning, and we tried to take into account traditional First Nations social values and architecture, including such features as tribal pit-housing. We chose to use renewable energy sources—including wind, sun, and geothermal—and only local, non-polluting materials appropriate for the climate and place. The project was built by local crews of First Nations people, and community members were trained in new skills, which in turn contributed to the economy of the Seabird Island First Nations. A "healing garden" provided a place for self-reflection, outdoor activity, and growing food.

At Mayo, in the Yukon Territory, we've worked with the First Nation of Na-Cho Nyäk Dun to develop housing and community facilities as part of plans to both expand and relocate to safer, higher ground. Many of the existing structures are deteriorating or are structurally unsafe due to the

Friendly Cove lighthouse. 1929?
Graphite on paper by Emily Carr.
Royal British Columbia Museum,
British Columbia Archives.
PDP05706

continual movement and shifting caused by the permafrost's degradation. Here, too, innovations in community planning are being combined with alternative energy sources and materials.

At Carmacks, in the Yukon Territory, a major diesel spill caused the displacement of the daycare, community healthcare, and social services offices of the Little Salmon Carmacks First Nation. The replacement buildings have been designed as super-green, energy-efficient facilities with double walls, triple- and quadruple-glazed windows, arctic roofs, and heavy timber for framing. Wood—the only major renewable, carbon-neutral building material—was used extensively in constructing the facilities. These choices will result in substantial reductions in greenhouse gas emissions and energy costs.

More and more, designs like those implemented at Mayo and Carmacks are needed to address the kinds of ecological distress that are appearing in the far north and elsewhere as a consequence of global climate change.

Chief Dan George asked us to walk softly on the earth. Under the leadership of his son, Leonard George, the Tsleil-Waututh have been nationally recognized for their economic development initiatives. These include lower-cost housing options on leased Aboriginal land that benefit the younger Vancouver urban dwellers nearby. Chief Justin George—Dan George's grandson—and the Tsleil-Waututh people are also active in the cleanup and rehabilitation of Burrard Inlet and Vancouver's working inner harbour. Continuing their tradition as stewards of the inlet, they advocate limiting tanker traffic that would cause irreparable damage to their ancestral home. These quietly activist First Nations people are leaders in the renewable energy sector as well, reinvesting funds—raised from their own residential housing projects—in wind-turbine power development in the U.S. This is the Tsleil-Waututh First Nation's updated version of walking softly on the land.

According to the United Nations Population Fund, "it now takes the Earth 18 months to regenerate the natural resources that we use in a year." The commonly promoted United Nations definition of sustainability as a tripartite, equal relationship among the environmental, social, and economic realms is therefore problematic. The adverse effects of greenhouse gases, the destruction of micro-ecosystems, and the rapid depletion of non-renewable energy sources are at critical levels. Compounding this is the potential for further environmental catastrophe through the employment of techniques like fracking in oil and gas exploration, particularly in sensitive regions like the Alaskan and Canadian Arctic. It is ironic that Chief George's final resting place on the shores of Burrard Inlet overlooks the proposed expansion route terminus for the controversial Kinder Morgan Trans-Mountain Pipeline, which will transport bitumen from the Alberta tar sands and threaten Pacific Northwest coastal waters.

Eco-citizenship in the twenty-first century obliges us to create a way of living that is based on less economic growth, personal consumption, and waste. This is the practical dimension of what spiritual and scientific leaders term "interconnectedness." Traditional First Nation teachings call for thinking seven generations ahead about the environmental consequences of our personal actions. They tell us we are entitled to only one handful of earth and have a responsibility to our children to return it the way we found it. In my work as an architect and planner, I have tried to practice the wisdom Chief Dan George shared with us young students more than forty years ago. Such wisdom is the foundation of what he called keeping the earth alive.

Six Poems *with One Title*_____

LANGUAGE POEM (1)

The heron has practised his silence longer
than time has been time. When he rises
and speaks, there is no one in the cove
who doesn't listen, there is no one
in the cove who couldn't translate what he says,
and no one in the cove who wouldn't realize
the heron had been lost in that translation.
Everything speaks for itself in this world,
and everything rests in what is unspoken.

Hairy woodpecker too, mystified, miffed,
or exasperated or pleased, utters
his one word and jumps or hunkers down
and squeezes hard: hanging on for dear life
to what is, or swimming right through it
as if it were there. And it is. And it is.

How many more words would it take
to make up a language? Does language
actually have to have words? What it must have
are meanings—and some way of saying,
These and not those are the meanings that stand here
uncovered—or covered. The meanings
a language must have are the meanings
it lacks: located outside it, like sunlight
and grass. So together with meaning
there has to be pointing at meaning.
A language, in other words, has to have
gestures and speakers. One each, let us say,
for a start. With a little bit more—
one speaker, two gestures; one gesture,
two speakers—along with the requisite

bedrock and fauna and flora of meanings—
it might make the first blunt lurch
toward a life of its own.
                                    The sounds of our speech
are nothing but gestures that reach around corners
and work in the dark, the sounds of our footsteps
nothing but gestures out hunting for meaning.

There are, as you know, languages spoken
by millions of humans in which there are
syllables, gestures, with dozens or hundreds
of meanings. Imagine a language
with only one word and five hundred meanings.
Imagine one finger and five hundred moons.
You are not so far now from the woodpecker's
language, and not so far now as you were
from the shuddering throat of the great
blue heron or the sandhill crane. If you tried,
you might cling for a moment or two
to those hollow-boned fingers of air
in which five million years' worth of watching
and thinking are caught like a fossilized
fish in one braided, eroded, unanalyzed word.

The invisible dictionary that sits
on a rickety, tilted shelf of air
there in the great blue heron's study,
open to the weather, perpetually
shredded and reprinted by the wind,
has only one entry, a thousand pages long.
What does it mean, this evergreen
book full of one-fingered meanings?

That words are like wind in the leaves
and leaves in the wind: scraps of reality.
And that we harness them nevertheless,
as the fishermen, far up the river
harness their cormorants, horsemen their horses,
and as the *go* players harness their stones.

That gestures are gestures only because
we employ them as gestures—and gestures,
like other things, are what they are. They are not
what they point at and not what we thought
we would get them to say, in the same way
that horses are not what they pull.

That the journey will tell you, whenever
it's ready, where you were heading.
                                    That meaning
was here before you were, or they were,
and will be long after.
                            That gestures,
like horses, are part of it, yes, but gestures
can never—no matter how beautiful
they may be—create what they say. What
gestures give life to, and birth to, are gestures,
and that is their value—the same as with
cormorants, humans, and horses.
                                    And this:
that what speaks from its heart is in that moment
spoken—a form of the language, a part
of the speech—swinging down and back up
and back down on the dangling
tongue in its mouth like a bell—sometimes moving
toward singing, and sometimes toward walking
and sometimes toward freezing
and holding its breath in the presence of meaning.

LANGUAGE POEM (2)

The gesture is open, the symbol is closed.
But not wide, and not tightly. The difference
is small: just a twist of the fingers, a shift
of the eyelid, a cinch of the claws.

LANGUAGE POEM (3)

Sure. But when you say a talking horse,
you mean a horse that speaks and understands
your language, not a horse who tries—or balks
and chooses not to try—to speak to you
in his. You mean that what you're keen
to know is what you mostly know
already, not the many things a horse
who spoke as horses really do
and spoke that way to you could teach you.

But suppose the roots of language are prehuman,
premammalian—or preorganic, maybe.
Could it be that they survive in human form
the way the eye, the ear, the shoulderblade,
the shinbone, and the skin do, every
species to its own, though underneath
those metamorphoses of meat and bone
the grammar is substantially the same?

Go down the well of words until there are no words.
Go down until there are no sounds or signs.
Perhaps you'll find, in different shapes,
with different names, the same thing everywhere—
in chromosomes or nucleons or wings or tongues—
the hunger of the one-armed man
who hears within his heart
the sound of clapping.

Where is the man, his heart's ear, or
his arm, among the intertwining helices
and snarled quarks? Where is his other hand?
Not there, of course. The man,
as all men are, is incidental: one
example of a transitory form for whom
there is no stable answer and in which
the reach is no match for the grasp.

Just thirst and hunger, first and last.
A hope, a gesture, sometimes, yes. A pulse
or wave or signal, once or sometimes, yes,
but often only groping. Yes, and often
even less. You know, the one-armed
man can never, with his own
hand in his own heart,
point to clapping.

LANGUAGE POEM (4)

The language sleeps and dreams
and wakes and dreams. It sometimes even
wakes completely—just as, now and then,
we all do, dreaming flawlessly
for a moment or two of reality—
and then slips back to dreaming,
as we all do, about dreaming.

Perhaps, like you and me, it dreams
of beauty and exposure, flight and fear.
More stubbornly, it dreams of being
language, light, and music, and it dreams
of being meaning, and it dreams
of being silence, and repeatedly
and helplessly it dreams of being true.

But it is language, and its dreams
keep coming out as nouns and moans
and shouts and verbs. There are
no victories. The truth is always
everything that's there, and that is
harder, even harder, said than done.

LANGUAGE POEM (5)

You take a step in their direction and
the chickadees ignore you but the flicker
buggers off. Meaning, Ludwig says, is not
like looking through the window or like
checking in the book but like our walking
up to someone. And the flicker doesn't care
for what you mean. If you get close enough,
the chickadees won't either.

Like our going up to someone.
Preternaturally cautious, like
a birder, he says nothing whatsoever
of their coming up to us. Ever hopeful,
like a birder, he never says a word
about the chances of their scattering
the instant we get near.

What is it the flicker was saying?
That meanings are wary. Curious, hungry,
and horny, of course—and on occasion
even talkative as chickadees—
but wary. That the real ones are untamed.
That you were once the same as they are, but
are not so any longer. That it may
not be exactly what you wanted, but
you've actually grafted yourself on
to your machinery, not the other way
around. There's no more you; there's only

you-and-it. You've tied the knot and done
the honeymoon and started making
plans. You mean to save the wild rivers
and the trees and spotted owls by building
wilderness hotels. You also mean to build,
in every tree, a nest that's bigger
than the tree. And that will be the end
of meaning.

Meaning is bigger than you are, it's true.
It can move a lot faster than you
if it has to: also true. The only
wrinkle is, it needs a place to go.

What is it then, this thing you're calling
meaning? Physiognomy, says Ludwig.
Meaning blooms the way a face does, or
a rose. Those anthers, petals, beaks, and eyes
are the nature of things declaring itself
in its features—as if it were someone.
Declaring itself and taking things in.
That is probably the key. If meaning
faces up to meaning, the nature
of things can know and be known.

Does that mean meaning came equipped
from the beginning with nostrils, ears, and eyes,
or the desire that underlies them?
Does meaning feel you, smell you? Was it
watching you before you had a clue
that something your fine words had never
heard of, and you had no way to speak of,
might be there?

These rocks, redcedars, hemlocks, mosses,
sharp-shinned hawks, those chickadees, that flicker,
and the air and light they breathe, their leaves
and cheekbones, pollen, feathers, talons, seeds
and seedcones, scales, scents, their songs and calls—
all these are meaning. They're the shapes that being
takes when pressing out and pushing on
or pushing back, not caving in, the shapes
it comes upon in trying not to die
where there is nothing being born. That's roughly
all there is to meaning.

Roughly, yes, but not exactly. Meaning
also has to rest. It has to feed.
It has to feed, in fact, on meaning,
because meaning is the only food.
So meaning faces itself squarely where
it can, and where it can't, it ducks and runs
or tries to hide. When trapped, it's often
poker-faced. That is, its physiognomy
becomes a fist, the eyes no longer
fingertips but knuckles—which are blind
and silent when they open, with the closing
of the hand, and watchful only when the hand
reopens and they close.

And meaning is as meaning does. It feeds
on meaning, which has learned, because it had to,
to be wary. So the world is as it is:
the nature of things, wherever meaning
ducks or hides, can know and be known only
imperfectly.

We go ourselves—no bodyguards or proxies—
up to everything we mean—and things
we mean come up to us, as if the things
we mean were persons. Somewhere near them,
Ludwig says—but not too near them—we are
sometimes capable of speaking.

Out beyond them—on the other side
of anything we mean—and probably
a little way this side of it as well,
it must be better just to listen.

We can, it seems, at times, get fairly close
to what we mean, or think we mean. At
any rate, we try. We also sit sometimes
and let the things that mean get close to us.
They do come close from time to time, then
scurry off. They cannot stay for long unless
we tame them, and to tame them costs them
almost everything they have.

Sometimes for a moment, too, they seem
to tame themselves—as if they'd half remembered
we were once among them, and had half

forgotten what has changed. They'll often
wait, then, or hesitate, a little.
Always, soon, they carry on. However
close they come or far away they go,
they don't stay long where you imagine
you have seen or heard or smelled them.

That, I saw the flicker, then the sharp-shin, say,
is roughly how it is.

LANGUAGE POEM (6)

It knows what's what but not what is,
and that's because it has no nose
for things outside itself. It sleeps at night
and stumbles through the day, but still
it smells your breath in everything
you say. It cannot see the sun
or smell it. So it does not know
what light and warmth are present in the meaning
of the word. But it can smell the gaping holes
between whatever words might mean
and what our fat-lipped mouths and thin-lipped
ears are out to make them mean.
The language may be blind, it may be dumb,
but it is older than you'll ever be.
It's been where it can go. So like a chisel
or a wagon or a human or a well-worn
horse, it mostly knows when it's misused.

The language does, that is, remember,
some days, most days, where it comes from.
Like the forest, it is used to being blamed
for crimes committed in and near it.
It's been told, with some conviction,
that it's guilty. Still, it skips and slogs along.
It also knows—the way it knows
its mother's footsteps—how the taste
of home-grown meanings stands apart
from all the other ones, imported or imposed.

All any language does, in any case—
and all it can do—is to try to nudge
the unsaid into place against
reality. It knows that it will rarely
find itself there. It's the one that does
the talking, after all, and talking stops
in the embrace of what there is.
But still it knows a friendly touch, the way
a human or a chisel or a horse does.
It understands what kind of touch it is
that starts, stops, or evens out the talking.
It can say much more than it can say,
as well as less, and often does.
The reason is, it's been around.
It even goes, when we're not using
or misusing it, to visit
with the ones who have no mouths,
who come so seldom to the surface
and who tell the language everything it knows.

Lew Welch: An Appreciation

Not everybody who writes poems knows what a poem is. Lew Welch knew. I'm glad I got to meet him before he disappeared. He's often called a San Francisco poet or a California poet. He studied music in Stockton. He lived with his wife, Magda, in a house on a slope in Marin City, which is a Black city.

They had been expecting Earll and me; Magda had made enough sandwiches for about ten people, then went outside to work in her garden. She probably fed lots of kid poets who came to see her husband. Being still young, we naturally expected food and attention from adults, and did not recognize largesse when we received it. Lew Welch then was working at the docks as a longshoremen's clerk, and now that I'm a worker and writer myself, I know better than to take up a man's time on his day off.

He had cut his red hair for the summer. He had written about that: "In summer I usually cut it all off. / I do it myself, with scissors and a / little Jim Beam." He looked exactly as he said in his poem:

> Not yet 40, my beard is already white.
> Not yet awake, my eyes are puffy and red,
> like a child who has cried too much.

Only, I think, he had reached forty already; he had lines in his face, but though his eyes were red, they opened wide. He looked at you out of bright blue eyes, but at a part of you that isn't your appearance or even your personality; he addressed that part of you that is like everybody. I would like to learn to look at people that way.

He went for his papers and books and got down to business. He read to us. He cried. He sang:

> She bared her bos'm
> I whupped out m'knife
> Carved my initials on her thin breast bone.

"I invented putting a note before and after the parts that need to be sung," he said. "The book has these fussy sixteenth notes because those

Totem pole with eagle, Skidegate. 1928. Graphite on paper by Emily Carr. Royal British Columbia Museum, British Columbia Archives. PDP08934

were the only notes the printer had. They should have been quarter notes." I admired his caring about detail, and have checked the editions of his work that were printed after he disappeared, to see if the notes had been changed. They had, and they do look better.

He read a poem about driving, written by one of his students, and said, "Now, there's a poem. There's a poet. I phoned him to come do a reading with me, but he had to work on his car." There was going to be a reading that weekend by the Bay Area's best-known poets. "That's cool. That's right. He ought to be working on his car."

From the window, you could see down the hill to a round space filled with motorcycles and cars with their hoods up. Kids were repairing them. "Somebody ought to subsidize garages all over the country, stocked with automotive tools," he said. "Kids can come and work on their cars, something real, when they drop out of school."

He had many ideas for things for you to do. There is a poem accompanied by a circle drawn in one brushstroke. The poem is in his clear handwriting. He read it as if it were a friendly but imperative suggestion:

> Step out onto the planet
> Draw a circle a hundred feet round.
> Inside the circle are
> 300 things nobody understands, and, maybe,
> nobody's ever really seen.
> How many can you find?

One of his ideas was to organize to feed poets "so poets could have babies and fix their wives' teeth and the other things we need." He planned a magazine to be called *Bread* that would discuss the economics of being a poet in America. Somebody still needs to carry out these plans.

He talked about being one of the young poets who had driven William Carlos Williams from the airport to Reed College. I love the way that car ride has become a part of literary history. Gary Snyder, Lew Welch, Philip Whalen, and William Carlos Williams were the poets in the car. Today, Welch told us that he had felt Williams giving the power of poetry to him. The two of them had agreed on their dislike of T. S. Eliot.

Then Lew Welch sang us "The Waste Land" to a jive beat, and it did not sound at all as if he disliked it.

He said that poetry has to be useful. He was very proud that the No Name Bar in Sausalito pasted in its window his poem for protecting the town, and the "innkeeper" published that poem, "Sausalito Trash Prayer," by duplicating forty copies of it and giving it to people. It was "pasted in the florist's window . . . carefully retyped and put right out there on Divisadero Street . . . that it might remind of love, that it might sell flowers."

He read "After Anacreon," a poem about cab driving. He said that he had also read it to his fellow Yellow Cab drivers, and was happy when they told him that that was exactly what being a cabby is like.

He didn't say it that day, but there's some practical advice of his that is told by one to another, a word-of-mouth poem: "Think Jewish, dress Black, drive Okie."

He was a wise and trustworthy man. He warned and comforted kid writers: "To become enamored of our powers is to lose them, at once!" and "full / full of my gift / I am only / left out and afraid." He wrote two poems he called the first American koans, "The Riddle of Hands" and "The Riddle of Bowing." He invited readers who solved these koans to have their answers confirmed by writing to him. There was flesh behind his words. I guess that's why he was willing to see us, and also why he looked so worn.

After about two hours, we had to go, a sense of urgency about the work to be done having come over us. We thanked him and Magda for the poems and the beer and sandwiches, and said goodbye.

I haven't told you much that you can't read for yourself. He had spoken exactly like his writing.

I encourage my own students to write in dialect, and give them Lew Welch's instructions on how to do it: "Dialect is only a regional and personal voiceprint . . . You can easily separate structure and meaning from dialect, and still be dealing with sound, with music, with speech, with another's Mind. Gertrude Stein perfectly mimicked the rhythms and structures of Baltimore Blacks in her story 'Melanctha' and she didn't transcribe the dialect at all—that is, didn't have to misspell a lot of words to get the work done. Nelson Algren has many many passages with no misspellings, but catches the real flow of regional speech."

I keep some Lew Welch advice over my desk: "When I write, my only concern is accuracy. I try to write accurately from the poise of mind which lets us see that things are exactly what they seem. I never worry about beauty, if it is accurate there is always beauty. I never worry about form, if it is accurate there is always form." I ditto this for my students at the beginnings of courses, and tell them I have not much more to teach them, but they don't believe me, and stay.

In the spring of 1971, Lew Welch walked away into the woods of Nevada County, and has not come back. Those woods are in the northwest—the direction of leina-a-ka-ʻuhane. I think there must be a jumping-off place in California, just as there is one on each of the islands of Hawaiʻi. And Lew Welch's soul leapt away.

REX WEYLER

Nature's Apprentice:
A Meta-narrative for Aging Empires

Rex Weyler is one of the early cofounders of Greenpeace, an independent direct-action environmental organization that began in Vancouver, British Columbia, in 1971, and later expanded to Greenpeace International. In an interview published earlier this year in The Cascade, *an autonomous student newspaper produced at the University of the Fraser Valley, Weyler stated, "I never set out in this world to be an activist. It was never particularly a goal of mine. I got active because I looked around and saw that the world I lived in was sick. The culture I lived in was contributing to the sickness. There was no way I was going to participate in that without resisting it. I think that's a natural instinct." In the spirit of the activist orientation of Greenpeace, Weyler stresses in the following essay a new urgency. "After a half-century of environmentalism," he says, "we must admit that the world is less sustainable than in 1962. Why?"*

Bear totem pole, Port Renfrew. 1929. Graphite on paper by Emily Carr. Royal British Columbia Museum, British Columbia Archives. PDP08806

The major problems in the world are the result of the difference between how nature works and the way people think.

Gregory Bateson

Piecemeal ecology isn't working. It's hard to save something when it isn't really a thing. Humanity, it appears, still has to learn how nature works. Future historians may mark the period from British Petroleum's 2010 oil-spill disaster, through the 2011 release of radioactivity at the Fukushima Daiichi Nuclear Power Plant, to the 2012 Rio+20 Climate Conference failure as the catalyst for an earth-shaking shift in ecological awareness. Veteran ecology activists are now rethinking strategies in the face of unrelenting ecological deterioration. The global Zeitgeist has shifted, at least within environmental discourse. Even before Rio, evidence indicated that our scant actions arrive too late to stop severe global heating and—more critically—that the heating itself appears as a symptom of a far more multifarious predicament.

In 2009, *Nature* journal published "Planetary Boundaries" by Earth systems scientist Johan Rockström and colleagues. They explained how human activity has pushed seven of nine essential life-support systems—climate change, biodiversity, ocean acidification, nitrogen and phosphorus cycles, land use, freshwater use, and ozone depletion—near or beyond critical tipping points. Meanwhile, system feedbacks drive additional change, push other limits, and prove more complex than our engineering can fathom. Troubling system feedbacks include methane chimneys rising from melting polar permafrost, dying coral reefs, shrinking forests, creeping deserts, and invigorated beetles that can swarm over the Rocky Mountains.

In 2012, *Nature* published "Approaching a State Shift in Earth's Biosphere" by twenty-two international scientists. The team warned that human activity is driving a planetary-scale transition "with the potential to transform Earth rapidly and irreversibly into a state unknown in human experience." Canadian coauthor and biologist Arne Mooers commented, "Humans have not done anything really important to stave off the worst. My colleagues . . . are terrified." In confirmation, William Rees, a University of British Columbia professor and creator of the "ecological footprint" concept, summarized our conundrum in "The Way Forward: Survival 2100" in *Solutions Journal:* "Climate change is just one symptom of generalized human ecological dysfunction. A virtual tsunami of evidence suggests that the global community is living beyond its ecological means . . . by about 50 percent."

Welcome to what ecologists call "habitat overshoot," now occurring on a global scale. Ecologists from Rachel Carson to Arne Næss, Gregory Bateson, Donella Meadows, Rees, and countless others have warned us. We live within a dynamic network of coevolving systems, and these processes impose restraints on all material growth. This realization is now seeping into our ecology movements. Humanity's industrial engine has hit the redline. The time has arrived to plan and prepare for the blunt realities of adaptation to a global biosphere that is in remedial crisis. The new ecology realism arises naturally from the evidence: oil and nuclear-radiation accidents, bank failures and bailouts, crop failures, famine in the Sahel, extreme weather events and fires, Arab Spring uprisings, Occupy protests, and so forth. However, after the Rio debacle, a collective gasp arose even among the more patient scientists, journalists, and believers in the political process. Britain's Deputy Prime Minister Nick Clegg pronounced the agreements "insipid." Former Irish president and UN High Commissioner for Human Rights Mary Robinson called the results "a failure of leadership." Ecology groups walked out. Indigenous leaders held their own meetings and called the official Rio Green Economy plan "a new wave of colonialism."

With implacable dismay, writer-farmer Sharon Astyk summed up the mood for *Scienceblog:* "Most of these events are about feeling good about pretending . . . [The] fundamental policy changes that would be necessary . . . aren't even on the table . . . caring is not enough."

"When will ordinary people rise up?" asks Share the World's Resources, a UN consultation group. "Leaders and policymakers [are] paying merely lip service." The group now advocates "public uprisings and mass occupations." While defending an enduring stretch of wild river in Canada, scientist David Suzuki remarked, "In elevating the economy above everything else, we fail to ask the most elementary questions: What is an economy for? How much is enough? Are there no limits?"

Fifty years ago, Carson published *Silent Spring.* Ten years later—inspired by Carson, John Muir, and others—ecology-minded pacifists in Vancouver, British Columbia, founded Greenpeace. People in the ecology movements are aware that today, with far more environmental groups, we actually have less wilderness; we have more environment ministers, conferences, and "protected areas," but we have fewer species; we levy more carbon taxes yet produce greater emissions; we have more "green" products yet have less green space. The most troubling trends—global warming, less species diversity, soil infertility, toxic dumps, shrinking forests, expanding deserts—are worsening. The testimony of our collective failure blows around us like a chilling polar wind. It is too late to save the 25,000 species that blinked out of existence last year, the 300,000 people who perished from global warming last year, or the equal number who will perish this year.

After a half-century of environmentalism, we must admit that the world is *less* sustainable than in 1962. Why?

Moving Beyond Hope

I am thankful for the environmentalists who have sounded an appropriate alarm and slowed the destruction of nature, but collectively we are not winning against the denialists, marketeers, thugs, and swindlers. Perhaps environmentalists have been so eager to appear optimistic that some forgot about being realistic. In the autumn, when leaves fall and the wind turns chilly, it is not pessimism to point out that winter is coming. Contemplating the Rio failure, George Monbiot lamented in *The Guardian* that the "promise to save the world keeps us dangling, not mobilising. . . . Hope is the rope on which we hang." Extending this blunt truth, University of Texas journalism professor Robert Jensen contends in *Counterpunch,* "We have to believe in something beyond hope."

Hope may be a useful state of mind, but it is not a strategy; going beyond hope to action is necessary for our social movements. Systems ecologist Pille Bunnell, a professor at Royal Roads University on Vancouver Island, says it must be turned into action: "Hope is a manner of living and acting in the present that does not foreclose the future we desire."

In his recent book *Leavings,* farmer-writer Wendell Berry continues to sing in the old voice grounded in the earth. He takes up the question of appropriate hope. In his poem "Sabbaths 2007," he insists, "Hope must not depend on feeling good . . . stop dithering." The poem reminds us to seek hope "on the ground under your feet."

The new mood among environmentalists encourages a return not only to urgency, but also to fundamentals, common decency, a respect for place, magnanimous values, indigenous voices, limits to economic growth, and genuine ecology as the bases for any authentic or enduring solutions for humanity.

Make Fun, Make Trouble

Artists—Bohemians, Beats, Punks, outcasts—usually lead social Zeitgeist changes. Rouget de Lisle's *La Marseillaise* rallied eighteenth-century French revolutionaries just as Tunisian hip-hop artist El General's "O Leader!" became the soundtrack for an uprising that toppled a regime and sparked a democracy movement. Virginia Woolf anticipated modern psychology, the Yes Men brought street theatre back to activism, and *Adbusters* magazine awakened the Occupy Movement.

The new temperament that we must strive for accepts bad news honestly. In North America, Justin Ritche and Seth Moser-Katz post the *Extra-environmentalists* podcast series, which they call "Doom without the Gloom"—the tough-love news with a sense of irony. "Is sustainability a farce," they ask, "when associated with a way of life that is out of touch with reality?"

From Etobicoke, Ontario, the singer Cold Speck writes "doom soul" music—realism with rhythm. "We fall from a dying tree," she sings in "Winter Solstice." The Occupy Movement—as did the Hippies and Beats before it—understands that our future has been mortgaged by the privileged and that we can't shop our way to sustainability. More and more urban young around the world practice voluntary simplicity: growing their own food, buying secondhand clothes, and making life about experience, not stuff. A fresh spirit moves globally, seeking new, low-impact ways for communities to live with each other and with nature. The youth feel it instinctively. Witness eleven-year-old Ta'kaiya Blaney's warning: "If we do nothing, it will all be gone," she sings in "Shallow Waters," which she composed and performed in the indigenous camp at Rio.

How to Boil a Frog, the funniest film ever made about collapsing ecosystems, advises people to "Make friends, make fun, and make trouble." These new movements are reminiscent of the ecology spirit that emerged in the early 1970s. "Ecology's a whole new kind of revolution," Greenpeace cofounder Bob Hunter used to say in a Vancouver pub, before Greenpeace ever had an office. "It's not about trading one political power structure for another. Ecology is a revolution inside our own consciousness that is going to wake us up to realize that humans are not the centre of life on Earth."

Nature is not a "thing," but a process, a set of relationships among dynamic systems that are co-creative, coevolutionary, and interdependent. Nature is a system of systems, and the complexity unfolds at orders of magnitude and in eons of time beyond our conventional awareness.

Degrowth

Human enterprise finds itself in what ecologist and systems-theory pioneer Gregory Bateson called a "double bind." Our conventional economic system demands growth, but Earth's capacity requires us to act with restraint. Bateson pointed out that when such an impasse occurs in nature, communities of organisms get creative, pulling options from the random roll of events to radically change their way of living. Those not up to the creative task simply perish.

No species—including humans—can grow out of habitat overshoot. Contraction or "degrowth" is thus not just a rallying cry from ecology realists, but also an important stage in all natural processes. In nature, all growth stops, reverses, and resolves into "dynamic homeostasis," a system of balance that oscillates within biophysical limits. The problem for modern society is not that these ideas are wrong or too complex, but that they threaten the operating principles of the wealthy and powerful. The denialists appear in history as the papal henchmen who refused to look through Galileo's telescope. Promulgating natural limits is the modern heresy.

In 2008, economists and scientists met in Paris for the First International Conference on Economic Degrowth for Ecological Sustainability and Social Equity, launching the degrowth *(décroissance)* movement. It wasn't an entirely new idea. Forty years earlier, then World Bank senior economist Herman Daly proposed ecological economics in the now-classic *Steady-State Economics*. In a recent essay, Daly cites the IBM corporate slogan, "Build a smarter planet," and scoffs, "one that is 'smart' enough to obey our mindless command to keep growing." Rather, Daly suggests, "Let's make a smarter adaptation to the wonderful gift of the Earth, out of which we were created."

The human impact on Earth's ecosystems follows from growing population and per-capita consumption. Added to these dual drivers are the unintended consequences of human technologies: oil spills, toxic rivers, acid rain, global warming, and so forth. Successful species typically overshoot habitat capacity, and nature's default solution is starvation. In the human community, if we wish to fashion a more dignified solution, we will have to manage a contraction of our numbers and consumption habits and accept limits on technology. We may want certain economic sectors to grow, such as renewable energy and developing economies, but we need to appreciate the magnitude of the transitions we contemplate. The rich 15 percent of Earth's people now consume about 85 percent of available resources. As developing-world ethicist Vandana Shiva says, "The world's poor are not poor because they've been left behind by industrialism. They're poor because they've been robbed." Africa is ecologically depleted and poor because Europe and North America plundered it to fuel their economic growth. The global population grows at about 1.1 percent annually, adding 75 million people each year. Nations expect economies to grow by 3 to 4 percent annually. Extrapolating these growth rates to 2050, we would have a world of 9 billion people. Providing social equity, consumer lifestyles, and renewable energy for 9 billion people would require about thirty times more resources than we consume today.

Is that possible? We have already leveled half the world's forests, depleted major commercial fish stocks by about 80 percent, filled the atmosphere with carbon dioxide, and drained aquifers; now we turn pristine boreal lakes in Canada into black sludge pits so we can extract the dregs of Earth's once-great stores of irreplaceable hydrocarbons. Species diversity is now collapsing faster than at any time since the asteroid hit Earth 64 million years ago. How will we multiply these resources by thirty times?

The Rebound Effect

Understandably, certain technical solutions—such as solar panels, windmills, ethanol, nuclear fuels, "green" products, "clean" coal, and so forth—appeal to our longing for a solution that we can control and that someone can profit from. These two motivations—control and profit—prove extremely limited in natural systems, but on a quite practical level, no human technology erases the limits on consumption that challenge our belligerent empires. "My beef with the whole 'solutions' thing," writes James Kunstler in *Rolling Stone,* is that "the subtext to that particular meme is, 'Give us the solutions that will allow us to keep running our stuff the same way.'. . . The mandates of reality are telling us something very different."

The late Japanese poet and eco-pioneer Nanao Sakaki warned that we can outsmart ourselves, getting trapped by "solution networks" that confine us within destructive habits. This idea is similar to the conclusions of historian Joseph Tainter, who asserts that collapsing civilizations invariably build more complex "solutions" to solve problems created by their earlier solutions.

In *The Collapse of Complex Societies,* Tainter explains that such multiplying complexity is itself limited. Our industrial idea of a "solution" presumes the end point of a linear process—but nature isn't linear. Real solutions will have to be dynamic and designed for the long term, not for quick profit. We need to learn how complex systems actually function. Solar panels and windmills require energy and materials—iron, rare-earth metals, copper, silicon—which we mine with hydrocarbon energy, which is sunlight energy compacted over the last 500 million years. Try operating a copper mine on real-time solar energy and you will soon understand the dilemma.

If we attempt to power a wasteful, consumer culture for 9 billion people, we encounter some inconveniences. For example, all mechanical energy systems have limited lifespans. If we build enough windmills and solar panels to power a world for 9 billion people, the life cycle of the infrastructure would have to be about the same as the duration of construction, if we are lucky. In other words, to sustain such a world, we would be building and rebuilding the infrastructure forever. And no: "recycling" would not save us. Used energy doesn't recycle. Materials do not entirely recycle in useable form, and the percentage that does recycle requires energy to recover. The reason human enterprise has such a poor recycling record is that more energy is required to recycle materials than to dig the stuff out of the ground. Solar energy isn't free. No energy transformation in the known universe is free.

We hear of "decoupling" economy from materials and energy, but there are no known examples of this. Material and energy remain the necessary sources of human enterprise. We hear of new electronic efficiencies, but historically we never leave the efficiency gains in the ground. We take it out in profits. We expand. We use efficiency to consume more resources, not less. William Jevons documented this in the coal era, and in economics "Jevons' paradox" later became "the rebound effect." Remember when computers were going to help us save paper? That never happened. We now use six times more paper than we did in 1960. Computers accelerated economic growth and increased paper use—the rebound effect at work.

Conservation strategies are the only solutions that do not require material and energy. In nature, capacity does not match desire. By starting with our desires, we have approached "sustainability" backwards. We have to start with Earth's productive capacity and then design our cultural transition based on it. We have to recognize nature's patterns, then design society to restore, maintain, and support those patterns.

The Long Apprenticeship

In natural systems, there exists a difference between growth and what we term development. Nonmaterial qualities—species diversity, innovation, and ideas—can grow, but this is quite different from the growth of material things, such as populations, cell phones, and windmills. Nature can produce five species of finches or fifty species, but nature imposes limits on the total biomass of finches. Forests reach a limit that we call "maturity": roughly stable biomass with shifting diversity. Likewise, culture can develop, but not necessarily grow forever. Humans can create virtually unlimited musical styles, but only a limited number of maple cellos with ebony fingerboards. Cultural diversity can flourish, but physical habitats restrain expansion. Historian and ecologist Kenneth Boulding pointed out that "imperialism always makes the empire poor"—as in the cases of Persia, Rome, Britain, and now America—because expansion and the cost of defense that goes with it drain resources. Growth never pays for itself. Growth always creates a demand for resources, which is the stimulus for imperialism in the first place.

Our knowledge can grow, but the infrastructure of knowledge that nurtures an environment of ideas requires material throughput. The Internet may feel like "free" information, but it requires massive materials, energy, and waste sinks. Growth of difference—diversity—is not the same as growth of stuff. To understand diversity growth in terms of human culture, we must understand two characteristics of the developing biosphere: growth rates and natural-collapse events.

First, nature's growth rates remain tiny compared to those of human economies. Since about 1750, human economies, and concomitant consumption, have grown at about 3 to 4 percent annually, doubling total resource consumption every twenty years. On the other hand, over the last 500 million years, Earth's biomass has doubled about every 50 million years, two million times slower than human economic and consumption growth. Yes, diversity growth is natural, but not nearly at the rate that bankers and neoclassical economists want economies to grow.

Second, collapse appears frequently in the fossil record. Biological diversity reached capacity limits not only during the "five extinctions" but also in thousands of minor extinctions. About 600 million years ago, free oxygen allowed cells to extract more energy from the ecosystem, unleashing tremendous diversity growth. However, many times over the next 300 million years, this growth reached habitat limits: species crashed, recovered, and crashed again. The *rate* of diversity growth peaked during the Cambrian era, about 500 million years ago, and has not been equaled since. Diversity is not a one-way progression: ecosystems grow, stutter, collapse, and recover based on environmental capacity and changing conditions.

Human social complexity has developed great variety over the last 100,000 years, punctuated with collapses—Mesopotamia, the Mayan civilization, Rome—and ecosystem decline. Keep in mind that only a few thousand years ago, the Syrian desert was a cedar forest and the Sahara was a productive green savanna. Human success incurs ecological costs. Wishful thinking won't change this. Our challenge during the next century will be to manage the contraction of our wasteful economies. Rich nations typically ignore the costs of growth by exporting those costs to poor nations and using nature as a dumping ground—sending city garbage to the country, disposing toxic waste at sea, and placing dangerous chemical plants in poor villages such as Bhopal, where wages are cheap and disasters kill people without lawyers. A large portion of China's carbon dioxide emissions, for example, are really Europe's and America's because those rich countries consume the products of that pollution.

Localization, the countertrend to globalization, is a key to conservation and sustainability. We trade, share our cultures, and remain interconnected, but old-fashioned self-reliance is a hallmark of genuine sustainability. The instinct to grow was forged in natural evolution, but that instinct doesn't make limits disappear. When the context changes, instincts can be harmful. Once a species reaches its habitat limits, the instinct to grow and expand becomes a liability. In nature, all debts get collected.

Our universities can help turn society back toward the genuine sustaining patterns of nature, but only if they embrace this spirit of learning from nature's ways and prepare young people for a world characterized by limits on cheap energy, less or no substantive economic growth, food and commodity restraints, and increased ecological pressures. Industrial business-as-usual is not an enduring option. We can get ecology right, but we must humble ourselves enough to learn from nature. We must, in fact, apprentice ourselves to nature, learn its patterns, its strategies, its limits. This does not mean returning "back to the caves" or living in a dismal world. In fact, we consumers could live much more creative, productive, and happy lives with a lot less stuff. Ecology pioneer Arne Næss put it most clearly: "Richer lives, simpler means."

Happiness does not come from consuming more stuff. Happiness comes from friends, family, community, creativity, leisure, love, companionship, and time spent in nature—all of which require emotional, spiritual, and intellectual effort, but modest material investment. These are the qualities of life we should be promoting and teaching our young and eager students. Genuine sustainability will require this long apprenticeship to nature. Nature is not a thing. Nature cannot be "fixed" or made "smarter" by humanity. The living processes in which we find ourselves remain forever a mixing and merging of countless systems, from electrons to the mystery at the edge of our highly buoyed senses. The realization of and negotiation with nature's limits and patterns may be the most important public dialogue of this century. And we had better get it right. Humanity may not get many more chances.

READINGS

Abram, David. *Spell of the Sensuous.* New York: Vintage, 1997.

———. *Becoming Animal: An Earthly Cosmology.* New York: Vintage, 2011.

Bateson, Gregory. *Mind and Nature.* New York: Hampton, 1979.

Benyus, Janine. *Biomimicry: Innovation Inspired by Nature.* New York: Morrow, 1997.

Boulding, Kenneth. "General Systems Theory: The Skeleton of Science." *Management Science* 2:3 (1956): 197–208.

Carson, Rachel. *Silent Spring.* Boston: Houghton Mifflin, 1962.

Catton, William. *Overshoot.* Champaign: Illini Books, 1982.

Daly, Herman. *Steady-State Economics.* New York: Freeman, 1977; Washington, DC: Island Press, 1991.

Georgescu-Roegen, Nicholas. *The Entropy Law and the Economic Process.* Cambridge: Harvard UP, 1971.

Meadows, Donella, Dennis L. Meadows, Jorgen Randers, and William W. Behrens III. *Limits to Growth.* New York: New American Library, 1972; 1977.

Meadows, Donella, Jorgen Randers, and Dennis L. Meadows. *Limits to Growth: The 30-Year Update.* White River Junction, VT: Chelsea Green, 2004.

Næss, Arne, in *Deep Ecology for the Twenty-First Century,* ed. George Sessions. Boston: Shambhala, 1995.

Odum, Howard T. *Environment, Power, and Society.* Hoboken, NJ: Wiley & Sons, 1971.

Odum, Howard T. and Elisabeth Odum. *A Prosperous Way Down: Principles and Policies.* Boulder: University of Colorado Press, 2001.

Rees, William and Mathis Wackernagel. *Our Ecological Footprint.* Gabriola Island, BC: New Society, 1996.

Tainter, Joseph. *The Collapse of Complex Societies.* Cambridge: Cambridge UP, 1990.

Lucky Truth

Opening statement to the Conference on Poetry and Philosophy, University of Warwick, 26 October 2007.

I.

Plato is wonderfully clear and insistent that love is the foundation of philosophy, even though for him and for everyone else in his tradition, this insistence is belaboring the obvious. Plato speaks a language in which philosophy is called *philo-sophia,* love of wisdom. So do we, of course—but Plato wants to think that, while misguided individuals may deliberately tell lies, words themselves—Greek words at least—would never do so.

If only, in his language, poetry had happened to be called something like ὀντοφιλία (*ontophilia,* love of being) or φιλογαῖα (*philogaia,* love of the earth)—something descriptive of poetry's posture. But poetry, in Greek, has a name that points to the joinery it involves and to what you might call the homesteading side of its nature. If Plato's language, in which he placed such trust, had given him a different cue, he might have thought more fruitfully and charitably about what poetry and philosophy have in common.

Plato is also wonderfully certain that music lies at the root of the moral life, and he loves the idea that it lies at the root of ontology too. It puzzles me that neither he nor Aristotle ever draws the corresponding link between music and logic. Given the overlap—plain to them both—between music and poetry, this might have solved a problem. All that was missing (or so it seems to me) is the simple admission that a musical mode or scale is a syllogistic form; that truth has a musical ring; that logical conclusion and tonic resolution are allotropes of one another, forms of the same thing.

I, at any rate, find it fruitless and unappealing to try to speak of poetry and philosophy without bringing music into the core of the discussion. These three domains seem to me to form a kind of conceptual nucleus, where the involvement of all three is what it takes to hold any two of them together. And I think that this is so for a good reason: because poetry, truth, and music are names for aspects of reality as well as names for things we make and do.

A musical education is now a rare thing in the so-called civilized world, and in its absence any conceptual or practical conjunction of poetry and philosophy is apt to be transitory or cold—or else a matter of blind luck. Luck and music, let us remember, have something to do with each other too. Music, you could say, is the lucky form of truth: truth in its most fortunate, favored condition. It may not be a universal or perpetual state of affairs, but it is a *natural* state of affairs—which we *naturally* try to emulate or replicate whenever we make music or write poetry or do philosophy.

II.

T. S. Eliot turned as a young man from the study of philosophy to the practice of poetry. In those days, he had some harsh ideas about the verse-writing philosopher-poets Parmenides, Xenophanes, and Empedokles. He was more tolerant of Lucretius, on the curious ground that Lucretius was less inventive. "The original form of a philosophy," Eliot wrote, "cannot be poetic." Then he goes further: "Without a doubt, the effort of the philosopher proper, the man who is trying to deal with ideas in themselves, and the effort of the poet, who may be trying to *realize* ideas, cannot be carried on at the same time."[1] I am here to quarrel with that claim.

Poetry is a word with several related senses. Most importantly, in my view, it is a name for a characteristic or condition of reality. Poetry is the lucky form of reality, not just the lucky form of language—in the same way that music is the lucky form of truth, not just the lucky form of sound. If poetry is indeed a characteristic of reality, and if philosophy is the attempt to understand and accept reality, then poetry isn't something philosophy needs to avoid (nor even something it can escape), and those "ideas in themselves," which the philosopher tries to deal with, ought not to be in need of protection from poetry. If poetry is an aspect of reality, then *the realization of the poetry of reality in the poetry of language*—which is really what is meant by "the writing of poetry"—might be a truly philosophical act. It might even be an *essential* philosophical act: an act without which philosophy isn't complete, isn't itself, isn't honest and faithful to what-is.

W. H. Auden held a view quite similar to Eliot's, though he put it less dogmatically. "We read Dante," Auden says, "for his poetry not for his theology because we have already met the theology elsewhere."[2]

Auden knew a lot more theology than I do, but my own experience doesn't quite jibe with his. I find that Dante's theology, like his moral philosophy, is embodied, reified, and personified in a way that no canonical and prosaic theologian's or moral philosopher's is, and I think that this is important. I don't believe the thought is independent of the embodiment. Nor do I think that disembodied thought is much of a standard by which to measure thought of other kinds, nor much of a target for serious thinkers to aim for.

A moral philosophy that is not put into practice is not much of a philosophy. A theology or metaphysics that is not put into practice may not be much of a theology or metaphysics either. How would one put a theology or metaphysics into practice? Just as one would a moral philosophy: by implying it in action; that is to say, *by behaving as if it were true.*

To behave as if your theology or your metaphysics were true would usually include trying to speak as if it were true. And that, it seems to me, could lead us pretty quickly and deeply into poetry. Poetry, again, is the name of something present in reality as well as the name of a corresponding kind of linguistic and intellectual behavior. Poetry gets written, or orally composed, because mind and language are trying to answer to the poetry of the real. How are we going to speak about the real without coming to grips with its character?

Perhaps we have, to some degree, met Dante's theology elsewhere—but maybe on the other hand we have never met a theology at all until we have met it embodied in poetry, in painting, in sculpture, or in some other behavioral or corporeal form. Is there a reason to think that abstract or discursive or desensualized or disembodied thinking is necessarily more accurate, more honest, more faithful to the truth than thought of other kinds? What would that reason be?

NOTES

1. Eliot, T. S. *The Sacred Wood,* 2nd ed. London: Methuen, 1928. p. 162 (in the essay on Dante).
2. Auden, W. H. *The Dyer's Hand.* New York: Random House, 1962. p. 277 (in the essay on D. H. Lawrence). There are, however, more and better things to be said about Auden's somewhat inconsistent view of poetry and thinking—and they have now been said quite handsomely in Jan Zwicky's *Auden as Philosopher: How Poets Think* (Nanaimo, BC: Institute for Coastal Research, 2012).

Solo

Afterthoughts from the Zen Poetry Festival, Enpuku-ji (円福寺), *Montreal,*
12 March 2011.

Some people love to climb rocks; they enjoy the exposure. Others are fasci-
nated by summits and delight in ticking them off. For some of us, though,
the rock is just part of the mountain; it is the mountain that draws us up;
the exposure is something we learn to endure; and a summit is just another
corner, where changing your direction is the only choice you have.

I cannot remember a time when I did not feel pulled—almost yanked—
upward by mountains—but I can remember not having the skill to get
pulled very far. Once, when I was young, my parents sent me to a camp in
western Alberta where climbing was taught, and once I tried joining a club
with a similar purpose. On both occasions I met people with skills I wanted
to learn, and they kindly taught me some things. But camps are camps, and
clubs are clubs, and the people who frequent such places have social agen-
das as well.

When people go into the mountains in groups, their identities are in
part absorbed and replaced by that of the team. They often assume, and
usually teach, that the group is an indispensable vehicle and a requisite
form of protection, like helmet and shoes. But as part of a group you are
not face to face with the mountain, nor with your life and eventual death,
in the way that you are when you go out alone. And climbing for me has
never been a recreation. So from early on, I turned to books for advice and
started testing this advice on solo expeditions.

People say you cannot learn from books alone, and I agree. You have to
bring experience to books—and you cannot always do this, especially
when you're young. Then you have to work the other way around, taking
your reading out into the world to see how it fares. This is good to do with
poems, novels, books on metaphysics and ethics, botanical textbooks,
rock-climbing manuals, and much else. You test some pages out and then
go back and read some more and then go out again. If the books are any
good and you are tolerably lucky, it will usually work. The reason it will
work in mountaineering is straightforward: the mountains are real.

Mountaineering as I understand it is a form of meditation, and meditation is a form of mountaineering. I would not encourage anyone to go into the mountains alone if they would prefer to go in a group. I would not encourage anyone to do zazen alone, either, if they would rather sit in a group. I only wish to say that such solo journeys are possible. One can find one's own way—or get truly lost—because in both cases the mountains are real.

It is true that you can do yourself real harm by meditating without a guide, just as you can by venturing carelessly into the mountains and getting trapped by a change of weather or by falling off a cliff. Close friends of mine have lost their lives in both pursuits. One who seemed to me especially alert and robust strayed into a spiritual crevasse during unguided or misguided meditation and soon committed suicide; others have frozen or fallen to their deaths. Still other friends, however, have died while eating dinner or walking down the sidewalk or waiting for a bus. There are no paths where danger does not lurk.

I do not for a moment believe one can learn what Zen is by reading a book. From *books alone,* it seems to me, one can actually learn nothing of any significance. Nor can one write a worthwhile sentence if all one knows are words. Words form groups the same as we do. Then, like humans, they start talking day and night to one another instead of addressing the facts at hand. To make any book useful, as writer or reader, one needs a little room between oneself and one's companions. In other words, one needs both a life and a death.

Teachers are also important, and I have had my share. Most, though not all, have been people I never met. Bill Reid, who taught me the grammar of Haida art and a great deal else, was a teacher I worked with in person for years—but Reid's most important teachers had died before he was born. The tradition of Haida art, when he encountered it, was well and truly broken. Through solitary study with dead masters, he brought it well and truly back to life. Traditions, in fact, are constantly breaking and being repaired. This is part of the truth of death and rebirth. Some of us, it seems, are actually better at dealing with breaks than with continuity, so we seek the fractures out—or even sometimes whack the tradition with a stick, looking for its weak spots.

My absentee teachers have included quite a number of writers and poets, and some of these writers and poets were monks. If I write their names here twice, in two different scripts, it is not to be troublesome or to show off, but as a gesture of thanks and respect, reaching out across the crevasses of time, language, and space. Wúmén Huìkai (無門慧開), author of *The Gateless Gate,* is one of those teachers. Xuědòu Zhòngxiǎn (雪竇重顯), the poet of *The Blue Cliff Record,* is another. Xuědòu's first editor, Yuánwù Kèqín (圜悟克勤), is a third. Dōgen (道元)—Old Man Trailhead, who never stopped looking and never stopped leaving—is a fourth. Some of these teachers lived most of their lives in monastic communities, engaging daily with other monks—but they had all known mountain monks or hermit monks who shied well away from human company. And all of them have taught me through the magic of simultaneous presence and absence, coming to visit in unbroken solitude, through their books. My local sangha also has a lot of members—rocks and trees, ravens and tree frogs, varied thrushes and black-tailed deer, the ocean, the air, the darkness, the light. One is never really alone. At the same time, one is never truly anything else.

Marine Air: Thinking about Fish, Weather, and Coastal Stories

"The kelp in amorous coils appear to pin down the Pacific"

In early summer, I spent an evening with my friend and my daughter, drifting on Oyster Bay in an old fiberglass canoe. Oyster Bay is a long body of water, part of Pender Harbour on the Sechelt Peninsula, which is dotted with small rocky islands. At low tide, almost the entire bay is a length of mud, the channels of the various creeks that empty into the bay articulating the bottom with rivulets of fresh water. Walking the bay at very low tide, you can see weather-worn stakes of cedar, indicating the location of a weir, driven in the last century or before by a Sechelt man or woman wielding a heavy pile driver, perhaps carved with the head of a dogfish looking away from the striking side.

But we were drifting at high tide, letting the currents take us to the head of the bay, where we planned to ease the canoe through the eelgrass and long strands of kelp, up to the cabin where Elizabeth Smart wrote *By Grand Central Station I Sat Down and Wept.* My friend's family owns much of the property on the northwest side of the bay, and the cabin belongs to them, along with various other outbuildings: another log cabin, an old net-shed, two cabins facing one another over a breezeway where a Japanese family lived until displacement in World War II. Occasionally, the cabin Elizabeth Smart lived in is rented out but not this summer. We headed in that direction to look at it and see if the inscription, THE CUT WORM FORGIVES THE PLOUGH, is still legible above the door. We glided past herons and dunlins on the muddy shore and past a pair of mergansers guarding their nesting site. We kept the canoe on course by pushing the paddles against the sides of the creek, where a Virginia rail *kick-kick-kick-ack*ed in the bullrushes and a blue-eyed snake swam strongly through the eelgrass. The surface of the creek was broken by the flipping of tiny salmon: coming down the creek from the gravel spawning beds further up, they were about to enter the ocean for the next part of their lives.

By Grand Central Station I Sat Down and Wept is not a quintessentially

*Sea monster, front figure on
great canoe. 1927. Graphite on
paper by Emily Carr. Royal
British Columbia Museum,
British Columbia Archives.*
PDP08832

West Coast book. Intense and passionate, it owes something of its cadences to the Bible and to Shakespeare, and its images of the natural world are subservient to the fierce emotional drama of the narrative. But the passages set in Monterey, where "the Pacific in blue spasms reaches all its superlatives" and "where the sea otters leave their playing under the cliff [and] the kelp in amorous coils appear to pin down the Pacific," are as keenly rendered as much of what we consider to be regional or specific to the Coast. The cabin by Oyster Bay crouches under several enormous broad-leafed maples, cool and green in summer, and Naples yellow, edged in burnt sienna, in fall. I like to think this was what Elizabeth Smart had in mind when she wrote of "the old gold of the October trees, the stunted cedars, the horizons, the chilly gullies with their red willow whips." I've imagined living in this cabin by myself, with the generous life of the estuary at my doorstep. Mornings, I'd drink my coffee and watch the eagles in the stand of firs on the other side of the bay, blackbirds loud in the reeds along the creek. Almost as good, I've begun a novel in which an Irish schoolmaster ends up in a cabin very like this one, on a bay very like Oyster; he scrawls a name for the cabin, "World's End," on a cedar shake with a piece of charcoal from his fire and rows a battered skiff out to the kelp beds to handline for bluebacks (coho salmon in their third year).

At the cabin, we found no sign of the inscription above the door, but my friend thinks that the front area was enlarged in the fifties and the original door used elsewhere. The newer part of the cabin is sheathed in cedar shakes, too, so the proverb might well still be scratched into the logs that are beneath. We looked around and I tried to imagine a writer's life in those years, a woman's life, awaiting the birth of her first child. "On August 26, she felt the first pangs of labour. Mr. Reid, a local fisherman, rowed her by boat to the Mission Hospital," reports Rosemary Sullivan in her biography of Smart. That was 1941. My own daughter, born forty-four years and two weeks later at that hospital's new location in Sechelt, was busy exploring the bluff where you could sit in perfect privacy and watch eagles fishing in the bay.

As far as salmon are concerned, the cedar piles in the bay indicate the very richness of this part of the world. Just up Anderson and Meyer Creeks, which both run into Oyster Bay, are spawning beds for chum and coho salmon. Every fall for the past fifteen years, I've stood by these creeks with my children, watching the mottled fish resting against the sides of the creek, pairing up, using their strong tails to excavate redds in the gravel. We've seen the eagles waiting in the tall cedars for the spent bodies, found ribs and backbones in the woods where bears and raccoons dragged the carcasses. The smell of dead salmon, rotting leaves, and cold water, tea-coloured and fast, is a signature of fall on the Coast.

"You may at once be smelled by Scenting-Woman"

If we'd gone in the other direction that evening, out to Georgia Strait, then north, if we'd had time, and provisions, and inclination, we'd have been heading toward the Kwakiutl fishing grounds. Not that we would make such a journey of an evening, but in the days I'm thinking about, people thought nothing of going great distances in their magnificent cedar canoes: families heading for fishing camps in sun and rain. The villages of Nawitti, Fort Rupert, Alert Bay, with their poles and planked housefronts, fish traps and racks for drying salmon, branches of kelp hung with herring roe, the smell of oolichans and wet cedar—these places had their own poetry, were purposeful and mindful of the importance of ceremony. In his books, ethnologist Franz Boas preserved some of the fishing chants. One ritual had the fisherman stringing nine river-caught sockeye salmon on a ring of cedar branch or withe while chanting:

> O Swimmers, this is the dream given by you, to be the way of my late grandfathers when they first caught you at your play. I do not club you twice, for I do not wish to club to death your souls so that you may go home to the place where you come from, Supernatural-Ones, you, givers of heavy weight. I mean this, Swimmers, why should I not go to the end of the dream given by you? Now I shall wear you as a neckring going to my house, Supernatural-Ones, you, Swimmers.

Then, placing the salmon on a mat in his house, the fisherman would continue:

> O Swimmers, now I come and take you into my house. Now I will go and lay you down on this mat which is spread on the floor for you, Swimmers. This is your own saying when you came and gave a dream to my late grandfathers. Now you will go.

I think of this prayer when I'm choosing my sockeye on Ron Malcolm's boat, the *Sapphire Sky,* each body a kind of frozen perfection lying in the hold. I like to think that the souls have left the fish and continued up the river, in this case the Skeena, perhaps as far as Babine Lake. We make a ceremony of the season's first salmon, cooking it outside and inviting friends to share the meal. I use a variation of Susan Musgrave's recipe: instead of marinating fillets in a dish, I brush the marinade over a whole five- to seven-pound sockeye laid out on heavy foil, putting lots of marinade in the body cavity. I then let it sit for an afternoon in the fridge. It takes about forty minutes to cook on a fairly low barbeque and tastes like the northern rivers: wild and sweet on the tongue. There's seldom any left: every morsel is plucked from the skeleton until the backbone lies on the platter like a delicate comb.

1/2 C unsalted butter
1/3 C honey
1/3 C brown sugar
2 T freshly squeezed lemon juice
1 T natural liquid-smoke flavouring
3/4 T crushed red-pepper flakes
pinch of allspice (optional)
2 LB salmon fillets, skin on, in two pieces

Combine all ingredients but salmon in saucepan. Cook over medium heat, stir-ring, for about 5 minutes or until smooth. Cool to room temperature. Arrange the salmon in a dish just large enough to hold it. Pour the cooled marinade over it and let stand for 15 minutes. Turn, baste with marinade, and let stand for another 15 minutes. Prepare hot coals for grilling (or gas barbeque). Oil the grill well and cook salmon, skin side up, over medium heat, for 5–7 minutes. Turn and cook until fish flakes easily, about another 5–7 minutes. Transfer fish to a platter and serve immediately.

The Kwakiutl halibut songs are also intriguing. The fishhooks, called Younger Brothers, were beaten with burning spruce branches as the fish-erman sang:

> Now, good Younger Brothers, I am putting on you this sweet smell, good Younger Brothers, that you may at once be smelled by Scenting-Woman, Old-Woman, Flabby-Skin-in-Mouth, Born-to-Be-Giver-in-House, when you first fall on the roof of their house, and then take hold of Scenting-Woman, Old-Woman, Flabby-Skin-in-Mouth, Born-to-Be-Giver-in-House when they come near you, good Younger Brothers, and do not let go of your hold when you take hold of them.

The hooks must have been tremendously strong, steam-bent wood—yew was used by the Makah, and other peoples used fir, balsam, spruce, hemlock—barbed with bone and later with iron. As the fisherman paid out a line made with spruce root, he exhorted the halibut to be quick about taking her meal, which consisted of octopus or small fish threaded onto the barb. When the fisherman made his catch, he hauled in the line until the head came out of the water. Striking the head with his club, he said,

> Indeed, this does not sound bad on your head, Old-Woman, you Flabby-Skin-in-Mouth, you Born-to-Be-Giver-in-House, for indeed, I came to do so to you with my club.

and then sent the soul of the halibut away to tell members of its family that it had the good luck of coming to the fisherman's canoe. The hooks were washed, and prayers said to them.

Our halibut comes from Ron Malcolm in autumn, one of a number of fish that he brings back on the *Sapphire Sky* intact but for the viscera. The call goes out from person to person—"Halibut's in!"—and we make our way to Ron's dock to pick up our fish, usually a sixty- or seventy-pounder. Halibut can be *really* huge, the females reaching four hundred pounds or more, and are odd to look at. More symmetrical at birth, they swim like salmon: dorsal fin upright. When they've achieved adulthood, they have adapted to lying on their left side, and their left eye has moved over the top of their head to a new position just above and slightly behind the right eye. Because they are bottom fish, living in very deep water, there is something of the ghost about them, their colouring, and their eerie gaze, even in death. I cut ours outside, on a piece of clean plywood, using a very sharp knife that will cut through the hard bones, portioning it into tough plastic bags. It freezes beautifully, keeping its good texture. The bones are simmered with shallots or an onion, some white wine or dry French vermouth, a bay leaf, and some black peppercorns for stock. Any scraps left after I've made steaks and thick slabs for barbequeing go into chowder. My friend Mary White uses clams and scallops in her recipe, which I've adapted for halibut:

GOOD FISH CHOWDER

about 1 LB of halibut, cut into bite-sized pieces
1 tin of clams or the equivalent fresh
1½ C fish stock or water
½ C white wine
2 T butter
2 T olive oil
¼ C flour
2 diced red or yellow onions or equivalent amount of scallions
4 large red potatoes (use other boiling potatoes if red ones are not available), unpeeled, scrubbed, and diced
2 C milk
2 C light cream
ground pepper to taste
lots of fresh minced parsley

In a large soup pot, cook onions in butter and oil until soft but not brown. Add potatoes and flour, and cook, stirring, for 5 minutes. Add stock and wine and simmer for about 10 minutes or until potatoes are tender. Add halibut and clams and simmer gently for about 10 minutes. (If you're using fresh clams, scrub them and steam them open in a heavy pan, shaking the pan, while the potatoes are cooking. Remove the meat from the shells, strain the juice, and add both meat and juice to the chowder.) Add milk, cream, and pepper. Heat through until steaming. Garnish with parsley.

Note: This is terrific with the addition of a little smoked salmon. Not mild cure or lox but the barbequed tips you can often get quite cheaply. A little—perhaps a quarter-pound?—will add great flavour.

In his comprehensive *Ethnology of the Kwakiutl,* Boas included many fish recipes collected and recorded by George Hunt, of Fort Rupert: roasted salmon, blistered salmon, dried salmon, old salmon, green salmon, and boiled salmon, among others. What is most impressive is the variety of methods for using every part of the fish in ways best suited for that part. There are recipes for salmon spawn with salmonberry sprouts (I've eaten these sprouts, and they taste a little like celery, a welcome early green on the Coast); boiled salmon guts, cheeks, tails, and fins; seal and porpoise; herring spawn, chitons, and sea slugs; and dried halibut head, the recipe for which calls for soaking the head in the bilge water of a fishing canoe. There are also recipes for lily bulbs, lupine roots, clover, crabapples, viburnum, elderberry, and huckleberry, among other succulent plant foods. Reading this lengthy section of Boas's book, one cannot help being impressed by the resourceful spirit of these cooks, preparing meals that were true reflections of the world around them. No wonder the feast dishes were so beautiful: they were created both to acknowledge the origin myths of the family and to provide suitable receptacles for honouring the food and family. One chant, recorded by Boas, exhorts the fish:

> Go now and tell your father, your mother, your uncle, your aunt, your elder brothers, and your younger brothers, that you had good luck, because you came into this, my fishing canoe.

"The sky is turning over"

In the Provincial Archives there is an 1868 photograph of salmon drying on racks by Hell's Gate: strung on poles, the fish catch the warm wind and sun funnelling through the canyon. There is evidence that people have lived for at least nine thousand years in this area, relying on rich runs of fish for sustenance. Cultures that depend upon something as intimately as the coastal and river First Nations peoples depended upon salmon generally express the dynamism of the relationship in every aspect of their lives, from practical fishing gear to songs and prayers to vessels that hold and cook the fish to ingenious methods of preserving fish for the winter months. One has only to look at the pile drivers, halibut hooks, tobacco bowls, clothing, baskets, and hilts of daggers, or to read some of the transcriptions of prayers to see how interwoven those cultures were with the means of their subsistence. Some modern authors have written out of a similar relationship. In those cases where a people's nourishment is not so dependent upon fish, it might be argued that fish and fishing, the life of the ocean, speak to a spiritual hunger for connection.

In my own community, Pender Harbour, Native fishermen have been netting salmon and digging clams for hundreds of years. My friend on Oyster Bay lives in a house constructed over and among shell middens, and when the tide is low, she can see the piles from the ancient salmon weirs sticking out of the mud like signposts. Digging in the garden, her family has found pieces of slate blades from fish knives. Once my friend's husband thought, as he sat on some rocks, that generations of people had likely been cutting up fish on the same rocks. Turning, he found a complete slate blade on a little shelf of rock where it had been placed and forgotten a century or more ago by someone sitting where he was sitting, perhaps pausing in his work to watch eagles pick off merganser chicks from the water near the small rocky islands. White fishermen have been leaving the harbour in boats for a hundred years, heading to various fishing grounds for herring, halibut, salmon, black cod, and prawns. Each fall, when all the boats are back from the north or from the west coast of Vancouver Island or from the mouth of the Fraser River, there is a homecoming dance in the community hall. All the old fishing families are represented (the white ones, that is, because the Native boats sail out of Sechelt now): the MacKays, the Malcolms, the Reids ("Mr. Reid, a local fisherman, rowed her by boat to the Mission Hospital . . . "), the Camerons, the Warnocks. And some years the boats are represented, too, by a photograph or a flotilla hung on the walls among the balloons and streamers: the *Sapphire Sky*, the *Gallivanter*, the *Scotia*, the *Belle Isle*, the *Ocean Viking*, all of them home safe and their skippers dancing on dry land for a change and not untangling gear in a storm or sitting in Prince Rupert in the rain, waiting for an opening.

Several years ago, my son Forrest conducted a census of the cutthroat population of the lake near our home. They are a rare population, spawning in the fall, while most freshwater cutthroat—as opposed to coastal cutthroat, which have a residency period in salt water—spawn in the spring. Forrest began his project as a result of spending a day with a Ministry of Environment technician who was clearing debris from the spawning area. The technician said no one had a clear idea of the number of fish in the lake and suggested that Forrest undertake a census, providing my son the forms and listing some steps to follow. Mostly the project involved regular visits to the creek that the fish spawned in to determine when they first migrated from the creek to the lake. After school each day, Forrest went to the creek at a set time and counted fish for half an hour. There was a way of extrapolating real numbers from this brief but regular count. The census was completed when there were no more fish to be seen in the creek. Most days I went there with Forrest and walked the shore, alert to the movement of trout in the clear water. Some idled under the low limbs of cedars and alders; some shot up the quick rapids and darted among the big rocks. We saw lots of cutthroat and were lucky enough to observe all sorts of birds, too: ouzels (or American dippers) running along the creek bottom, a heron waiting on the bridge rails, a kingfisher squawking from a high tree. A neighbour, out with his dog, told us he'd been walking the creek all fall and one day had seen seven otters feeding off the carcasses of trout. We kept our eyes open for otters but didn't see one. When the census was complete, Forrest turned his findings into a project for his school's science fair. What I remember most about those days we walked the creek and counted cutthroat, often in rain, was the fresh smell and the damp air, our hair and skin jeweled with mist.

When we go to look at the salmon spawning, it's always the smell of fish, the living and the dead, that I notice the most. The living fish, on the final stretch of the long swim home, have shredded tails and patches of deteriorating tissue all over their bodies, and the dead fish have been pulled from the creek to be eaten by birds and mammals. But the cutthroat spawn a number of times and return to the lake after depositing eggs in the gravel. We found on the bank of the creek, perhaps carefully removed by an otter, one perfect specimen, dead but with no sign on its body of a struggle, no eye nipped out, its belly intact. Leaning over to rearrange it slightly for a photograph, I could smell only the earth it reposed on, mossy and rich, and the wet stones of the creek bank.

Last fall we took to walking the creek again, watching for cutthroat. For some days, nothing. Then one Sunday we pushed through salmonberry and thimbleberry bushes to an area just up the creek from the lake. A deep pool, formed by a natural dam of fallen trees that painted turtles reclined upon in summer, was hung over by a few huge cedars. Looking closely we could see at least a dozen big trout idling in the shadows cast by the limbs of cedar. Shafts of sunlight poured through the higher branches, the light refracting as it hit the surface of the creek. I thought I'd never seen anything so lovely. Occasionally another trout would swim up to join the others in the deep pool, and sometimes one would suddenly dart away to the faster water racing under the bridge. We watched for some time and then walked to the trail that leads along the creek to where the water races and tumbles on its urgent way to another lake a mile or two away. We could smell, just faintly, the heavy sea air coming in from Agamemnon Channel on the wind. I knew in the deepest possible way why there are poems for fish. Hilary Stewart, in her book *Indian Fishing: Early Methods on the Northwest Coast,* gives us one such poem:

> I will sing the song of the sky.
> This is the song of the tired—
> the salmon panting as they swim up the swift current.
> I walk around where the water runs into whirlpools.
> They talk quickly, as if they are in a hurry.
> The sky is turning over. They call me.

Great Haida canoe, Ottawa. 1927.
Graphite on paper by Emily Carr.
Royal British Columbia Museum,
British Columbia Archives.
PDP08831

About the Contributors

Robert Bringhurst is a poet, typographer, translator, cultural historian, and linguist. He studied comparative literature at Indiana University and poetry at the University of British Columbia. He has published over a dozen collections of poetry, including *The Beauty of the Weapons: Selected Poems 1972–1982* (1982), *The Blue Roofs of Japan* (1986), *Conversations with a Toad* (1987), *The Calling: Selected Poems 1970–1995* (1995), and *Selected Poems* (2009). His recent books of prose include *The Tree of Meaning: Language, Mind and Ecology* (2006) and *Everywhere Being Is Dancing: Twenty Pieces of Thinking* (2009). His books on Haida mythology and storytelling include *The Raven Steals the Light* (1984), *A Story as Sharp as a Knife: The Classical Haida Mythtellers and Their World* (second edition, 2012), and *Nine Visits to the Mythworld* (2000). He lives on Quadra Island in British Columbia.

Hugh Brody was born in the north of England and educated at Trinity College, Oxford. He taught at Queen's University, Belfast, and the University of Cambridge before moving to Canada in 1969. An anthropologist, writer, and filmmaker, he has been involved in land rights and aboriginal research in the U.S., India, Australia, and South Africa, as well as Canada. His books include *Maps and Dreams* (1983), *Living Arctic* (1987), and *The Other Side of Eden: Hunter-Gatherers, Farmers and the Shaping of the World* (2000). His films include *Nineteen Nineteen* (1985), *Time Immemorial* (1991), *A Washing of Tears* (1993), *Inside Australia* (2004), and *The Meaning of Life* (2008). He is currently Canada Research Chair in Aboriginal Studies at University of the Fraser Valley.

Trevor Carolan is a longtime campaigner and advocate on behalf of Aboriginal land claims and British Columbia watershed issues. A former elected councillor in North Vancouver, he holds a doctorate from Bond University, Queensland, in Literature, Ecology, and the Sacred in International Relations. His publications include the novel *The Pillow Book of Dr. Jazz* (1999); *Celtic Highway: Poems & Texts* (2002); the nonfiction book *Return to Stillness: Twenty Years with a Tai Chi Master* (2003); a co-translation of *The Supreme Way: Inner Teachings of the Southern Mountain Tao* (1997); and the anthology *Making Waves: Reading British Columbia and Pacific Northwest Literature* (2010). He teaches English and writing at University of the Fraser Valley.

Emily Carr was born in 1871 in Victoria, British Columbia. A celebrated Canadian painter, she was deeply inspired by the indigenous peoples of the Pacific

Northwest Coast. Often on her own, Carr journeyed around Vancouver Island, Haida Gwaii (Queen Charlotte Islands), the Skeena-Nass River country, and the rugged Pemberton-Lillooet region. In 1927, she was embraced by the Group of Seven, the leading modernist painters in Canada. At age sixty-nine, she published *Klee Wyck* (1941), the first in a series of autobiographical memoirs. The book was a bestseller and winner of the 1941 Governor General's Award that year. Her other books include *The Book of Small* (1942) and *The House of All Sorts* (1944). Carr died in 1945. Most of her books have been handsomely reprinted by Douglas & McIntyre, of Vancouver.

Wade Davis is a native of British Columbia, where he worked as a park ranger, forestry engineer, logger, big-game hunting guide, and ethnographic field worker, studying several indigenous societies of northern Canada. He received his doctorate from Harvard in ethnobotany and is a scientist, advocate for bio-cultural diversity, filmmaker, and writer. His many books include *The Serpent and the Rainbow* (1986), *Penan: Voice for the Borneo Rain Forest* (1990), *Shadows in the Sun* (1993), *Nomads of the Dawn* (1995), *One River* (1996), *Light at the Edge of the World* (2001), *The Wayfinders: Why Ancient Wisdom Matters in the Modern World* (2009), *The Sacred Headwaters* (2011), and *Into the Silence: The Great War, Mallory, and the Conquest of Everest* (2012). An explorer-in-residence at the National Geographic Society, he lives in Washington, DC.

Chief Dan George was born in 1899 on the Tsleil-Waututh Reserve at Burrard Inlet in North Vancouver, British Columbia. He was raised for eleven years in St. Paul's Roman Catholic Residential School, where he was forbidden to speak his family's Halq'eméylem language or engage in traditional indigenous practices. He worked first in logging, then as a longshoreman for twenty-seven years. For twelve years, he served as Chief of the Tsleil-Waututh people. Later in life, he was an award-winning actor and became known as a spokesman for First Nations peoples and as a beloved Canadian elder. He died in 1981.

Tom Jay is a sculptor, essayist, poet, and, as cofounder of the citizen group Wild Olympic Salmon, an advocate for the riverine ecology of the Pacific Northwest. His essays have been included in *Reaching Home: Pacific Salmon, Pacific People* (1995), winner of the 1995 Pacific Northwest Booksellers Association Book Award, and *Working the Woods, Working the Sea: An Anthology of Northwest Writings* (2008). His poetry is collected in *The Blossoms Are Ghosts at the Wedding: Selected Poems and Essays* (2006). He lives with his wife, Sara Mall, also a sculptor, on the Olympic Peninsula of Washington State.

Eve Joseph grew up in North Vancouver. Her first book of poetry, *The Startled Heart* (2004), was nominated for the Dorothy Livesay Award. Her second book, *The Secret Signature of Things* (2010), was shortlisted for the Victoria Butler Prize and the Dorothy Livesay Award. She received the 2010 P. K. Page Founder's Award for poetry and the 2010 Malahat Creative Nonfiction Prize.

Maxine Hong Kingston is the author of *The Woman Warrior: Memoirs of a Girlhood Among Ghosts* (1976), which received the National Book Critics Circle Award; *China*

Men (1980), which received the National Book Award; *Hawai'i One Summer* (1987); *Tripmaster Monkey: His Fake Book* (1989); *To Be the Poet* (2002); *The Fifth Book of Peace* (2003); and *I Love a Broad Margin to My Life* (2012). She received the National Humanities Medal in 1997 from President Bill Clinton. In 2007, the Northern California Book Reviewers gave *Veterans of War, Veterans of Peace* (2006), edited by Kingston, a special recognition award in publishing.

Theresa Kishkan was born in Victoria, British Columbia, and now lives near Sakinaw Lake. She is the author of the poetry collections *Arranging the Gallery* (1976), *Ikons of the Hunt* (1978), and *Black Cup* (1992); the books of essays *Red Laredo Boots* (1996) and *Phantom Limb* (2007); the novels *Sisters of Grass* (2000), *A Man in the Distant Field* (2004), and *The Age of Water Lillies* (2009); the novella *Inishbream* (2001); and the memoir *Mnemonic: A Book of Trees* (2011).

Charles Lillard was a highly regarded poet and historian with an extensive and intimate knowledge of British Columbia and the Northwest Coast, from Alaska to Puget Sound. He published twenty books of fiction, nonfiction, and poetry. *Shadow Weather: Poems Selected and New* (1996), the last of his seven books of poetry, was nominated for the Governor General's Award. He was born in 1944 and died in 1997.

Barry Lopez is the author of the acclaimed *Arctic Dreams: Imagination and Desire in a Northern Landscape* (1986), for which he received the National Book Award. Among his thirteen books are eight works of fiction, including *Field Notes: The Grace Note of the Canyon Wren* (1994), *Light Action in the Caribbean* (2000), and *Resistance* (2004). His nonfiction includes *Of Wolves and Men* (1978), a National Book Award finalist, for which he received the John Burroughs and Christopher medals; *Crossing Open Ground* (1988); and *About This Life: Journeys on the Threshold of Memory* (1998). He is a recipient of the Award in Literature from the American Academy of Arts and Letters, the John Hay Medal, Guggenheim, Lannan, and National Science Foundation fellowships, and other literary and cultural honors. In 2004 he was elected a Fellow of The Explorers Club.

Lee Maracle was born and raised in Vancouver, British Columbia, and is a keeper/mythmaker among the Stó:lō First Nations people. In 1981, she helped found the En'owkin International School of Writing, in Penticton, British Columbia, a learning institute with an Indigenous Fine Arts Program and an Okanagan Language Program. In 2001, she was appointed distinguished visiting professor of Canadian culture at Western Washington University, focusing on promoting awareness of Canadian culture. She has also been the traditional cultural director of The Centre for Indigenous Theatre. Her books of fiction include *Sojourner's Truth* (1990), *Sundogs: A Novel* (1992), *Ravensong* (1995), *Will's Garden* (2002), *Daughters Are Forever* (2002), and *First Wives Club: Coast Salish Style* (2010). She has also published poetry, biography, criticism, and collaborations.

Susan Musgrave has published almost thirty books, including the following: the poetry collections *Origami Dove* (2011) and *What the Small Day Cannot Hold: Collected Poems 1970–1985* (2000); three novels, including the recent *Given* (2012);

three books of essays, including *You're in Canada Now . . . A Memoir of Sorts* (2005); four books for children; and seven edited collections. She lives in Haida Gwaii (the Queen Charlotte Islands).

Mike O'Connor was born in Aberdeen, Washington. He studied at the University of Washington, the Universidad de las Americas, in Mexico City, and the University of California at Berkeley. In the seventies, after working for the U.S. Forest Service, he farmed in the Dungeness-Sequim River Valley and engaged in selective logging and reforestation in the Olympic Mountains. Beginning in 1979, he worked as a journalist and editor in Taiwan, and in 1995, he returned to the U.S. He has published nine books of poetry, including *Immortality* (2010); a memoir, *Unnecessary Talking: The Montesano Stories* (2009); and translations of Chinese literature, including *When I Find You Again, It Will Be in Mountains: The Selected Poems of Chia Tao* (2000).

Louis Owens was born in 1948. Of Choctaw, Cherokee, and Irish descent, he grew up in Mississippi and California and worked as a forest ranger and firefighter for the U.S. Forest Service. A writer as well as scholar, he is the author of the novels *Wolfsong* (1995); *The Sharpest Sight* (1995), which received the Roman Noir Award, France's equivalent of the Edgar Award; *Bone Game* (1996), which received the Julian J. Rothbaum Prize; and *Nightland* (1996), which received the American Book Award. He was a professor of English and Native American Studies at the University of California at Davis, and the director of creative writing. He died in 2002.

Red Pine is the pen name used by Bill Porter in his translations from Chinese. As Red Pine, he has published such books as *The Collected Songs of Cold Mountain* (2000), *Diamond Sutra* (2001), *Poems of the Masters* (2003), *The Heart Sutra* (2004), *In Such Hard Times* (2009), and *Tao Te Ching* (2009). Under his own name, he has published the books *Road to Heaven: Encounters with Chinese Hermits* (1993) and *Zen Baggage* (2008). His work in this volume of *Mānoa* will be published in 2014 by Copper Canyon Press in *The Mountain Poems of Stonehouse*. He lives in Port Townsend, Washington.

Robert Rice has stories and poems in numerous literary magazines, including *Hayden's Ferry, New Letters, The North American Review, The Saint Ann's Review, Quiddity,* and *West Wind Review.* He has also published three novels, including the highly acclaimed *The Last Pendragon* (1992). He lives in Montana.

Eden Robinson was born in Kitamaat, British Columbia, and is a member of the Haisla and Heiltsuk First Nations. She studied creative writing at the University of British Columbia and the University of Victoria. Her books include a collection of short stories, *Traplines* (1995); two novels, *Monkey Beach* (2000) and *Bloodsports* (2006); and a book of nonfiction, *The Sasquatch at Home: Traditional Protocols & Modern Storytelling* (2011). *Sasquatch* is about family, culture, and place and was the basis of her 2010 Henry Kreisel Lecture. Robinson is one of Canada's first female Native writers to gain international attention.

Judith Roche is the author of three poetry collections, most recently *Wisdom of the Body* (2007), and co-editor of *First Fish, First People: Salmon Tales of the North*

Pacific Rim (2003), both of which received the American Book Award. Her writing is included in permanent art installations in the Seattle area. She was the distinguished Northwest writer-in-residence at Seattle University in 2007 and has taught at the Richard Hugo House in Seattle. She is also literary director emeritus for One Reel, an arts-producing agency, and is a fellow in the Black Earth Institute, a think tank dedicated to strengthening the links between art and spirit, earth and society.

John Schreiber was raised in British Columbia, has worked in such jobs as logging, commercial fishing, and mining, and has had a stint with the Union of BC Indian Chiefs. He later became a teacher-counselor in Victoria, British Columbia. He is the author of two books of short nonfiction: *Stranger Wycott's Place* (2008) and *Old Lives: In the Chilcotin Backcountry* (2011). *Old Lives* was shortlisted for the 2011 Victoria Butler Book Prize. His third book, *The Junction*, will be published by Caitlin Press this summer. Schreiber lives in Victoria, British Columbia.

Chief William K'HHalserten Sepass was born of a Thompson mother and a Stó:lō father around 1841. He lived on the Skowkale Reserve in Sardis, British Columbia, and was chief of the Skowkale for over sixty years. He died in 1943.

Robert Sieniuc is a Canadian architect and environmental designer. The founding principal of Broadway Architects, he specializes in environmentally sensitive commercial, recreational, and residential architecture. His firm also does eco-planning projects for communities, government, resorts, and First Nations throughout Western and Northern Canada. He lives in Vancouver, British Columbia.

Gary Snyder grew up in the Puget Sound country on a small subsistence farm during the Depression. His father and uncles worked at sea or in the woods most of their lives. He started snow-peak mountaineering as a teenager, and then went to Reed College. During his twenties, he worked in logging camps or for the U.S. Forest Service in the summers: two seasons on fire lookouts; two seasons on trail crews. Winters he studied East Asian languages as a graduate student in Berkeley. He lived over ten years in Japan. The last forty years, he has lived in a handmade house in the northern Sierra. His poems and prose explore many cultural and bioregional dimensions of the whole West Coast.

Richard Van Camp is a member of the Dogrib (Tlicho) Nation from Fort Smith, Northwest Territories. He is the author of two children's books with the Cree artist George Littlechild: *A Man Called Raven* (1997) and *What's the Most Beautiful Thing You Know About Horses?* (1998). He has published a novel, *The Lesser Blessed* (1996), which is now a feature film with First Generation Films. His collections of short fiction include *Angel Wing Splash Pattern* (2002), *The Moon of Letting Go and Other Stories* (2010), and *Godless but Loyal to Heaven* (2012). He is the author of three baby books: *Welcome Song for Baby: A Lullaby for Newborns, Nighty Night: A Bedtime Song for Babies,* and *Little You.* He is also the author of two comic books published by Healthy Aboriginal Network: *Kiss Me Deadly* and *Path of the Warrior.*

Richard Wagamese is Ojibway from the Sturgeon Clan. After a youth spent in foster homes and with a family as an adoptee, he reestablished connection with his people and began a lengthy career as a newspaper and electronic journalist. His novels include *Keeper'n Me* (1994), *A Quality of Light* (1997), *Dream Wheels* (2006), *Ragged Company* (2009), *The Next Sure Thing* (2011), and *Indian Horse* (2012). He has published two autobiographical works, *For Joshua: An Ojibway Father Teaches His Son* (2003) and *One Native Life* (2009); a collection of short fiction, *One Story One Song* (2011); and a book of poetry, *Runaway Dreams* (2011). The recipient of national writing awards and honorary degrees, he lives near Kamloops, British Columbia.

Rex Weyler is a writer, photographer, ecologist, and activist. A co-founder of Greenpeace International, he is the author of *Greenpeace: How a Group of Ecologists, Journalists and Visionaries Changed the World* (2004), the organization's definitive history. He is also the co-author of *Chop Wood, Carry Water: A Guide to Finding Spiritual Fulfillment in Everyday Life* (1984). His other books include *The Story of Harmony* (1997), the history of musical knowledge and technology; *Blood of the Land: The Government and Corporate War against First Nations* (2007), a history of indigenous American struggle; and *The Jesus Sayings: The Quest for His Authentic Message* (2008), a deconstruction of first-century history. He is a freelance journalist and writes the monthly *Deep Green* column for Greenpeace International.

Jan Zwicky is a poet, essayist, philosopher, and musician. She is the author of seven collections of poetry, including *Songs for Relinquishing the Earth* (1998), *Robinson's Crossing* (2004), and *Forge* (2011). Her books of philosophy include *Wisdom & Metaphor* (2003), *Plato as Artist* (2009), and *Lyric Philosophy* (2011). A native of Alberta, she now lives on the West Coast of Canada.

The mask on the back cover of this volume was collected around 1883 by ethnologist and explorer Johan Adrian Jacobsen, likely at Ft. Rupert, for the Berlin Museum. At the time, he identified it merely as a "Large black opening animal mask, a grinning black and white human face," suggesting that the inner face represented "Masmasmalanix," a culture hero of the Nuxalk (Bella Coola) people. The anthropologist Franz Boas made his own drawings of this mask (in its open and closed aspects) around 1886, which he took with him on his earliest fieldwork in an attempt to better identify it, though he does not seem to have had much success at this time. Prior to his 1894-1895 winter field trip to Ft. Rupert, Boas requested more detailed, full-color paintings from Albert Grünwedel, a curator and artist at the Berlin Museum. Likely on this trip, Boas recorded on the painting itself a number of notes, suggesting the mask belonged to a Hamshamt'sas privilege and depicts a Bear on the outside and Baxwbakwalanuxwsiwi' on the inside; indicating that the rights to the mask belonged to the "Lō'yalswiwe" (presumably the Loyalaława 'na̱'mima, or kin group) of the Ma'a̱mtagila Band (which he claimed to have "corroborated"), while giving the owner's ceremonial position title; and recording symbolic interpretations of many painted motifs and colors. On the reverse of the painting are song lyrics in Kwak'wala with brief English glosses.

Perhaps around 1895, Boas transferred many of his notes for this object from the research painting to the Berlin museum catalogue card. Here he provided expanded song lyrics in German that translate as: "1. He searches for food in the whole world. 2. He searches for men in the whole world. 3. Consuming the living in the whole world. 4. He nods for cut-off heads in the whole world."

Boas's description of the mask in the 1897 report is drawn primarily from his notes on the Grünwedel painting, though he provides a slightly different English gloss on the lyrics and he omits the crucial information regarding 'na̱'mima and Band ownership. In the appendix, Boas provides an interlinear translation of the Kwak'wala song lyrics as well as musical notation for a tune he recorded. This is the only mask illustrated in the 1897 report that has specific colors described for it, and subsequent authors have returned to this description as indication of Kwakw<u>a</u>k<u>a</u>'wakw symbolism. Boas states that the animals depicted on H<u>a</u>msh<u>a</u>mt's<u>a</u>s masks represent "protectors" of the dancer, but this is a vague and ethnographically imprecise term. They more likely represent spirit beings that figured in ancestral encounters resulting in the acquisition of the dance/mask/song privilege itself.

At some point, likely in the early 1920s, George Hunt recorded the following terms in his own personal copy of the 1897 book: "Dałdałag<small>Em</small> n<small>En</small>; H<small>E</small>msh<small>E</small>mts! <small>Es</small>ēwe; Ḻoyalaława." Soon after, he added the following notes to his manuscript on the 1897 captions: "Dałałā n<small>En</small> H<small>E</small>msh<small>E</small>mts! <small>Es</small> Hem^εsē^εwe open up grizzle Bear eater on forehead mask of the forhead this mask with a man inside of the grizzly Bear is Lo^εya^εlał the first man of the n<small>E</small>memot of the Lo^εy^εlała^εwa of Kwagoł." This corroborates Boas's identification of the mask as a Bear H<u>a</u>msh<u>a</u>mt's<u>a</u>s belonging to a specific Band, although he lists a different Band at Ft. Rupert as being its owner and he identifies the inner, humanoid face as depicting a 'n<u>a</u>'mima ancestor rather than Baxwbakwalanuxwsiwi', which is more consistent with other transformation masks of this kind and with the contemporary Kwakwaka'wakw understanding that Baxwbakwalanuxwsiwi' itself was not generally depicted on masks. Boas accepted these revisions in his 1924 typescript revisions to the 1897 text.

In the 1930s, Hunt returned to this object again, confirming much of the previous identification but adding details to its use in performance and a new transcription for its song. In his 1933 manuscript to Boas, he wrote: "this mask cover the face and when the Dancer is ready to come in the mask comes inside of the Door about two steps in . . . and he wiggles about as though he try to shake off his [mask] . . . while [they] Beat fast time without singing for about one minute . . . <u>nawes</u> only one on earth. this name Belong to the <u>Loyalaława</u> clan. this name is Hereditary no other clan can use it … the <u>Hamshamts!</u><small>Es</small> of that clan always called <u>nawes</u> . . . . and the man who made him Hamshamts!<small>Es</small> Dancer is <u>Lagusdes<small>E</small>las</u> or <u>copper comes to his Beach</u>."

The mask was pilfered by the Soviets at the end of WWII and sent first to Leningrad and later to Leipzig, from where it was returned to Berlin in 1992.

The above is adapted from an annotation that is part of the project "The Distributed Text: An Annotated Digital Edition of Franz Boas's Pioneering Ethnography." This project will reprint and annotate Boas's important 1897 monograph *The Social Organization and the Secret Societies of the Kwakiutl Indians* and create a multimedia website, in a partnership headed by project coordinators/editors Judith Berman (U. Victoria) and Aaron Glass (Bard Graduate Center). Framed with critical essays and contemporary Kwakw<u>a</u>k<u>a</u>'wakw perspectives, these new editions of Boas's monograph—print and online—will reunite the original text with the diverse, but widely distributed archival resources and museum collections associated with the original monograph. The project is under the rubric of a proposed Franz Boas Critical Edition book series, edited by Regna Darnell.

The 1897 monograph was arguably the single-most substantive and holistic ethnographic publication produced by Boas during his lifetime, as well as one of the first fieldwork-based monographs in the history of North American anthropology. A collaborative product of Boas's own observations in British Columbia (and at the 1893 Chicago World's Fair) and extensive materials provided by his long-time indigenous co-worker George Hunt, the text was the first systematic attempt to document all sociocultural, spiritual and aesthetic aspects of a spectacular and vital Native American ceremonial structure. Boas and Hunt recorded (through texts, photographs, museum collections, and wax cylinders) not only masks, myths, music, and dances tied to individual and lineage-bound rituals, but also the larger social context of all of these expressions of what Boas called "mental life." A pioneering achievement on many levels, it was the immediate inspiration for subsequent texts, images, and museum displays, and has been the subject of an ever-lengthening body of secondary literature. However, both Boas and Hunt were dissatisfied with the book and immediately began compiling corrections and additional materials, most of which have been lost in the archive ever since (these include hundreds of pages of annotations produced by Hunt in the last years of his life).

While the publishing technology of the day could not accommodate the diverse materials available even then to document Kwakwaka'wakw culture, digital media present new opportunities to enhance the historiography of this important volume, and to provide models for similar annotations across the humanities. This collaborative project has numerous goals: to reunite widely distributed archival materials necessary for a deep reading of the book, which will help achieve Boas and Hunt's long-deferred vision for it; to reveal the nature and process of co-authorship in Boas's foundational anthropological research; to use multimedia to help return a sense of sensory richness to ethnography as an immersive genre; and to bring this historic scholarship into dialogue with contemporary indigenous communities for whom the knowledge it conveys is still socially, aesthetically, and ceremonially relevant.

See www.bgc.bard.edu/news/bgc-press-room/bgc-receives-neh.html for additional information.

Permissions and Acknowledgements

DISCOVER MĀNOA

INLAND SHORES

Guest-edited by Charlene Gilmore

This collection features writing from Western Canada, from British Columbia's coast to Manitoba's wetlands. Includes poetry by Jan Zwicky, Tim Lilburn, Elizabeth Philips, and Monty Reid; fiction by Kevin Van Tighem and Susan Haley; essays by Don Gayton, Dave Carpenter, Sid Marty, and Alan Haig-Brown; and an epic Haida tale retold by Charles Lillard.

MAPS OF RECONCILIATION

Guest-edited by Barry Lopez

Some of the world's most thoughtful authors in fiction, essay, poetry, drama, and parable ask important questions about the future, to give us moral direction and individual courage. In many voices and dialects, they urge us to be compassionate and attentive and to bring hope to bear on the challenges before us.

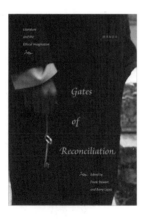

GATES OF RECONCILIATION

Guest-edited by Barry Lopez

Writers from South America, Europe, Australia, the Middle East, Asia, the U.S., and elsewhere explore the role of literature in addressing the most pressing issue of our time: how individuals, communities, and nations can reconcile differences and grievances and forge a future with a renewed sense of dignity and mutual respect.

available online at

http://www.jstor.org • http://muse.jhu.edu